I0902365

IMAGES
of America

ROSELLE PARK

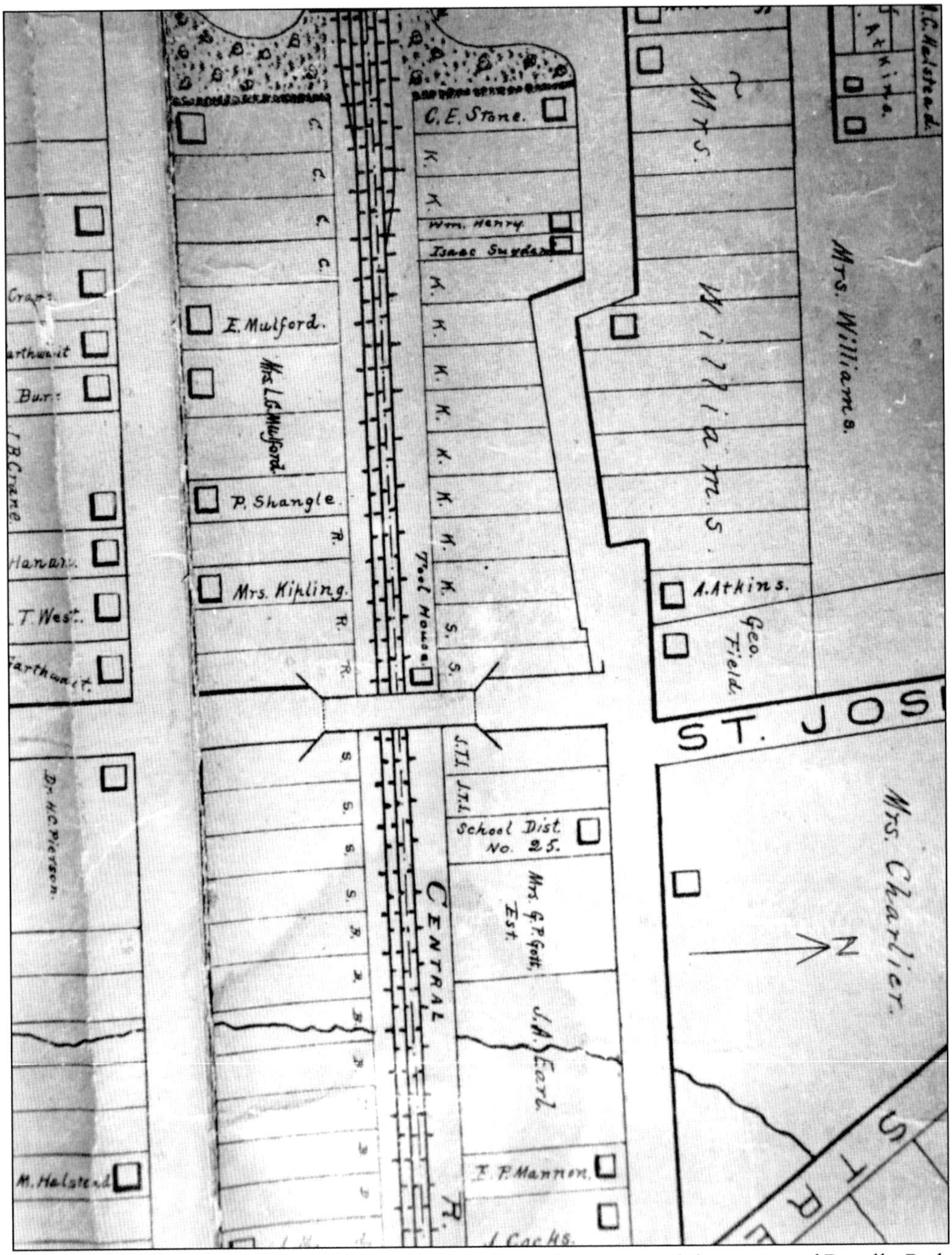

This section of an 1887 map of Union County shows how some of the streets of Roselle Park came to be named.

IMAGES *of America*

ROSELLE PARK

Audrey Morgan, Patricia Pagnetti, and Barbara Sokol

ARCADIA PUBLISHING

ISBN 978-0-7385-0430-8

Published by Arcadia Publishing
Charleston, South Carolina

Printed in the United States of America

Library of Congress Catalog Card Number: 00104050

For all general information contact Arcadia Publishing at:
Telephone 843-853-2070
Fax 843-853-0044
E-mail sales@arcadiapublishing.com
For customer service and orders:
Toll-Free 1-888-313-2665

Visit us on the Internet at www.arcadiapublishing.com

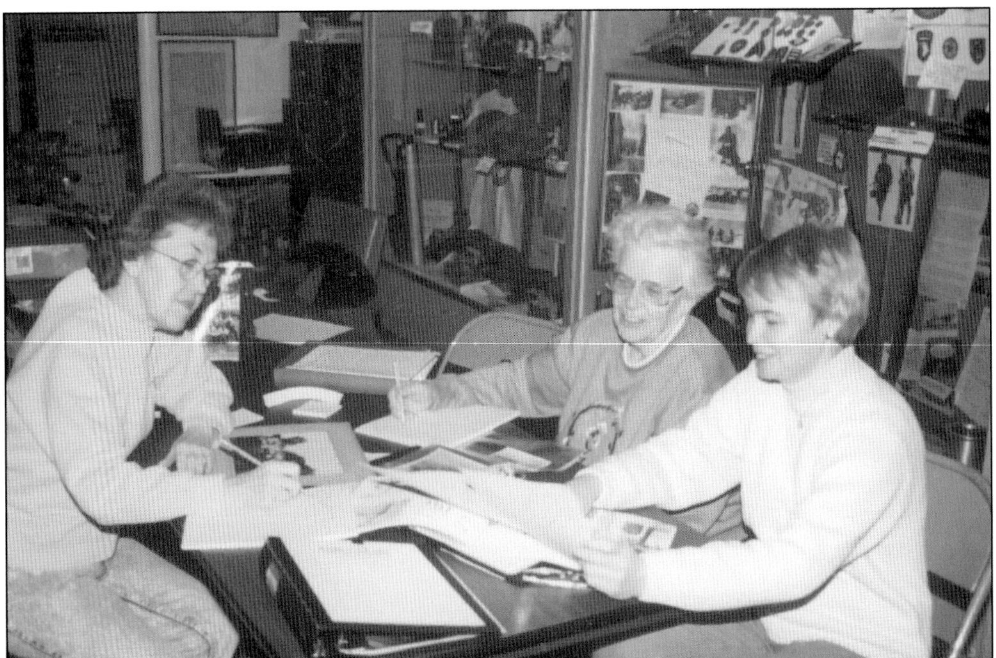

Authors Patricia Pagnetti, Audrey Morgan, and Barbara Sokol, who collaborated on the writing of *Roselle Park*, are surrounded by historic photographs, documents, and memorabilia at the Roselle Park Museum, which is operated by the Roselle Park Historical Society.

Contents

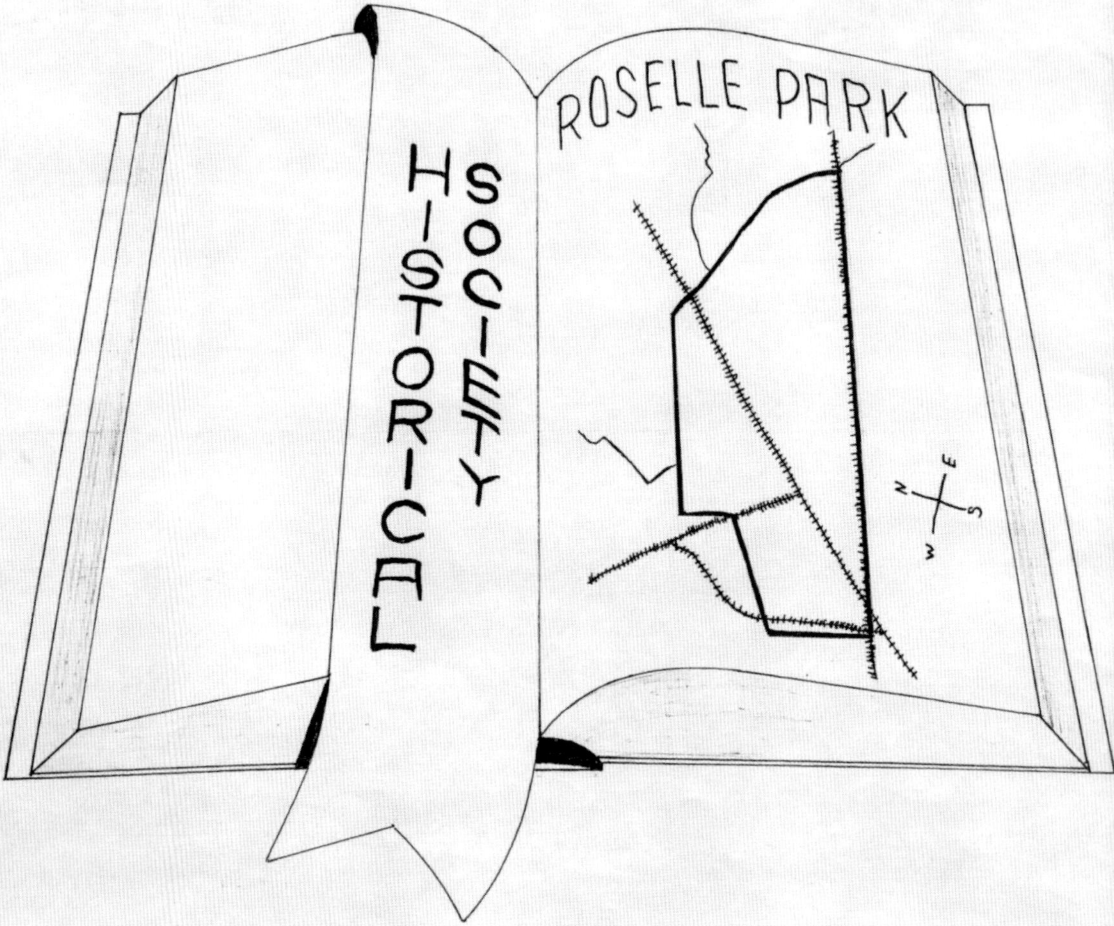

The Roselle Park Historical Society was incorporated in 1972 and is dedicated to discovering, collecting, preserving, and exhibiting the history of the borough of Roselle Park in photographs, documents, and memorabilia. The society's logo depicts a book representing education and opened to a map of the borough. The map is crisscrossed by the early railroads that helped develop this small rural village into a busy 21st-century community. The Roselle Park Historical Society operates the Roselle Park Museum.

This book is dedicated to the memory of David L. Keenan, whose foresight in accumulating and preserving photographs from the borough's early years formed the foundation for the Roselle Park Historical Society collection. Dave was the charter president of the society, first borough historian, and chairman of the Bicentennial and 75th Anniversary Committee.

INTRODUCTION

Incorporated in 1901, Roselle Park observes its centennial celebration in 2001. The 1.3-square-mile area in Union County was originally a part of Elizabethtown. In 1808, the area became part of Union Township and then an independent borough on March 22, 1901. The new borough consisted of 790 acres with 225 homes and a population of approximately 1,000. It was governed by a newly elected mayor and council.

The earliest recorded residents were the members of the Williams family. In the early 1700s, Samuel Williams, his wife, five sons, and three daughters built a home and farm on the road to the West Fields. At that time, there were three dirt roads, possibly old Native American trails, winding through the area. One was the road to the West Fields. The second was Galloping Hill Road. The third started with Union Road and ran diagonally northwest through Five Points to Springfield.

During the Revolutionary War, soldiers marched up Galloping Hill Road on their way to the Battle of Springfield. Some skirmishes were encountered there, and a monument on Galloping Hill Road marks the place where the son of Gen. William Crane was bayoneted by the British. The Hospital Oak on the corner of Westfield Avenue and Colonial Road marked the location of a field hospital where wounded soldiers were treated.

Several prosperous farms dotted the area for many years, and in 1839 the railroad connected the borough to Elizabeth and Somerville. As the area expanded with its growing population, more streets, small stores, and businesses were established. Charles Stone operated a general store and post office on Westfield Avenue near Chestnut Street that welcomed the 20th century as the world's first electrically lighted store. In 1912, Marconi set up a company that manufactured wireless equipment for the U.S. Navy. It was here that Marconi made the first successful transatlantic broadcast. On December 15, 1921, in this same building, WDY, the second licensed radio station in the United States, made its debut.

From its inception, the borough of Roselle Park has owed its development and character to the energy of its many volunteers, a tradition that has continued for over 100 years. It is the fervent hope that this book will inspire memories and discussions that will provide additional information back to the historical society. Readers are invited to contact the Roselle Park Museum to share their photographs and recollections.

ACKNOWLEDGMENTS

We sincerely acknowledge the contributions of all the members of the Roselle Park Historical Society who have contributed their time, photographs, and expertise toward the completion of this book. Special thanks to those who served as consultants and photographers and who donated their photographs to be included in this anniversary collection: Paul Endler, Pat DeMarco, Charles Helfrich, Bill Frolich, Charles Florio, Nicholas Pagnetti, Donna Pagnetti-Mulvihill, Sandy Thompson, Lyman Thompson Jr., George Blaskewicz, Marie Roth, Angelo Capone, John Lyle, Bob Lehr, Bob Kluge, Barbara Cooley, Matthew J. Ryan, Carol Delloiacano, Andy Rubilla, Pat Riley, Fortunate Salerno, the Riccitelli family, Tara Delnero, Dick Ahle, Carl Hokanson, the Roselle Park Police Department, the Roselle Park Fire Department, mayor Joseph DeIorio, and the 1999 and 2000 council. We are also grateful to all those who donated any photographs and information to the Roselle Park Historical Society and Museum over the many years, some of which may have been incorporated into this book.

One

Early Settlers

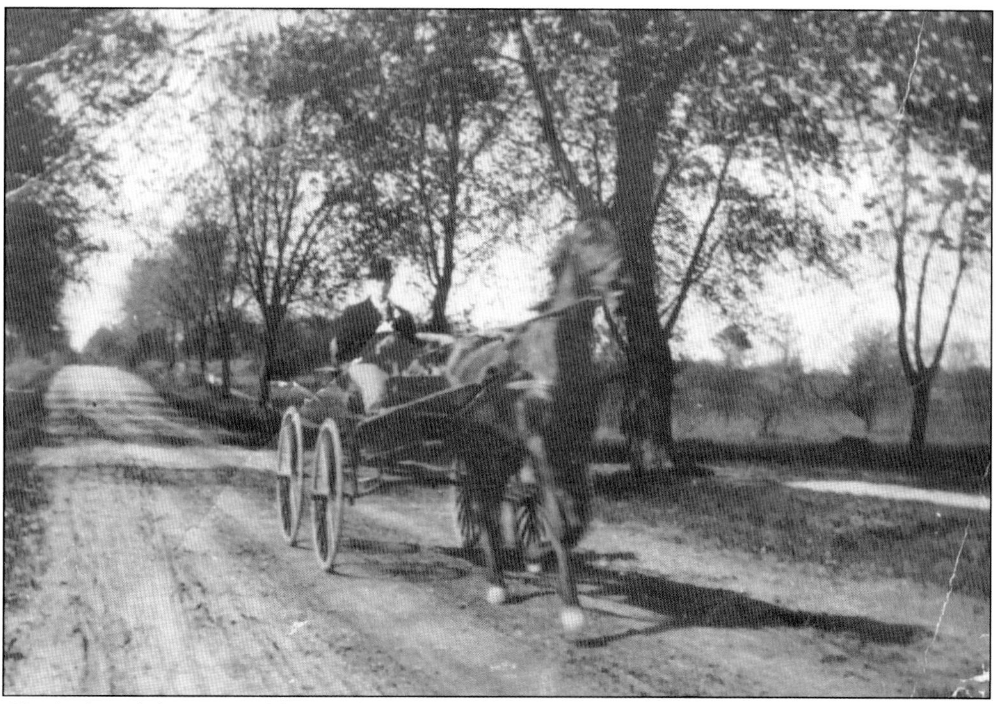

Climb aboard the Honorable Joseph Morgan's buggy as he guides his horse past open fields on the narrow, dirt, country road that was Chestnut Street, *c.* 1901. He will take you on a trip into the past, stopping along the way to point out local landmarks, places of interest, thriving businesses, and the folks around town. Behind him is a view looking toward Five Points, Union.

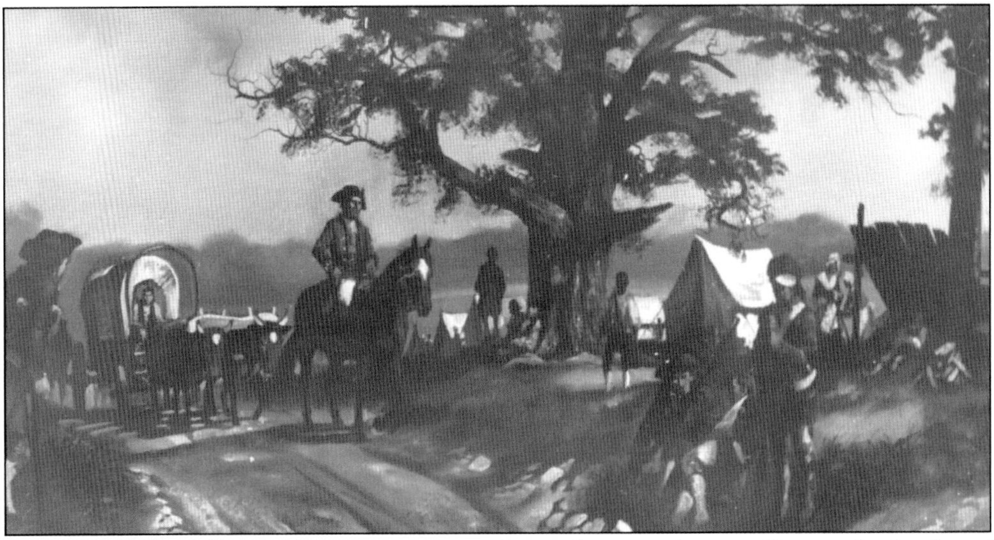

In a borough long known for its trees, one oak stands out in history. During the battles of the Revolutionary War, the Continental Army established a field hospital, located under the massive and spreading branches of the Hospital Oak, where wounded and dying soldiers were treated. It stood near the corner of Westfield Avenue and Galloping Hill Road. The junction was on the main route used by Washington's troops traveling to and from the famous battles of Springfield and Connecticut Farms. The tree lasted until the early 1900s. This is an artist's rendition of the field hospital.

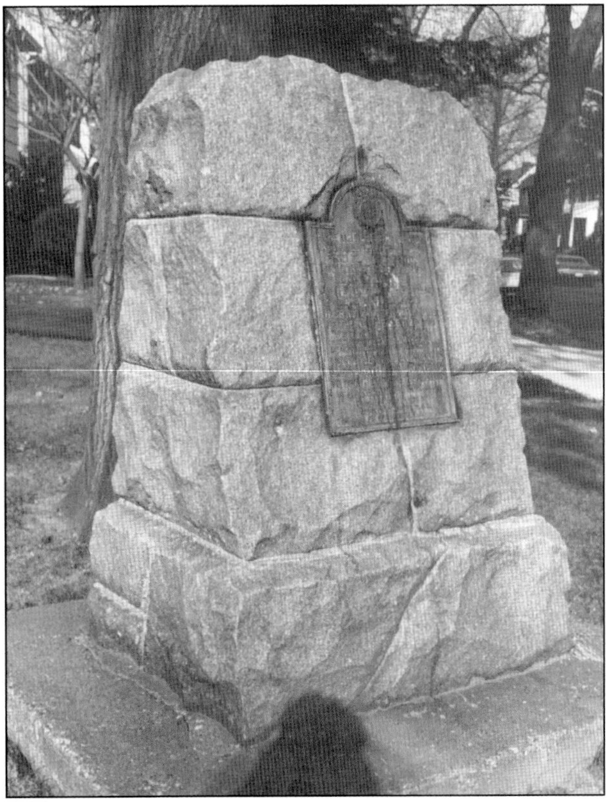

The British turned into Galloping Hill Road from Elizabethtown to Connecticut Farms and Springfield during the Revolutionary War battles of June 7 and 23, 1780. Afterward, Washington said of the New Jersey Militia, "They flew to arms universally, and acted with a spirit equal to anything I have seen during the war." A son of Gen. William Crane is said to have been bayoneted to death by British soldiers nearby. The monument at Galloping Hill Road and Colonial Road was erected June 10, 1913, by the Daughters of the American Revolution, Boudinot Chapter.

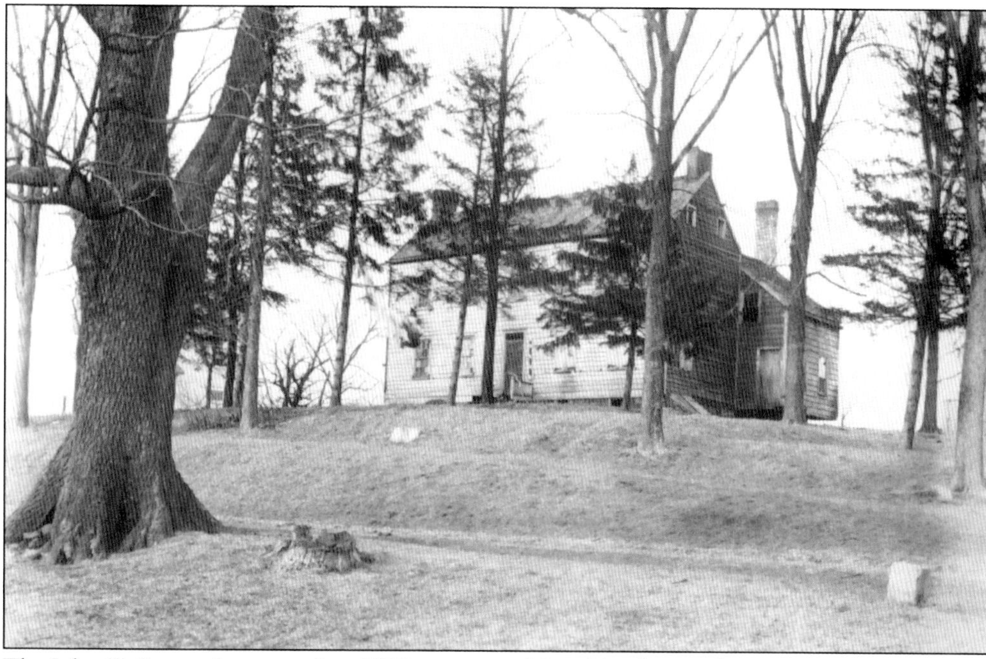

The John C. Seaton homestead, *c.* 1810, was one of the oldest known homes of its type in Roselle Park in the mid-1990s. When Lehigh Valley Railroad tracks were laid across Seaton Avenue property in 1888, it was said that two Seaton sisters sat vigil on their lawn in rocking chairs. They eventually fell asleep and railroad workers quietly completed rail construction that night.

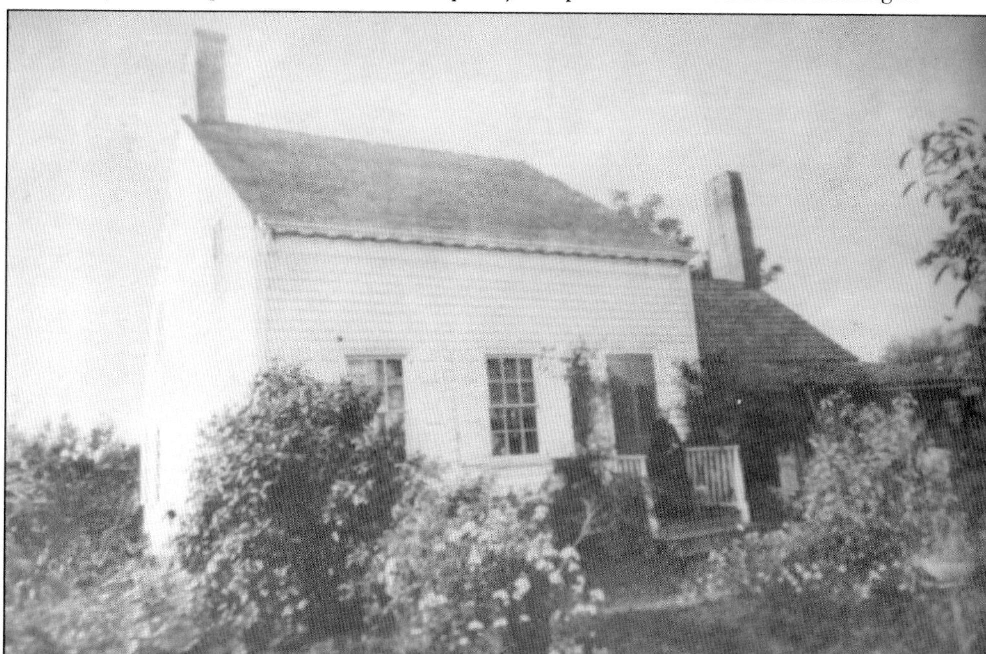

According to Sadie Wilson, "Aunt" Williams never married, but the family gave her this *c.* 1721 house on the Williams farm. Her home and lovely garden was on a little road off East Westfield Avenue near the Parkway Ford Company.

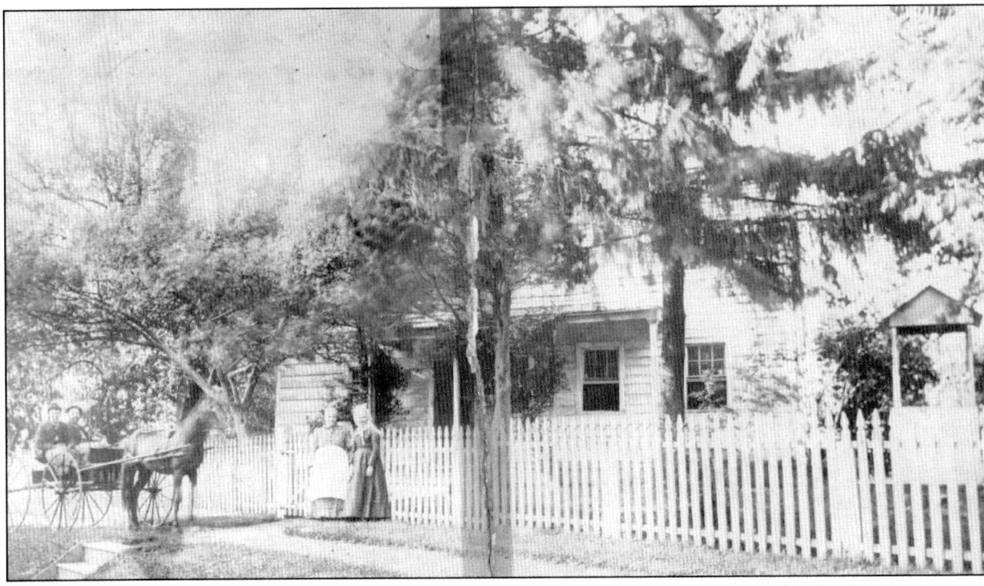

The Earl family homestead on Union Road, between Westfield Avenue and Charles Street, was located on an 1860 map of Union Township. Other families nearby were J. Allen, J. Krieg, J.S. Winans, E. Sauer, C.P. Gott, D.B. Thompson, S. Mills, and I. Board. A 1906 map attributes the property to James A. Earl. During the Revolutionary War, this road was a main link between Elizabethtown and Springfield, crossing Walnut Street to Tucker Avenue in what is now Union.

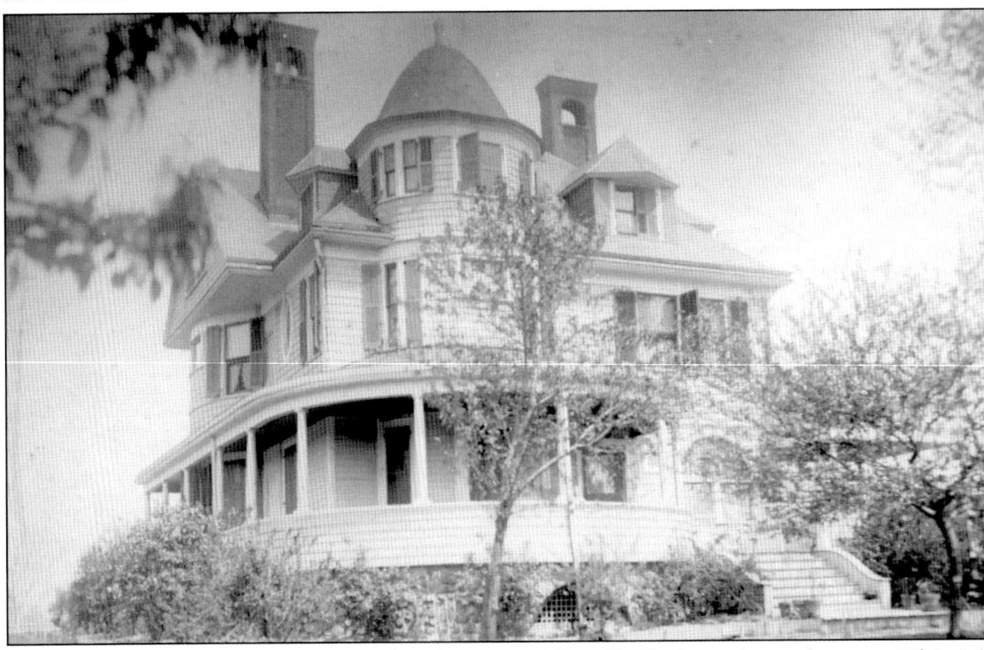

Many lovely homes graced the tree-lined streets of Roselle Park in the early years. This 16-room house was located on Lincoln Avenue between Chester and Roosevelt Streets. Built in 1881 by Mr. Condit as a residence, it later served as a rooming house and a minister's retreat house. There was a windmill on the property that pumped water from the well. A victim of the depression, it was demolished in 1933 and replaced with six homes.

Ann Williams, dressed in a typical ladies outfit of the day, relaxes in the backyard of the Williams property.

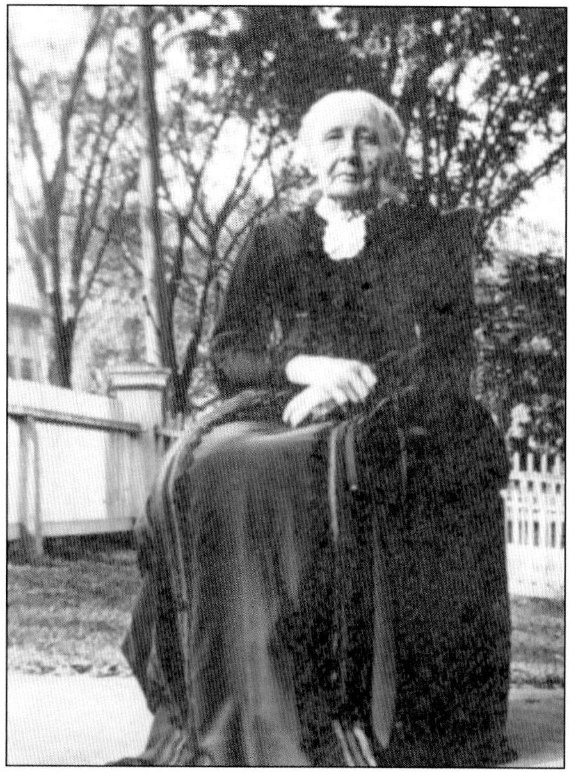

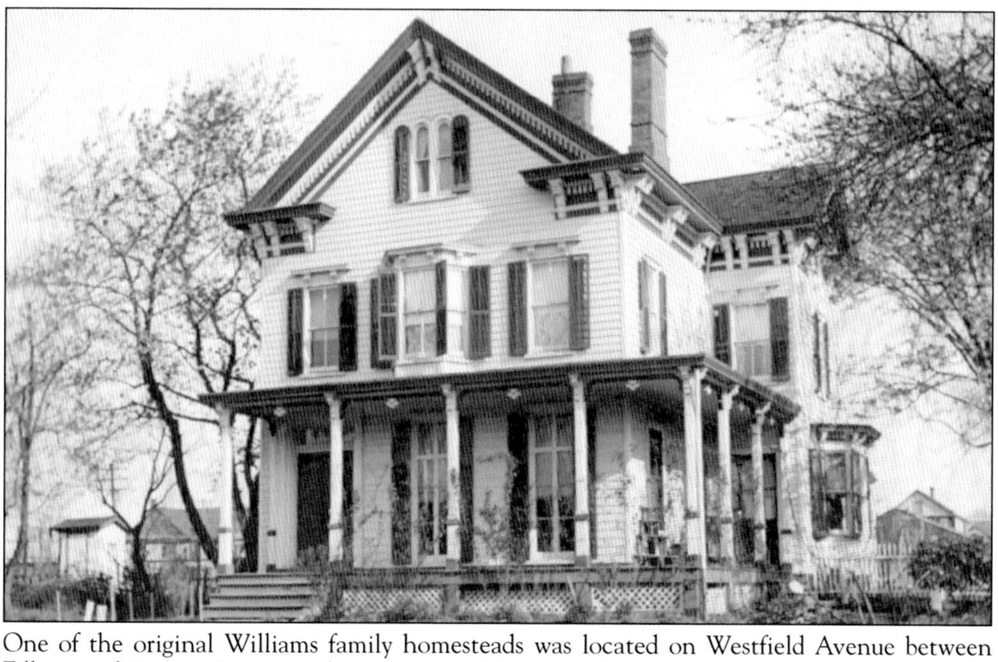

One of the original Williams family homesteads was located on Westfield Avenue between Filbert and Locust Streets and was occupied by David Williams and Ann Crane Williams. The Victorian architecture features floor-to-ceiling windows, a wrap-around front porch, gingerbread trim, and shuttered windows. It was later occupied by the Balnicki family and was demolished in the early 1960s.

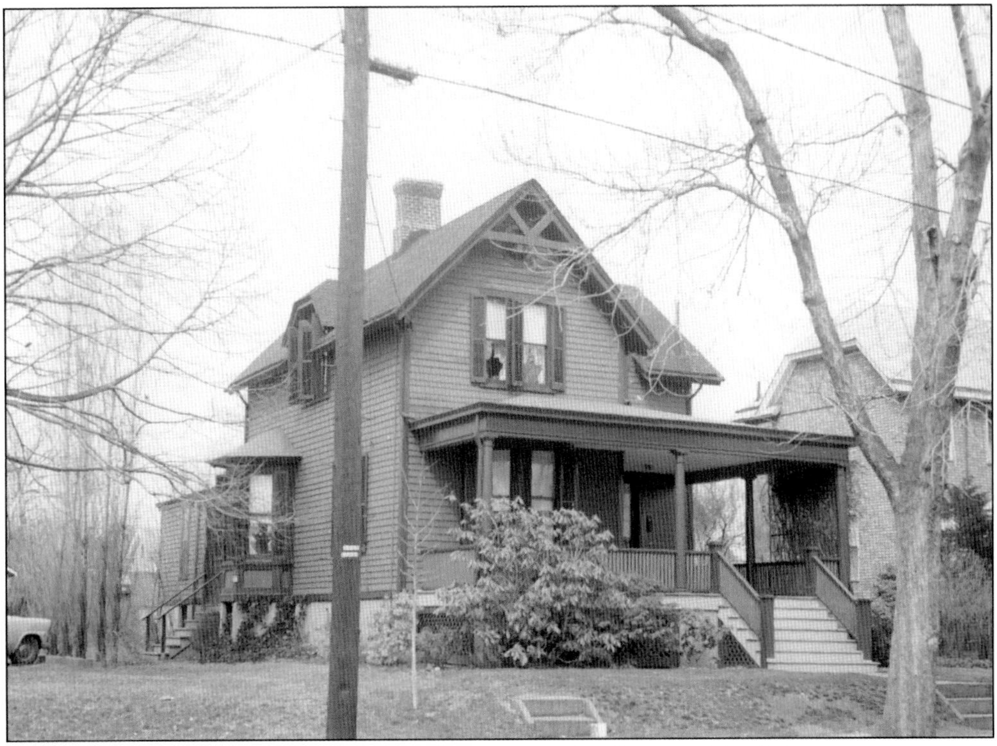

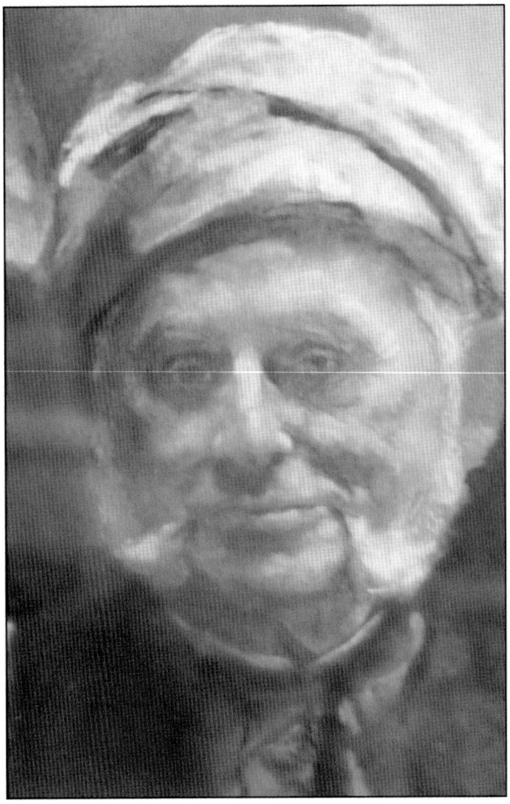

In 1867, Capt. Alfred Atkins, a distinguished Civil War hero, was smitten by the charms of Hannah W. Williams, daughter of William Sayre and Abigail (Mulford) Williams. William Sayre Williams, who was born in October 1807 and died May 1, 1873, owned one of the large farms forming the site of what later became Roselle Park. Abigail Mulford was born November 25, 1818, and died in 1890. Alfred and Hannah Atkins married on November 1, 1867, and settled here in 1871 shortly before her father's death. This home was their residence, adjoining her father's house. Transplanted from Poughkipsie, New York, Atkins brought with him the leadership qualities that enabled him to become one of the founding fathers of Roselle Park.

This is the home of the Cooley family on West Westfield Avenue. John Cooley was born in 1888 and died in 1951. The lady at the gate is the grandmother of Barbara Cooley.

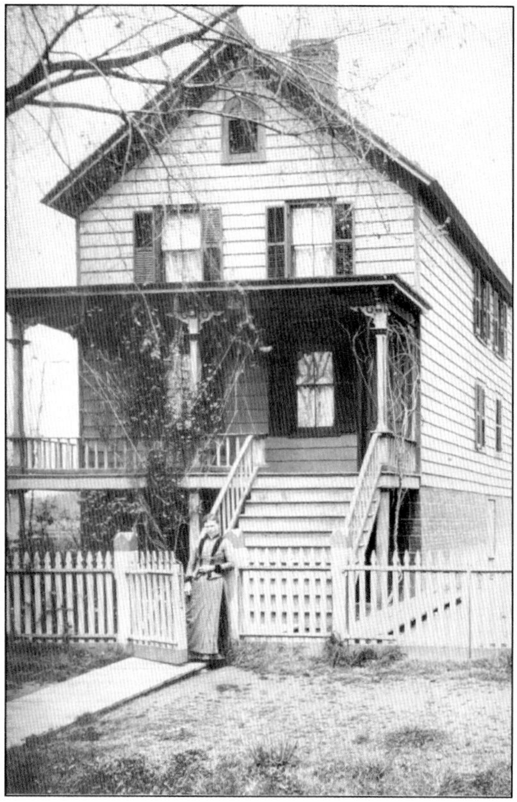

The Weissleder's porch, *c.* 1906, on Pershing Avenue, was the perfect spot to gather for a family birthday celebration. The two children sitting on the railing are Helen Weissleder, later Helen Moyle, and Clara Mauthe, later Claire Kluge, who resided in the borough until her death at age 99 in March 2000. Shown, from left to right, are Martha Opitz, Ida Hoeh, Emily Opitz, Agnes Weissleder, Sophie Weissleder, Helen Weissleder, Clara Louisa Mauthe, Clara Mauthe, and Anton Weissleder.

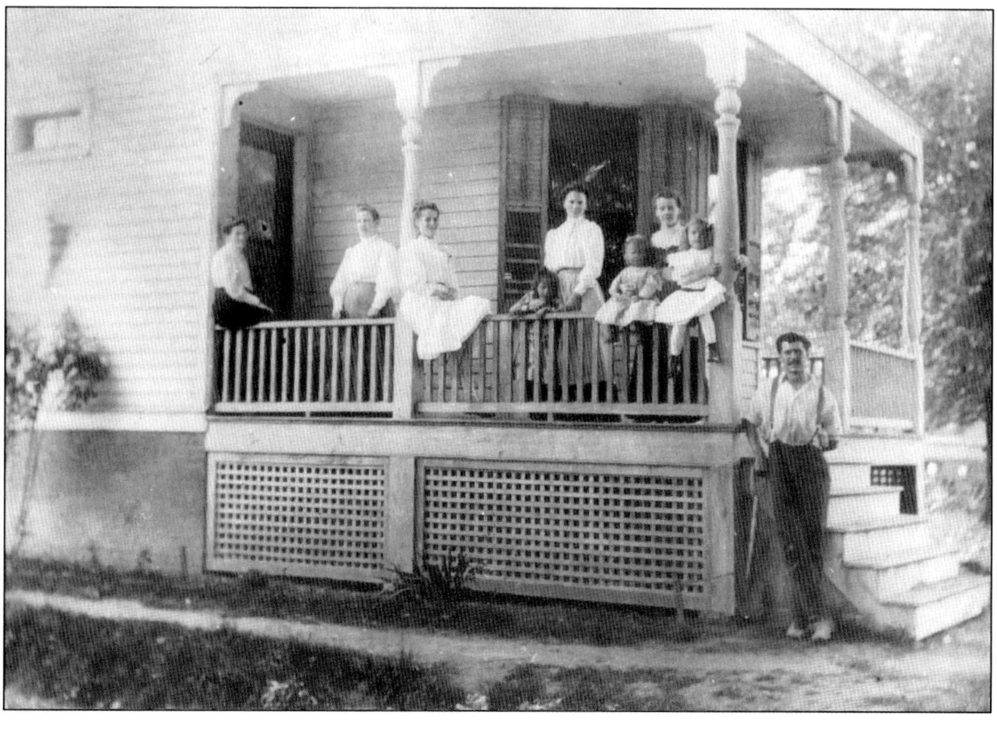

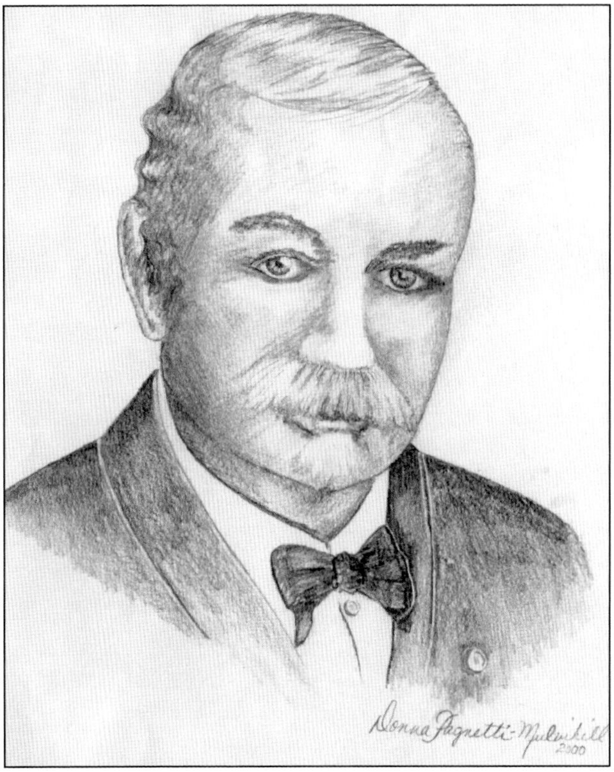

John Christian Bender, known to all as Honest John, was a driving force in the establishment of a new community. Active in civic affairs, he donated land and paid for many improvements in the Sherman area. Bender, a councilman and freeholder, was instrumental in naming Westfield Avenue as the first county road. The Lorraine Hotel, Bender's picnic grove, slaughter house, and meat market are now only memories of bygone days.

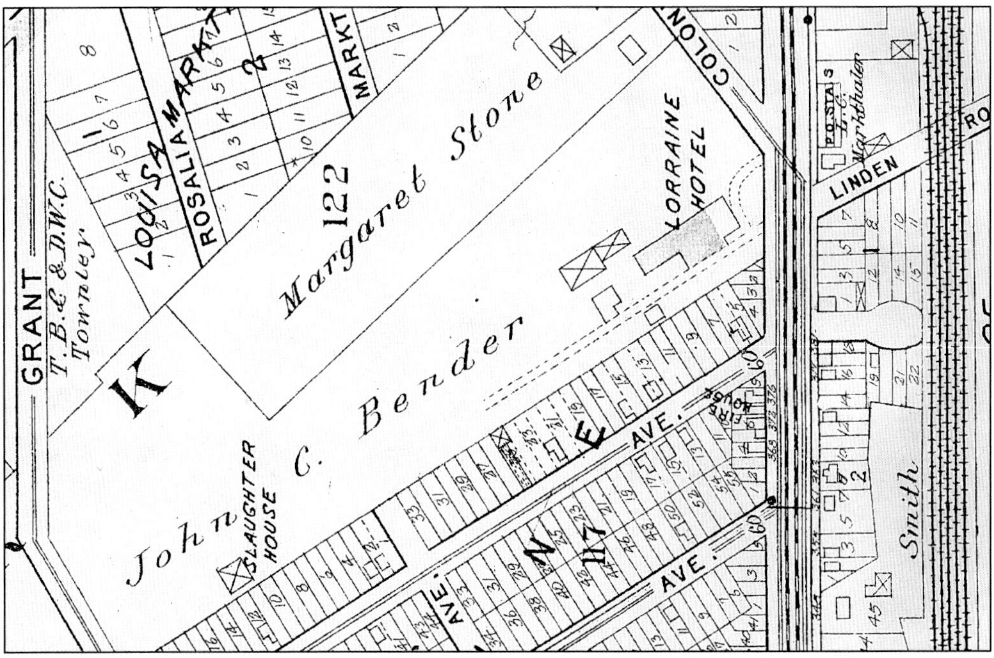

In 1891, John Christian Bender purchased 21 acres of land and built his residence on East Westfield Avenue near Colonial Road. There, he and his wife, Josephine Peters Bender, raised their seven children. This 1901 map indicates the building in the rear as the Lorraine Hotel, which he operated for many years. This area is now known as the "Bender Section."

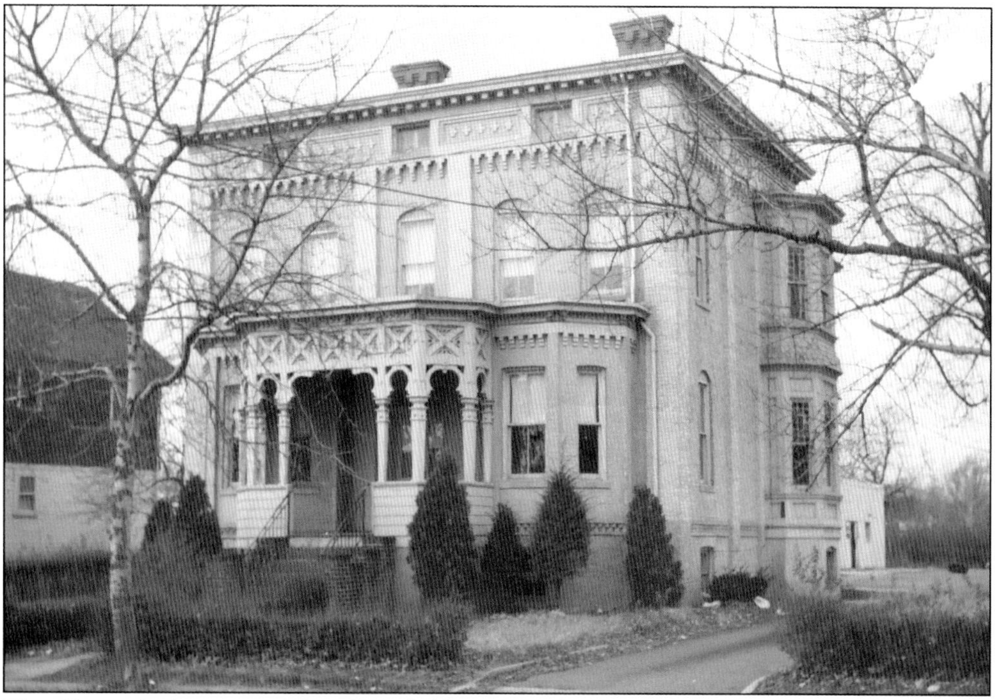

The Tomasulo home on West Westfield Avenue became the site of the Sunrise Village apartments. Antonio and Vincenza Tomasulo left San Fele, Italy, in 1892 and immigrated to New York City. Antonio had a shoeshine stand on Wall Street. They moved to Roselle Park in 1906, where they raised six sons.

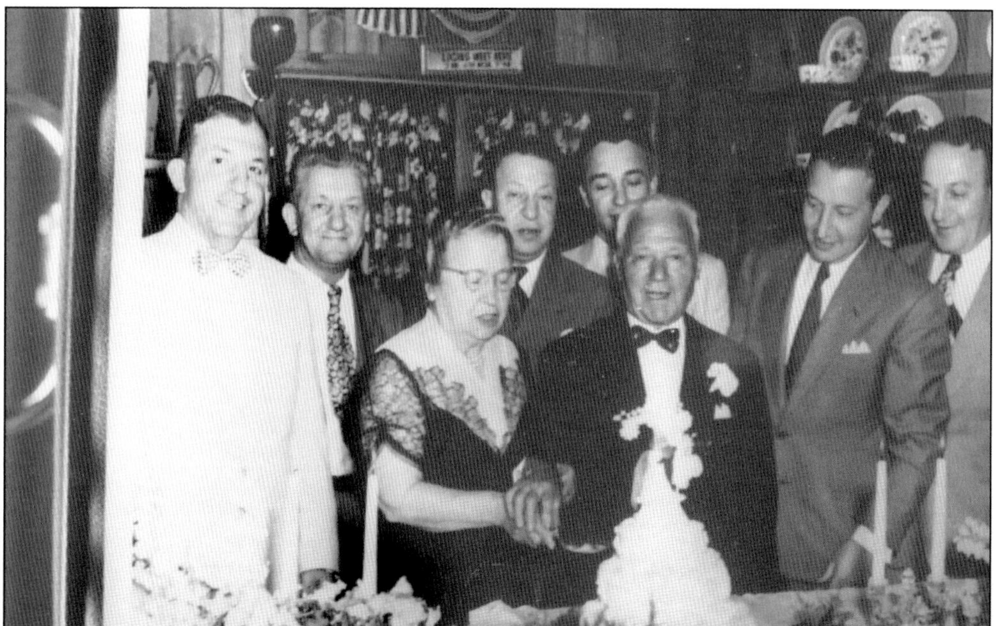

At a family gathering celebrating their 50th wedding anniversary, Mr. and Mrs. Tomasulo are surrounded by their sons. From left to right, the sons are Joseph, James, Michael, Frank, Nicholas, and Louis. All of the sons became professionals in various fields of endeavor.

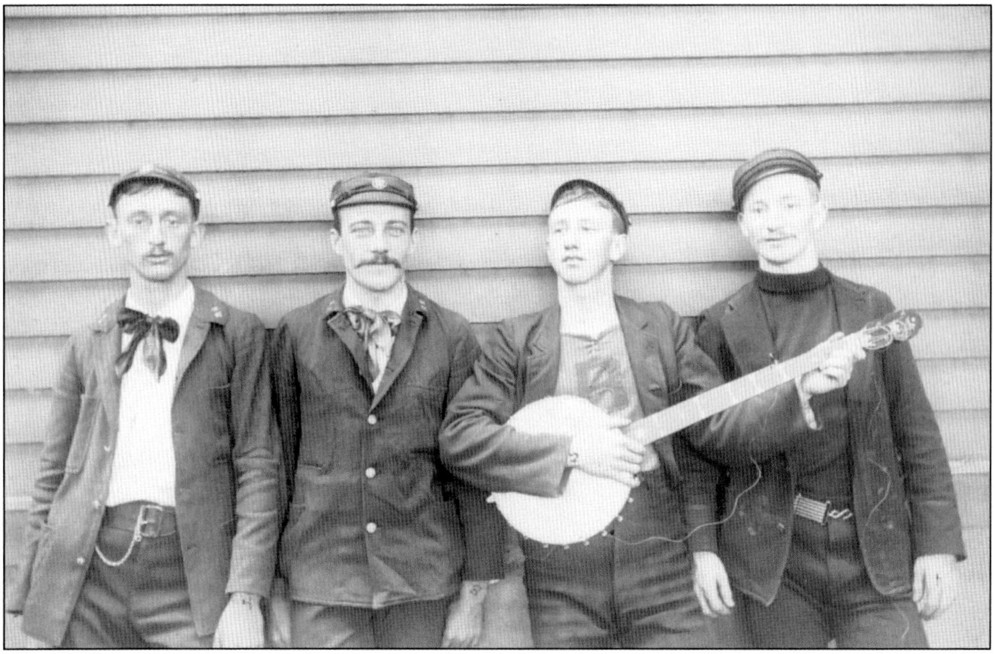

In these 1889 images (12 years before their hometown became Roselle Park), these young friends who were to call themselves "the Roselle Ramblers" demonstrate their musical and athletic prowess. Shown above are, from left to right, Arthur Pope, Edward Kingsland, George Pope (playing the banjo), and George Bogart. Below, the same four set out for a day of cycle racing, wearing fashionable biking uniforms of the day.

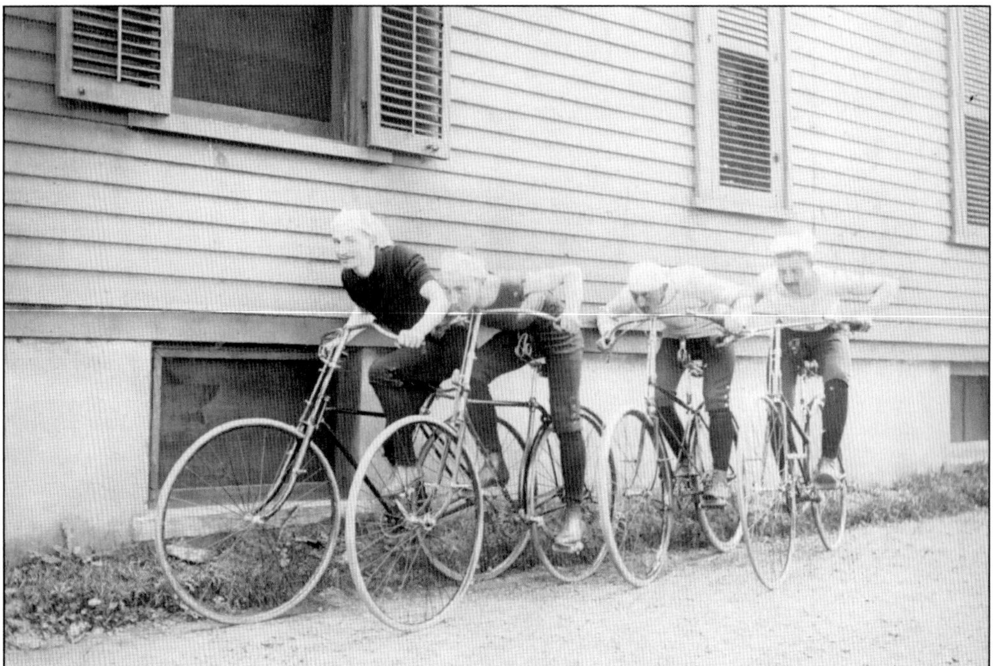

Two

Neighbors

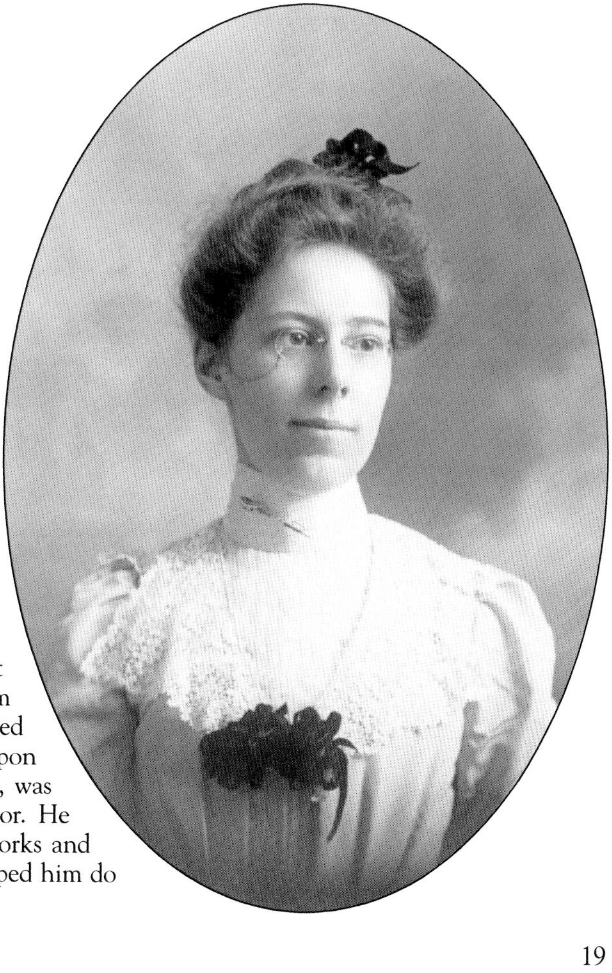

Annie Wilson, born December 16, 1892, graduated from Livingston School in June 1908. She later recalled that the blacksmith shop was where New Park Cinema stands today. Sidewalks then were boardwalks, and "streets were so swampy" that she could ice-skate in winter. Starting as a library volunteer, she became assistant librarian, working at the library from 1943 to 1957 and beyond. She willed money to the town and library upon her death. Her father, John Wilson, was the borough's first building inspector. He headed the department of public works and was also the tax assessor. Annie helped him do the books.

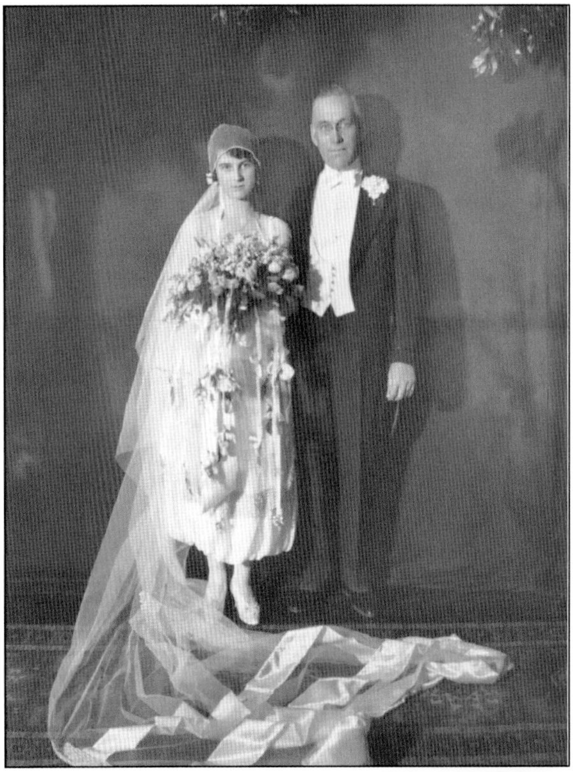

Dr. William R. Smith married Mary Etta Roe on October 22, 1891. They lived on East Westfield Avenue, where he practiced family medicine. Mary was born November 24, 1867, and died August 18, 1946. Her ancestors, Jonas and Benjamin Roe, fought in the American Revolution, and her family can be traced back to the mid-1600s in this country.

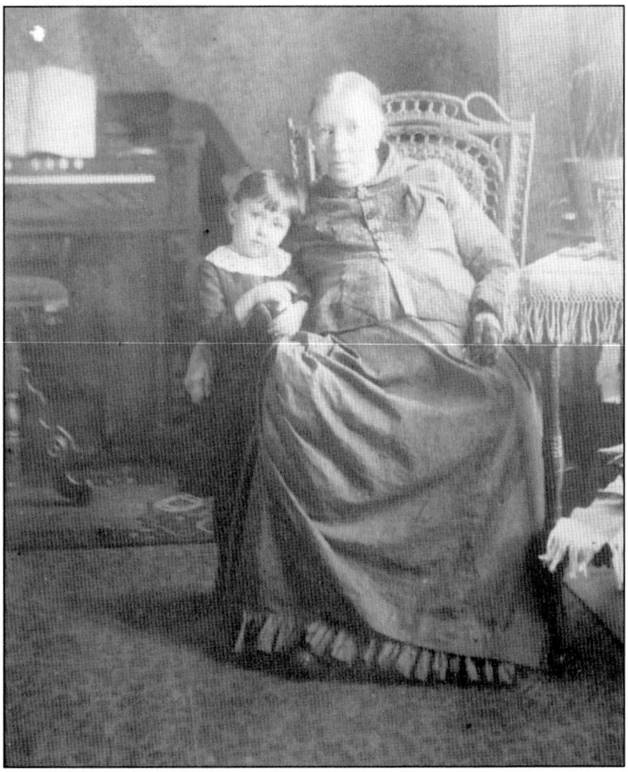

Martha McCloud and Robert Morse McCloud pose for a professional photograph taken on "Monday evening November 5, 1900." The background shows a typical Victorian parlor with a pump organ and fringed doilies on the table. The McCloud family was prominent in Roselle Park, and residents enjoyed the many tastes and aromas emanating from the McCloud's bakery on Chestnut Street.

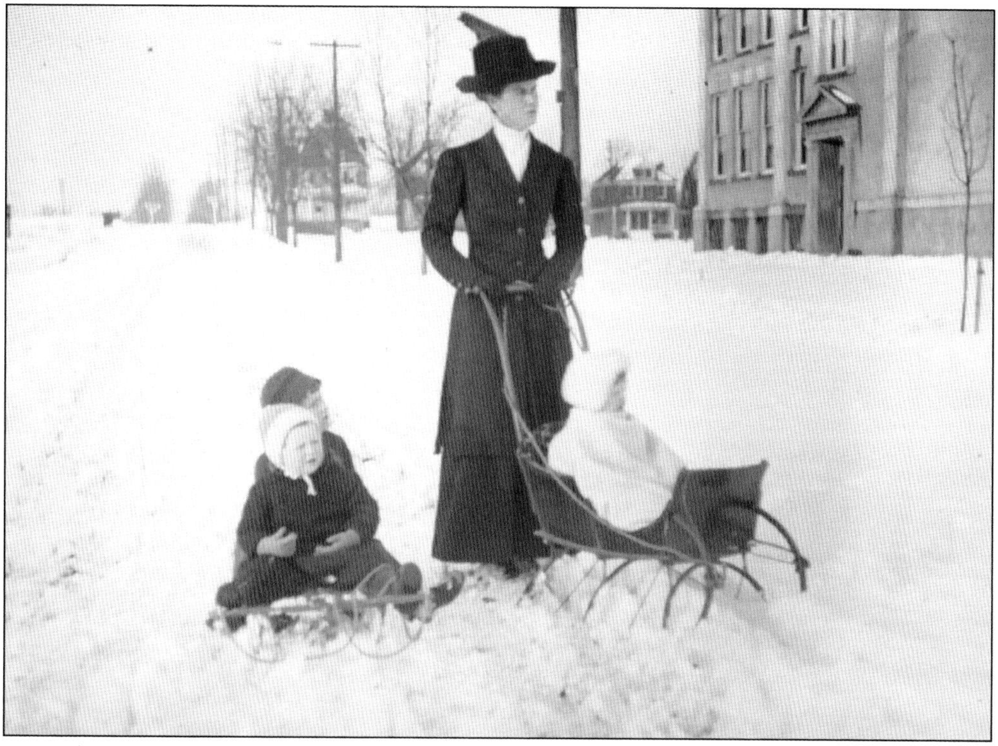

Mrs. Charles Waite walks with her children on a snowy winter day, *c.* 1912. Looking north on Locust Street, Robert Gordon School is on the right. The homes in the background are on West Clay Avenue; distant railroad signs warn of Lehigh Valley train tracks that were then at ground level. This photograph predates the former Junior High School (later known as Woods School). Many homes and trees later lined Locust Street, a county road.

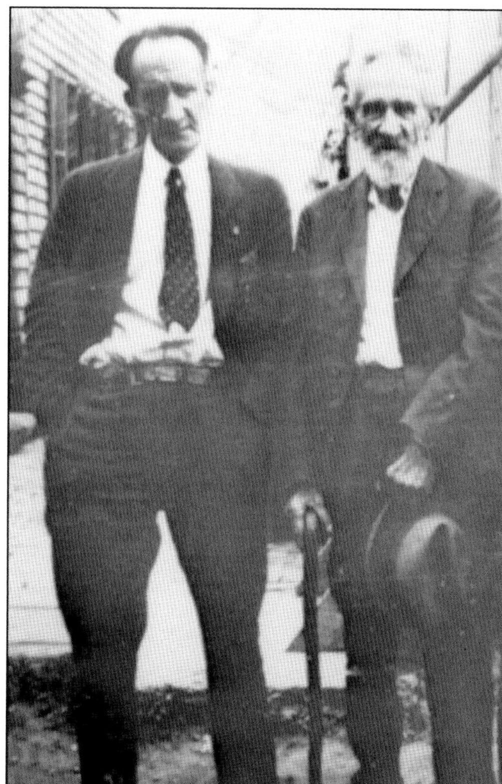

Dr. Frank Halsted Brown, left, was the longtime physician for the Roselle Park public school system and was the surgeon for the police and fire departments. He and his wife, Marie Ufland, a registered nurse, ran a general medical practice as well as a maternity hospital at their residence, 327 Chestnut Street. His children distinctly recall being assigned the duty of changing newborns' diapers. The bearded gentleman on the right is Dr. Brown's father, C.H. Brown.

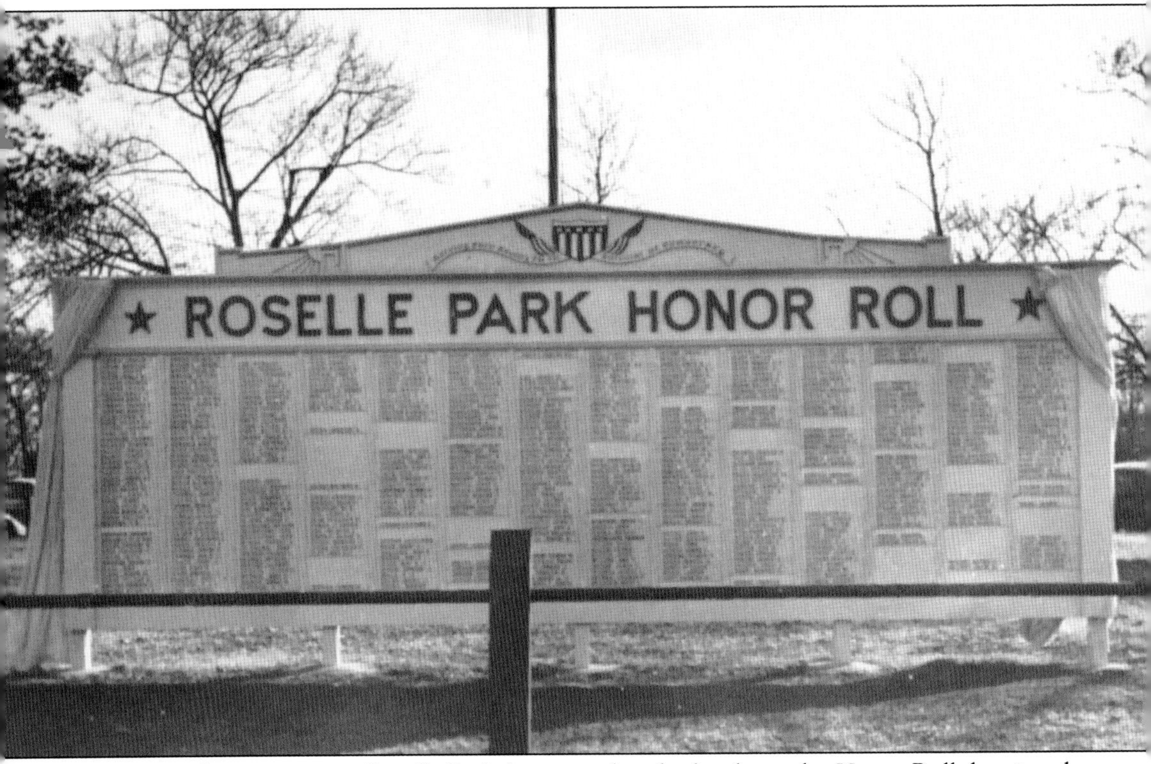

A revered monument in Roselle Park for many decades has been the Honor Roll, bearing the names of sons and daughters in the armed forces during wartime. This wooden structure in the Oval Park at the Central Railroad station proclaimed the borough's pride in those who served. Although most returned, many were killed in action. The following are those who never returned: (World War I) Samuel Damiano, Pietro DiPalma, Clarence V. Fanning, Edward A. Fanning, Joseph Macedo, Charles Montgomery, Thomas Paulson Jr., S.J. Peluso, Betram A. Rowe, Oscar Swanson, and John E. Williams; (World War II) Walter T. Byram, Samuel Capiello, Carl F. Cooke, Robert M. Corwin, Percy Donak, Joseph T. Donahue, Kenneth H. Flath, Elliott Goodman, Robert J. Jones, Alfred A. Keimig, Vernon J. Kempson, Paul E. Kessler, Charles M. Mooney, Charles G. Norbert, Helen M. Otto, Jack W. Ragland, Lee C. Ragland, John W. Reindel Jr., William W. Roberts, John A. Salinardo, Richard F. Selk, Frank J. Stallone, Arthur W. Swanson, John G. Swanson, John J. Szostak, Michael J. Tirone, Raymond L. Turner, Glenn Williams, Eric Wittman, William H. Wolfskeil, and Andrew Z. Yeaple. The Vietnam War claimed the lives of Roger J. Spence and Robert M. Worshinski.

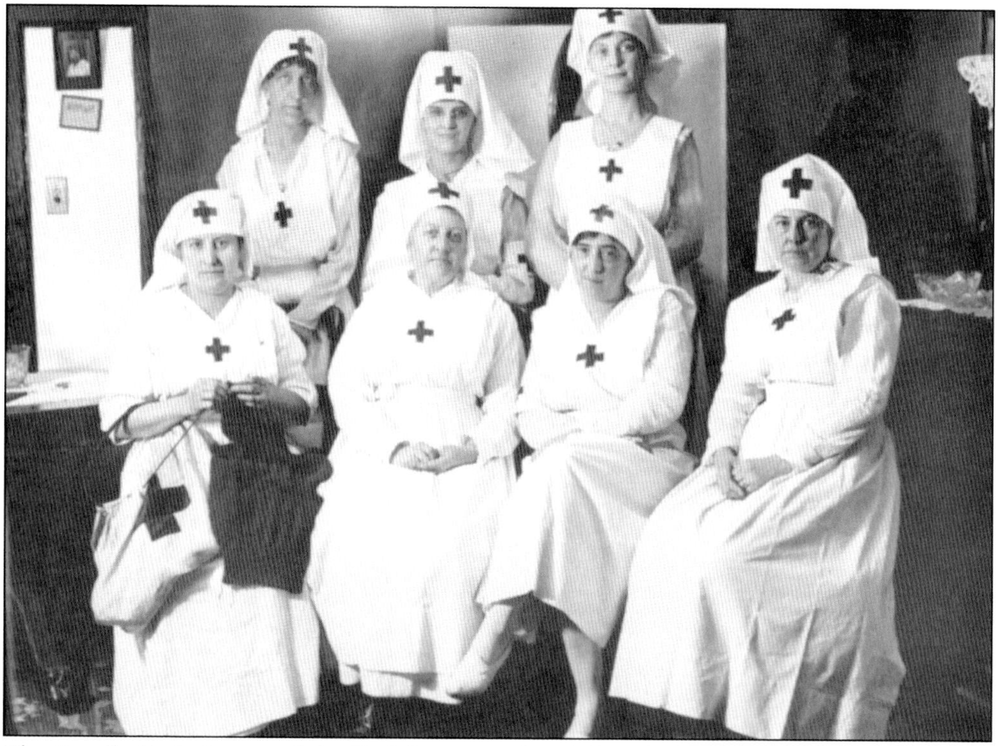

The Roselle Park chapter of the Red Cross was founded in 1916 by Anne Eberle. The ladies shown, from left to right, are as follows: (front row) Mrs. L. Eberle (knitting), Mrs. O. Peck, Mrs. A. Crane, and Mrs. E. Shopp; (back row) Mrs. Hammond, Mrs. W. Hall, and Mrs. Polhemus.

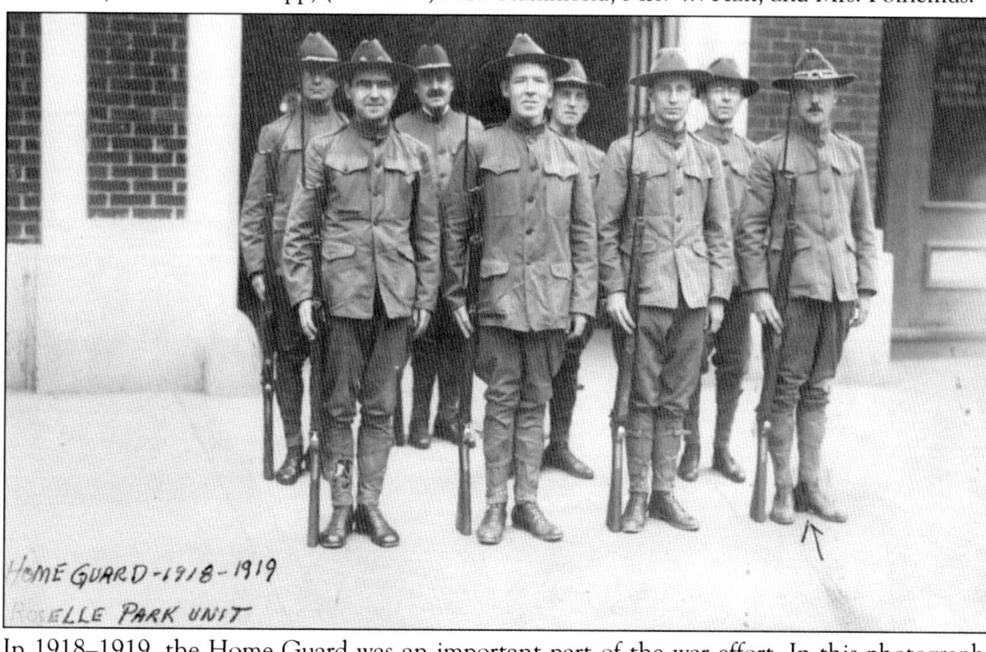

In 1918–1919, the Home Guard was an important part of the war effort. In this photograph, they demonstrate their readiness for action as they stand at attention in front of the firehouse on Chestnut Street.

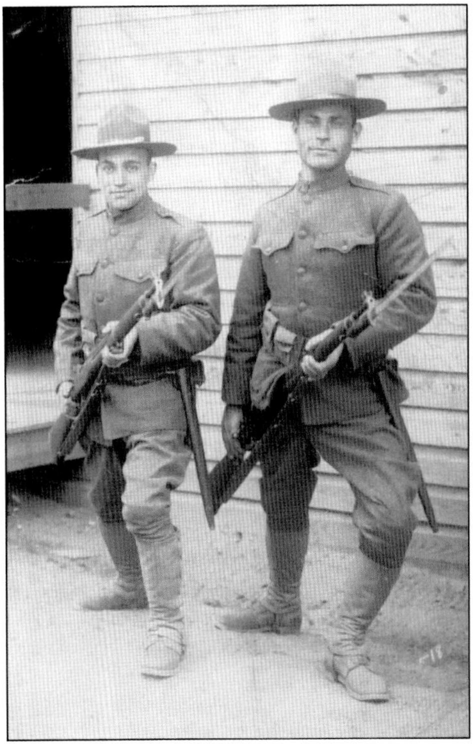

During World War I, close friends Nicholas DeMarco and Peter DePalma served together in France with the 311th Infantry, 78th Division. Peter was killed at Argone and Nick returned to marry Josephine Crecco and started DeMarco's Shoe Service.

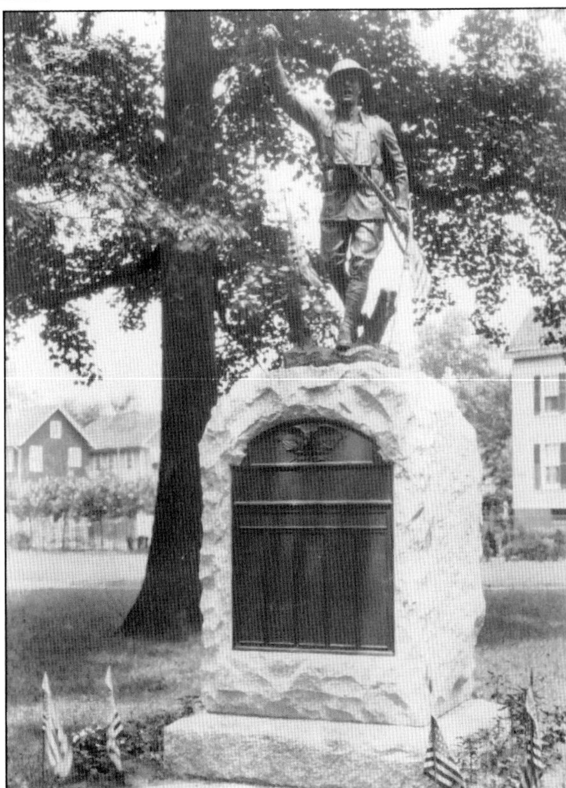

Grateful citizens donated funds to erect a doughboy statue to honor 11 servicemen who gave their lives in World War I. Tragically, later wars were to add dozens more names to the plaque.

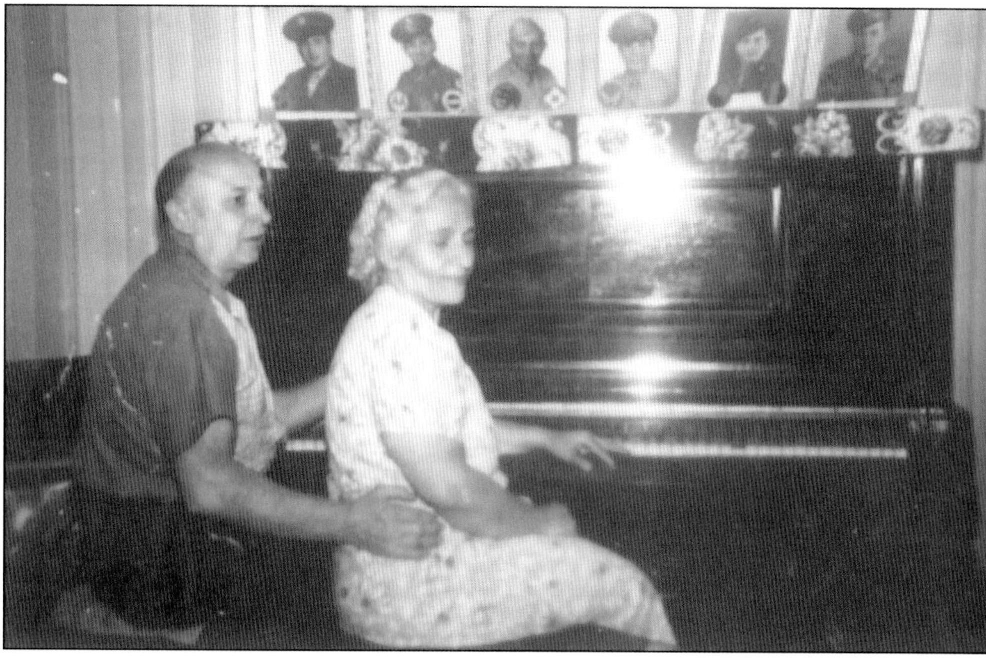

No greater love of country was shown by a family when Felice and Carmel Delloiacono sent their six sons to serve in the U.S. Army during World War II. Benjamin, a private first class, served in the coast artillery. John, also a private first class, was burned at Aachen, Germany. Joel, a sergeant, was with an antiaircraft unit in Germany. Private first class Emilio "Amey" served with an infantry outfit overseas. Nicholas was a corporal with a medical unit in Mississippi. Staff sergeant Carmine served as a scout during the D-Day invasion and received the Purple Heart, the Silver Star, and the Bronze Star. They marched as Honor Guard in the Memorial Day parade in 1946.

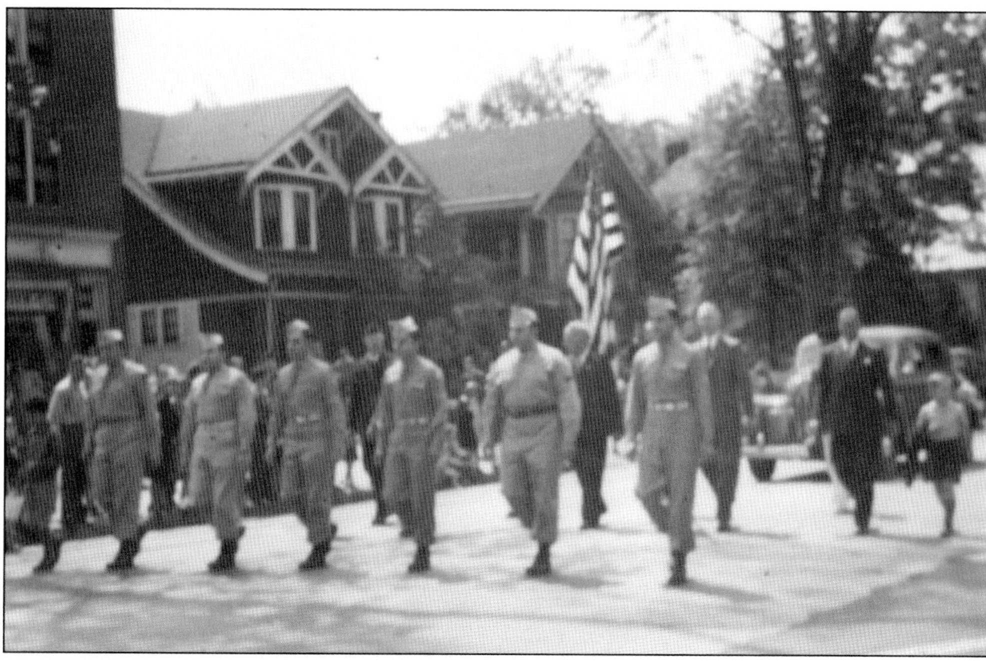

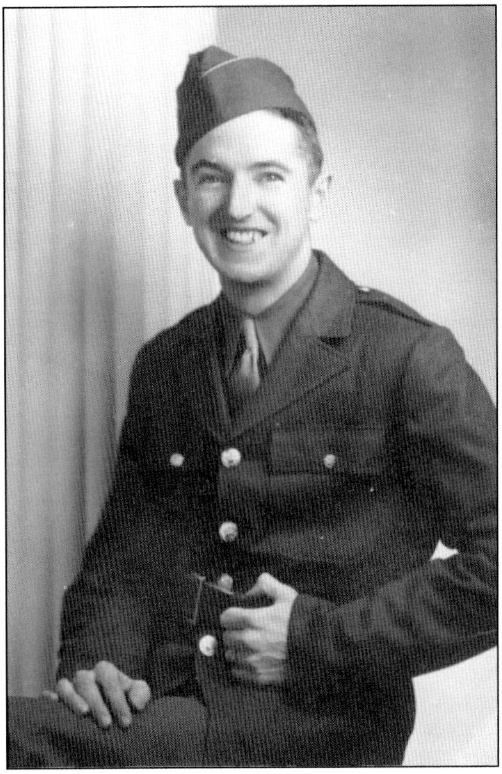

Volunteerism and politics dominated Robert "Bob" Lehr's life after his World War II tour with the U.S. Army Air Corps in the Pacific Theater. He was an Esso accountant, Union County coroner, borough councilman for 9 years, and held offices in the American Legion, Veterans of Foreign Wars, Disabled American Veterans, the Air Force Association, Republican Club, Historical Society, Library Board, Retired Associates, and Senior Citizens. Bob visited all 50 states, and every continent except one.

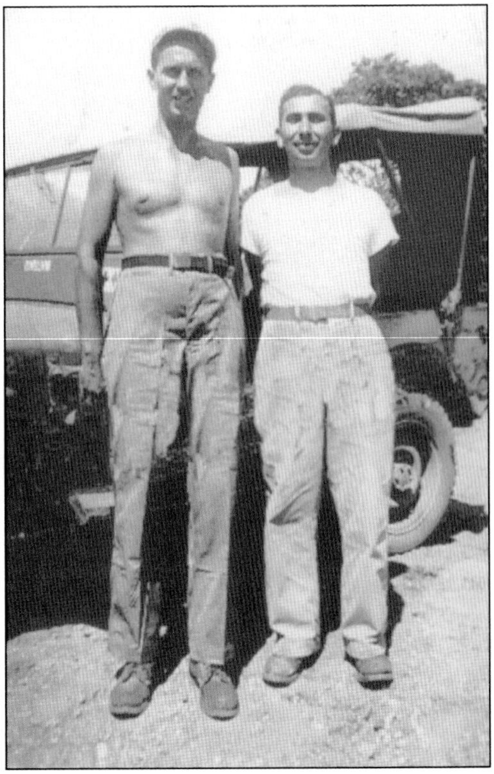

Halfway around the world, two buddies from Roselle Park met at Guadalcanal in 1943. Sgt. Charles DiStefano (right), who served with the 425th Malaria Survey Detachment, 1st Marine Division, ran into James Grinrod (left). After the war, James became co-owner of Grinrod and Hazelhurst Hardware, and Charles became owner of Charlie's Liquor and Grocery Store

Little could they foresee what illustrious dual careers they would embark upon when Herm and Dorothy Shaw honeymooned in the 1920s. Soon they were both well-known and influential teachers of Roselle Park students. Herm became the athletic coach and all sports director, leading many of his varied teams to championships. Dorothy taught high school Spanish for 38 years, including 15 years as head of the Foreign Language Department.

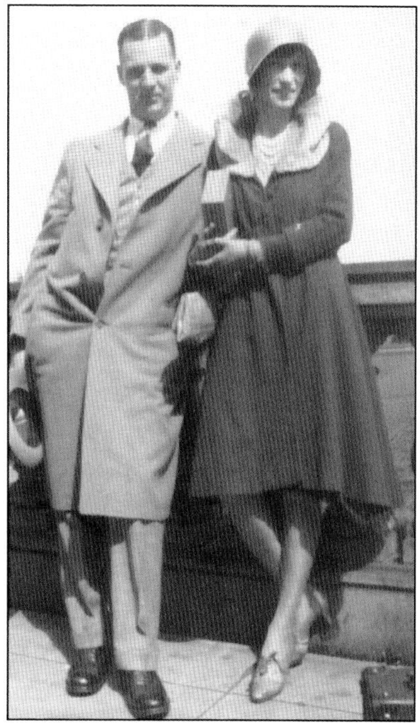

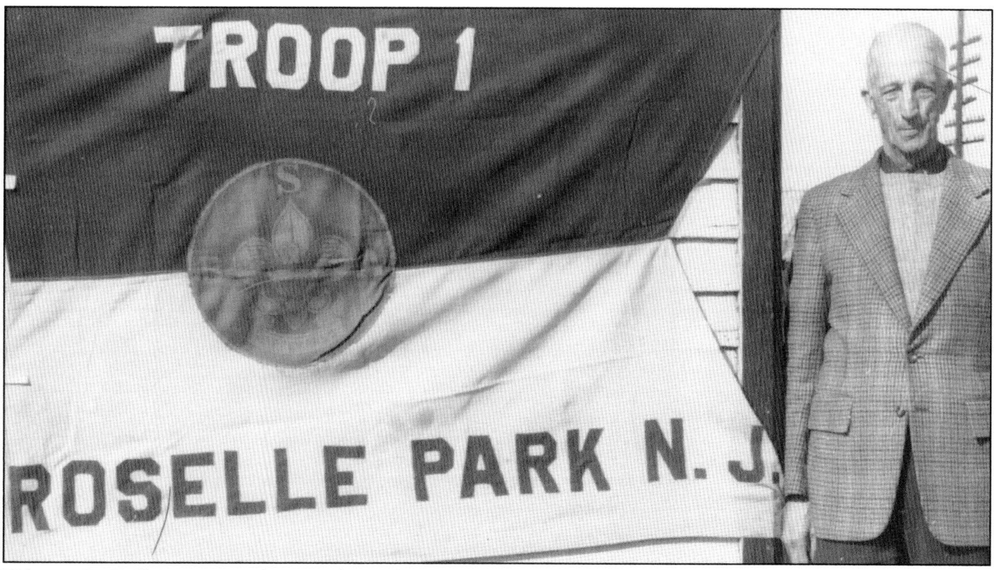

Elliott C. Dill Jr., an early member of Boy Scout Troop No. 1, was awarded the Distinguished Eagle Award, an honor bestowed on a person who has been an Eagle Scout for at least 25 years and has distinguished himself in his career and public life. He lived by the Boy Scout philosophy of working hard and being active in community service. Boy Scout Troop No. 1 was chartered in Roselle Park on February 12, 1912. During World War I, only 32 members raised $85,600 in five liberty loan drives. In 1926, the troop lost its coveted No. 1 designation due to redistricting, and was reassigned the number 52. Elliott and Gertrude Dill were active members of the community. Mrs. Dill is warmly remembered by Woods School alumni as their fifth grade teacher. Mr. Dill owned Bachman-Veghte Fuel, located on the historic site of Thomas A. Edison's laboratory in Roselle.

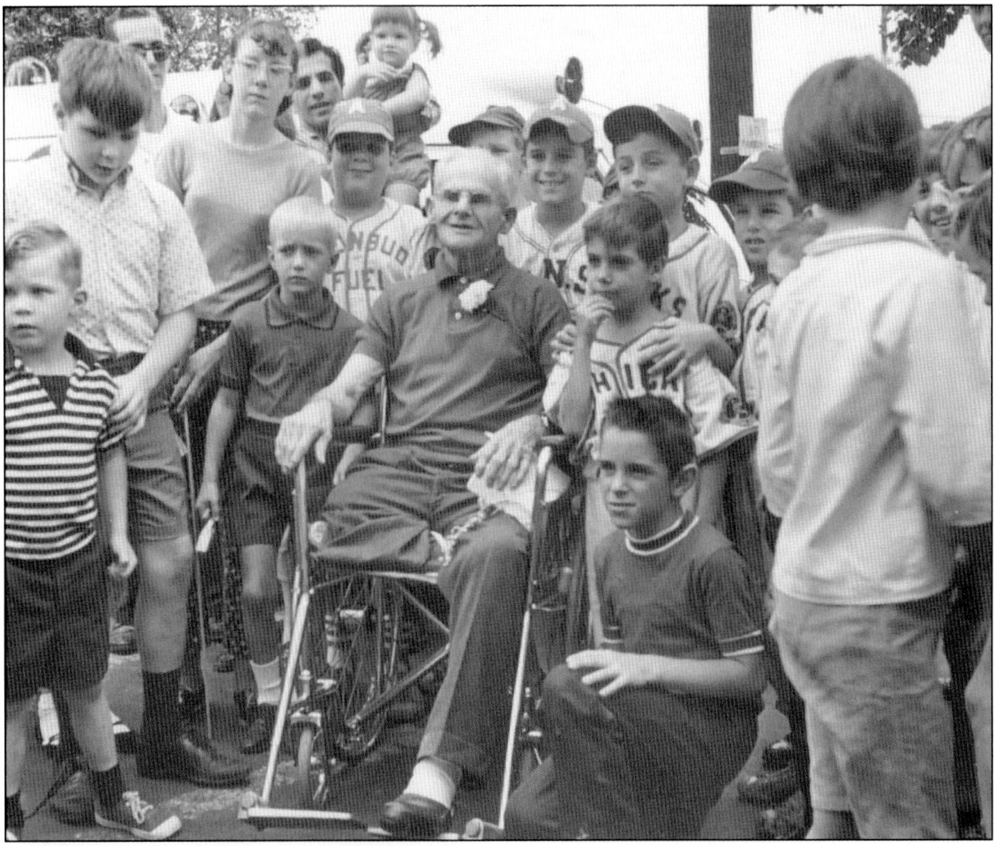

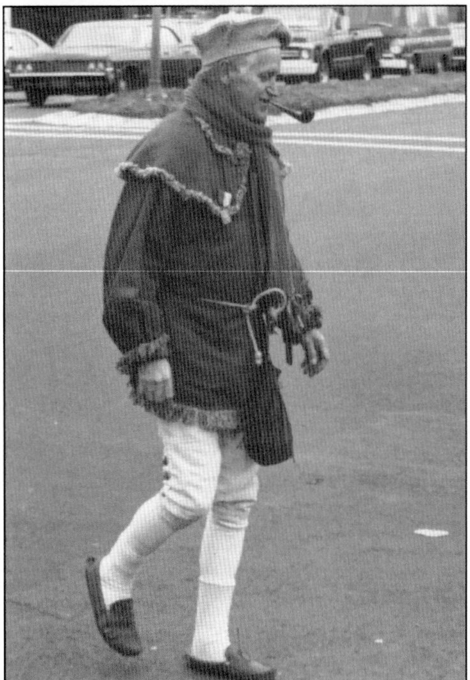

Always surrounded by youngsters, Eddie "Hot Dog" Acker was proud of his lifelong popularity with children. He could be seen driving boys and girls to and from softball games, and in parades in his Model A Ford Woody station wagon. In 1966, "Hot Dog" Acker Park was dedicated to him. Some of his devoted young friends who were there included Tom and Jim Cummings, Gene Antonucci, and Jim, Joe, and John Tumblety.

Oblivious to 20th-century traffic crawling along East Westfield Avenue and Walnut Street behind him, Dave Keenan, dressed in colonial garb, leads fellow historians in a reenactment of Washington's retreat through the borough.

Three

Learning and Praying

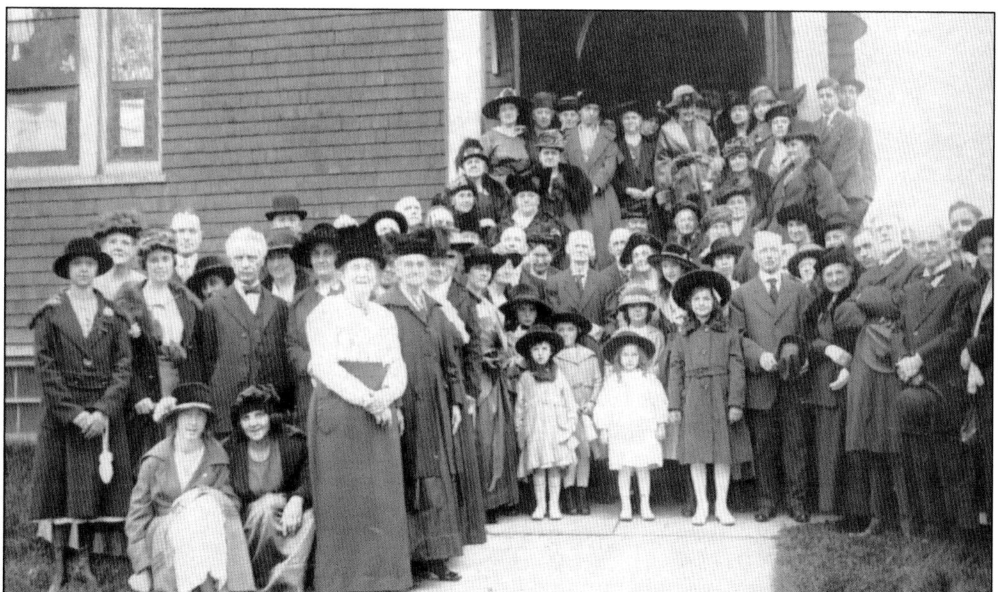

The members of the congregation gathered in their Sunday best at the East Grant Avenue entrance of the First Methodist Episcopal Church. The earliest founders met on Sunday afternoons in private living rooms. In 1871, members worshiped under the leadership of the Rev. L.R. Dunn of Elizabeth at the Cedar Grove District School No. 4. A year later, their first chapel was built at Chestnut Street and East Grant Avenue. Within a few decades, 175 parishioners and 226 Sunday schoolers regularly attended services. In 1968, the church combined with the Evangelical United Brethren Church and changed the name to Community United Methodist Church of Roselle Park.

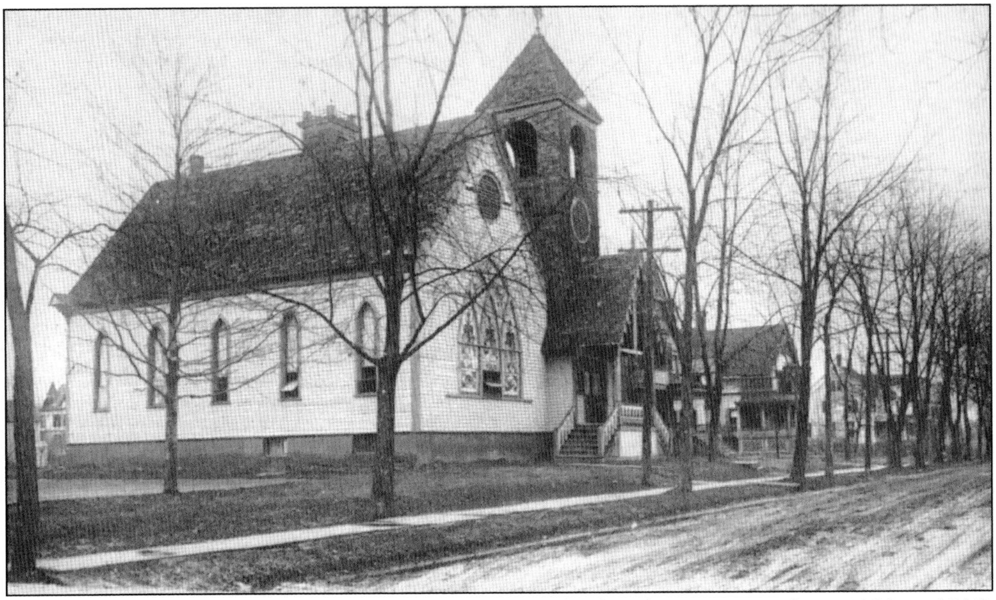

The second building of the First Methodist Episcopal Church was in use from 1900 to 1915. Originally, property had been donated by Jeremiah Eighnue, and its first building was dedicated in 1873. Homes on the right were residences of the Potter and Shipman families, leaders in the fledgling community. Grant Avenue was still a dirt road. A note on this postcard addressed to Rev. Ralph E. Pearce reads, "Showing a corner of the tennis courts where I will play this summer. ME."

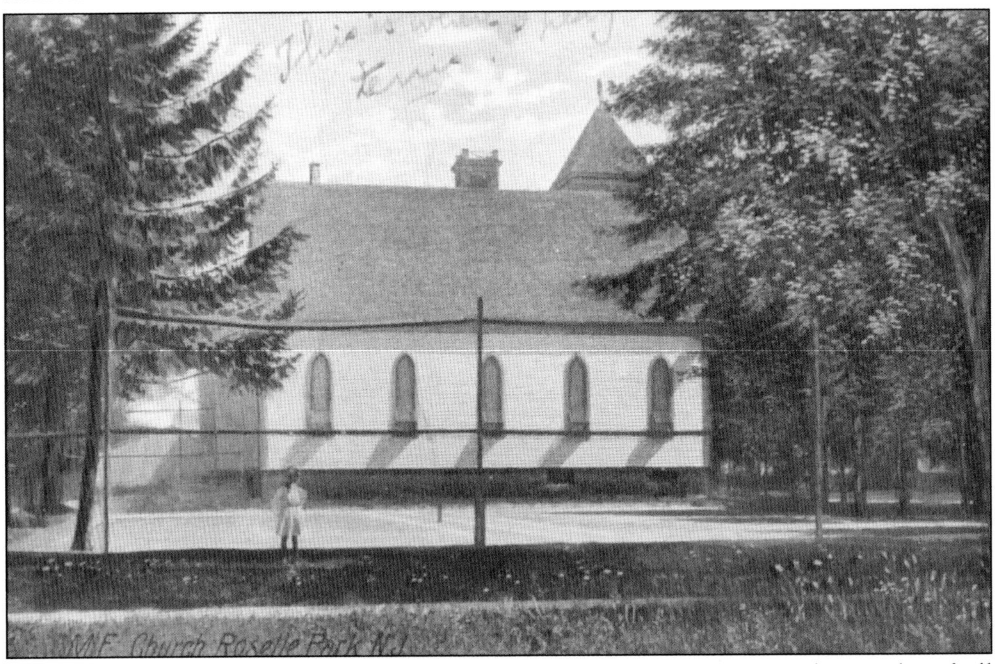

Varied sports activities were offered by the Methodist Church to keep the youths of all denominations busy. Many old-timers from all sections of town remember playing basketball in their gymnasium. This postcard, dated September 14, 1907, shows the tennis courts on property that later became the parking lot.

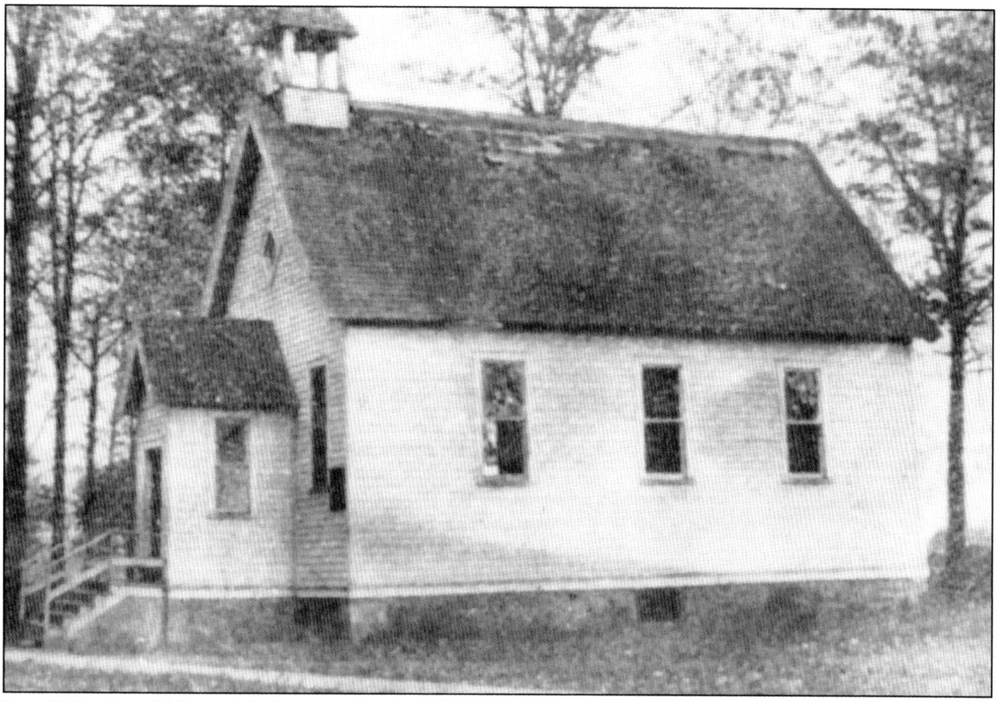

In 1893, the Aldene Methodist Episcopal Church was erected at the corner of Faitoute and Webster Avenues on property donated by Silas Condict (his son's name was Alden). He also donated adjoining property known as Lincoln Park. The frame structure was partially destroyed by fire on October 10, 1905, and the property was sold.

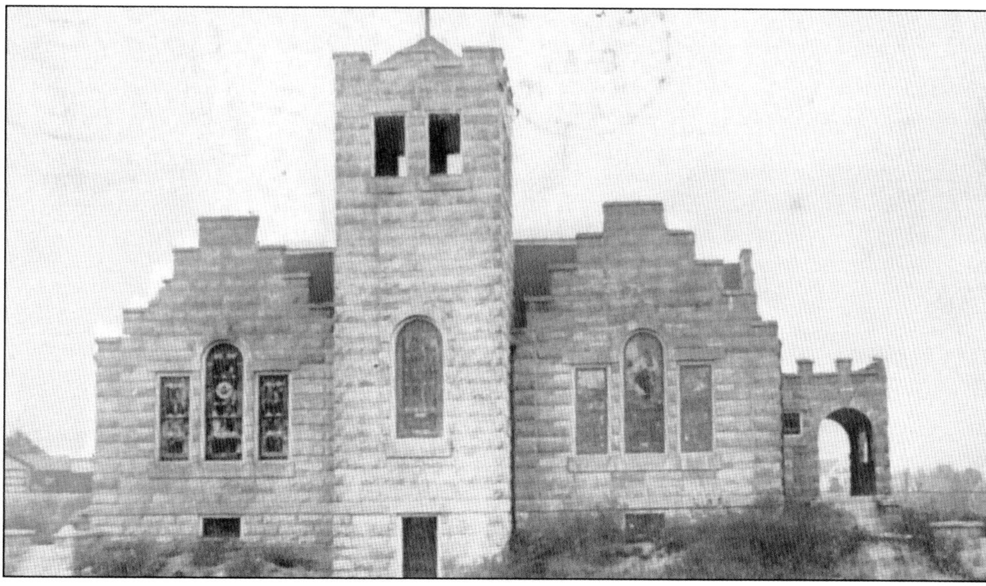

In 1908, a new Aldene Methodist Episcopal Church was erected at Faitoute and Westfield Avenues at a cost of $5,000. By the time the mortgage was paid in 1914, the building had aged due to poor construction, faulty wiring, inferior roof and walls, and its proximity to railroad and highway traffic. The church and property were sold in 1928 for $14,500, and the congregation moved to Roselle to form St. Paul's Methodist Church.

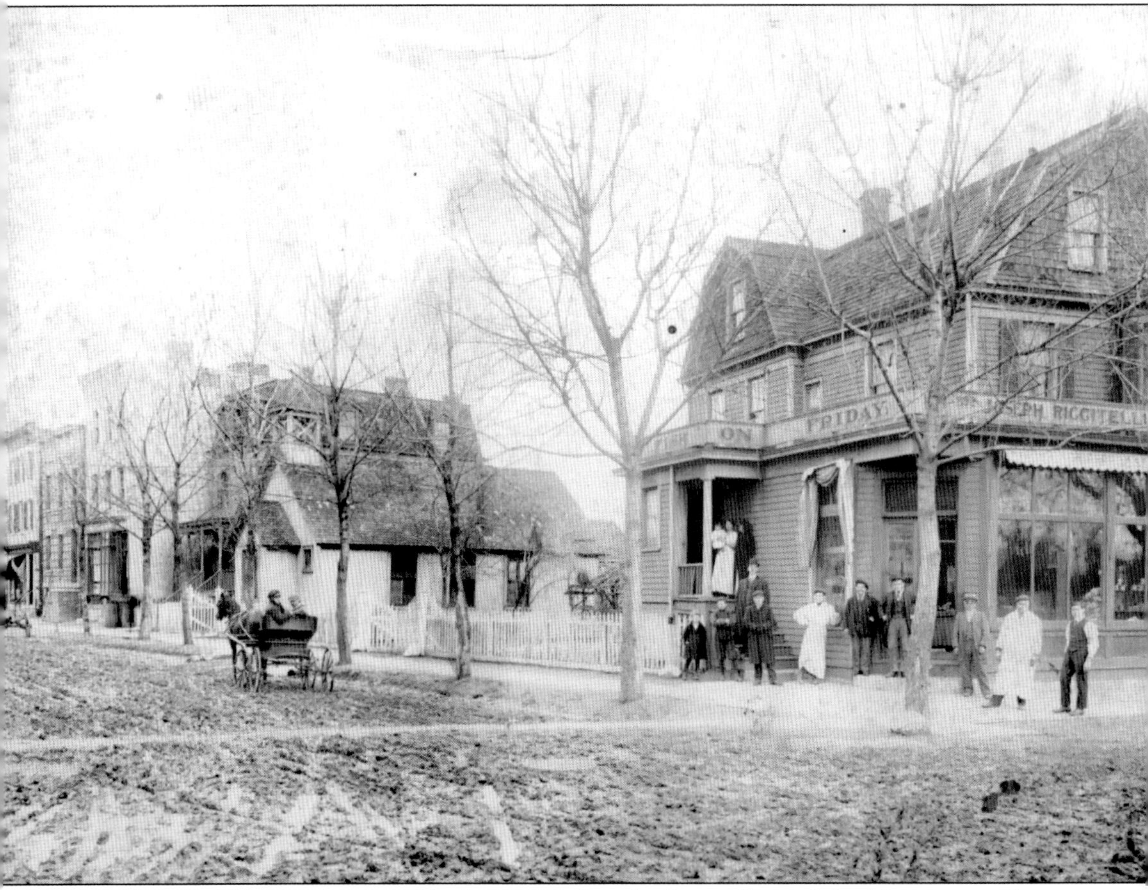

Italian Catholic families, notably the Tomasulos, the Riccitellis and the Marianos, wishing to practice their faith, felt the need of a priest speaking their native language. A tiny building on Chestnut Place behind Riccitelli's meat market was donated by him to start the parish. The Church of Assumption parish was incorporated on January 15, 1907, with Fr. Cataldo Alessi as pastor. Note the "Fish on Friday" sign. The street was renamed Columbus Place, and the church building was later occupied by the Viking Plumbing and Heating Supply Company.

As the parish grew, the next Church of Assumption was a frame building that seated 200 worshippers. It was erected in 1911 on then unpaved West Westfield Avenue at Coolidge Place (later renamed Chiego Place). Here, the First Holy Communion Day is recorded in that year. The gentleman at the far right has been identified as the first police chief, Simon Bermingham. The Feast of Assumption was an annual event celebrated with a week-long carnival in Riccatelli's field behind the meat market, under the direction of Rev. Salvatore J. LoVecchio, who served from 1910 to 1943.

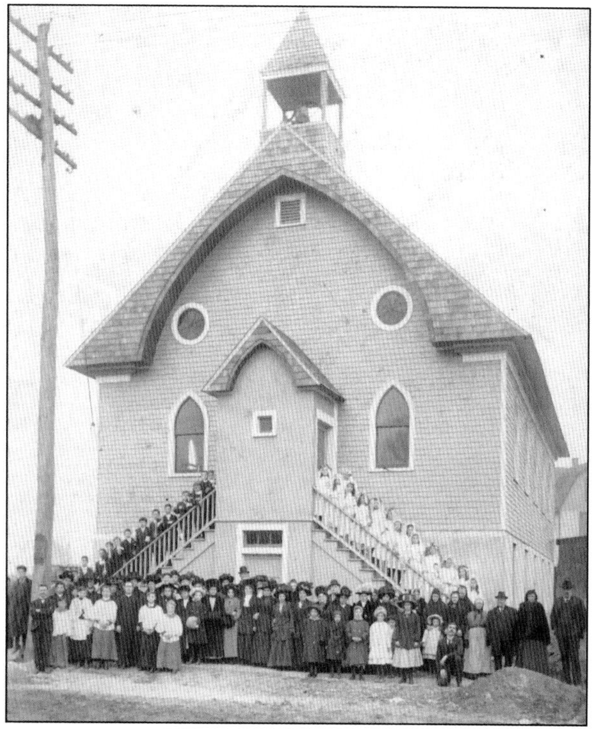

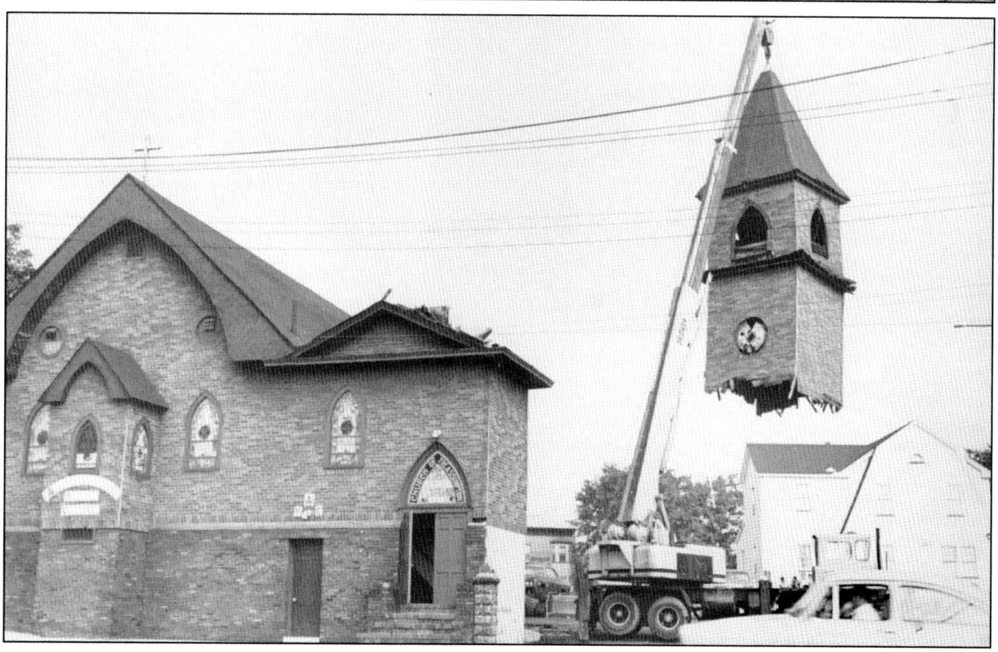

An enclosed staircase replaced the outside stairs in 1916. In 1971, the bell tower was removed. On August 20, 1955, a larger, modern, brick edifice was dedicated across the street, which replaced this building . This structure was modified to accommodate the Father Chiego Youth Center, and later served as a senior citizens center. The white frame house in the right background, which once served as the rectory, later saw use as a Catechism instruction center, after a rectory was added to the modern church.

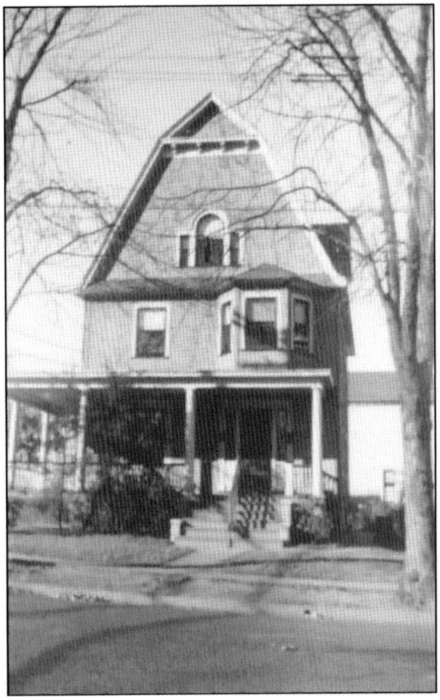

The Cornerstone Mission was incorporated on April 8, 1938, under the direction of Florence Ely, who preached at meetings held in a house at 63 West Clay Avenue. The Sunday school was well attended. The congregation supported missions for the blind, missions to the Jews, missions in India, and Rev. James Riccatelli's mission in West Africa. The Cornerstone Mission later became a Christian Jewish mission.

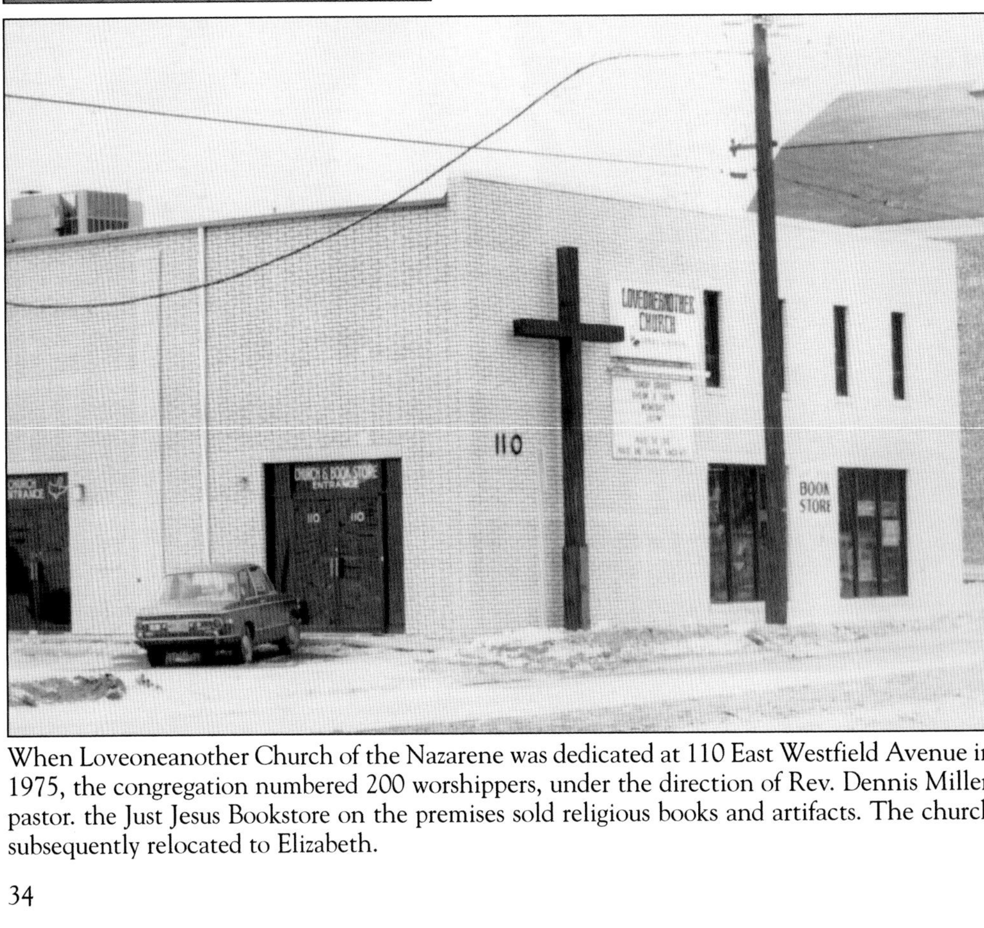

When Loveoneanother Church of the Nazarene was dedicated at 110 East Westfield Avenue in 1975, the congregation numbered 200 worshippers, under the direction of Rev. Dennis Miller, pastor. the Just Jesus Bookstore on the premises sold religious books and artifacts. The church subsequently relocated to Elizabeth.

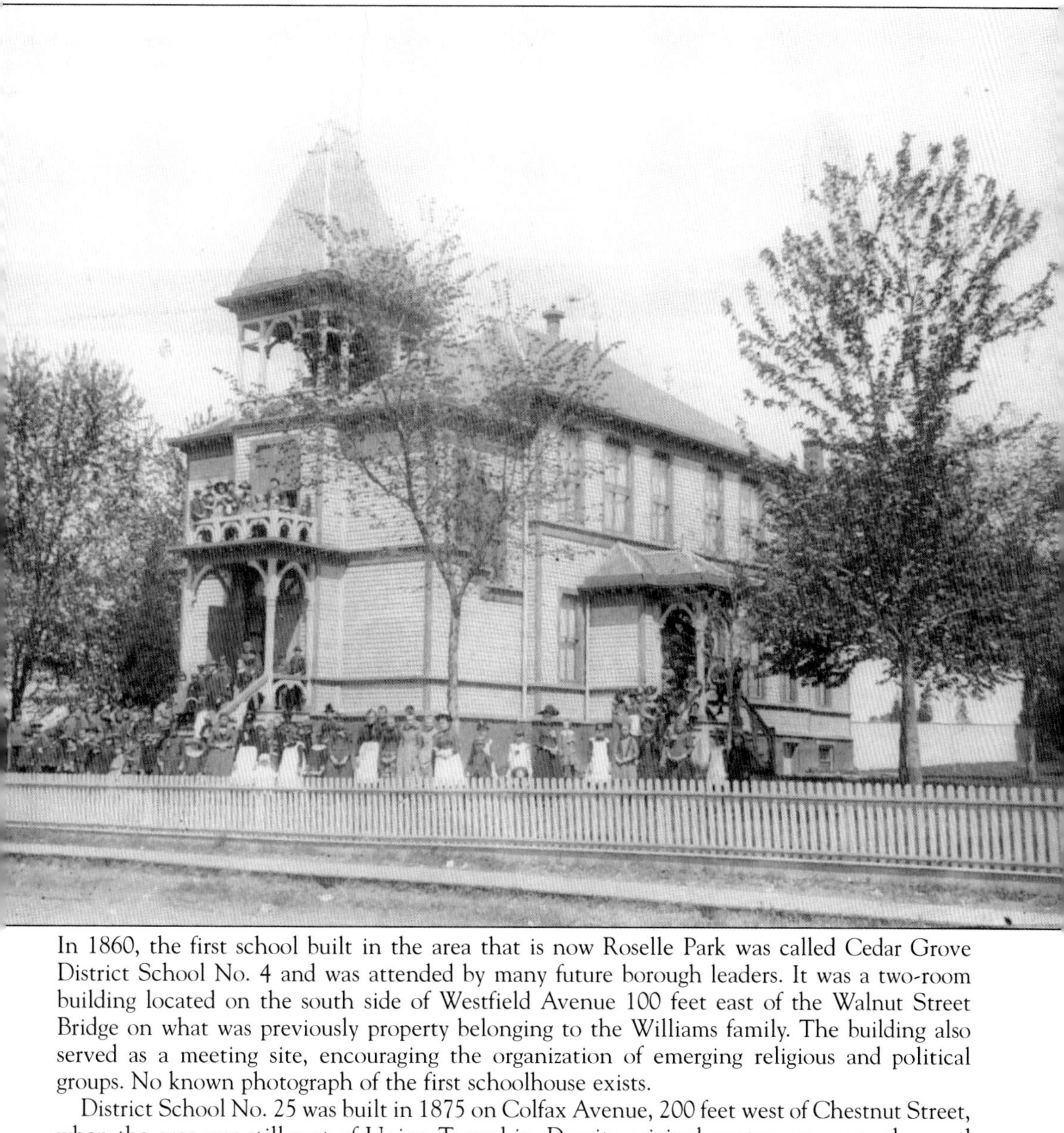

In 1860, the first school built in the area that is now Roselle Park was called Cedar Grove District School No. 4 and was attended by many future borough leaders. It was a two-room building located on the south side of Westfield Avenue 100 feet east of the Walnut Street Bridge on what was previously property belonging to the Williams family. The building also served as a meeting site, encouraging the organization of emerging religious and political groups. No known photograph of the first schoolhouse exists.

District School No. 25 was built in 1875 on Colfax Avenue, 200 feet west of Chestnut Street, when the area was still part of Union Township. Despite original controversy as to the need for a large school in this remote section, expanding population demanded that a two-room wing be added in 1890. It was renamed Livingston School in honor of one of New Jersey's first governors. By 1901, some 350 students were enrolled—elementary through a two-year high school. Teachers included Esther Shilton, Jeannette Clark, and Lydia Waite. The last graduating class, in 1908, consisted of six pupils.

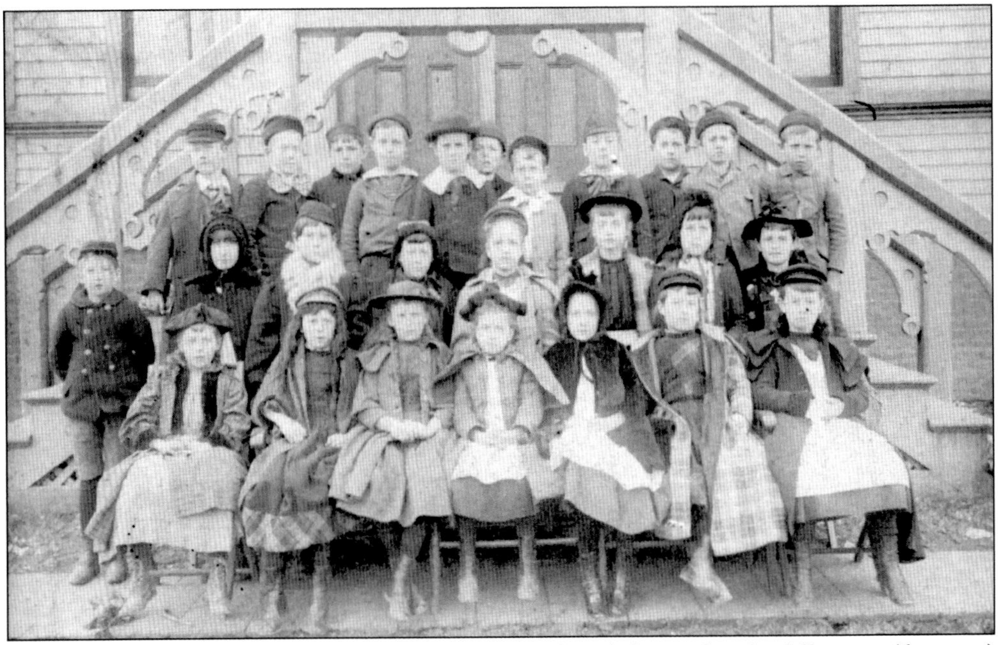

This c. 1889 class at the Livingston School includes, from left to right, the following: (first row) Ida Crane, Millie Hart, Effie McCloud, Grace Cummings, Hattie Swick, Bessie TenEyck, and Grace Earl; (second row) Arthur Cook, Susy Willis, Ida Bonnell, A. Edith Kingsland, Helen Andrus, Elsie Bender, Annie Ratchford, and Florence Stryker; (third row) Willie Potter, Alfred Abrams, Douglas Cook, Louis Bogart, Alec Cummings, Bertram Hart, Ernest Ostermann, Arthur Oakley, Harry Klein, John Stryker, and Ernest Fidler.

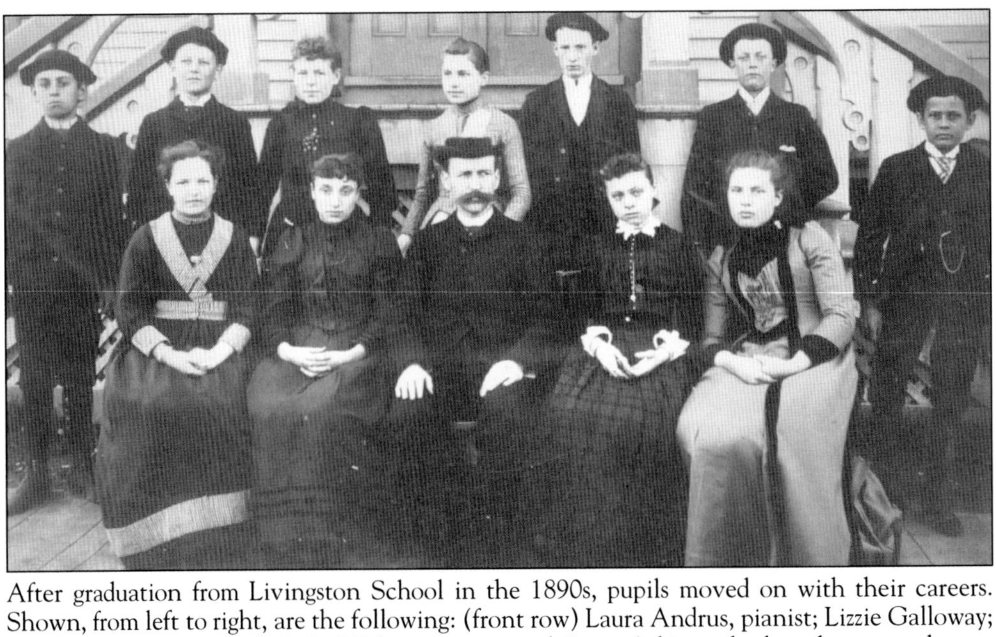

After graduation from Livingston School in the 1890s, pupils moved on with their careers. Shown, from left to right, are the following: (front row) Laura Andrus, pianist; Lizzie Galloway; Mr. Armstrong, principal; Sadie Welton, pianist; and Grace Atkins, who later became a doctor; (back row) Spencer Higgins, who later became a doctor; Waldo Denton; Marion Hunt; Agnes Bogart; Ed Ming; George Peck, who became a Baptist minister; and Sam Paterson.

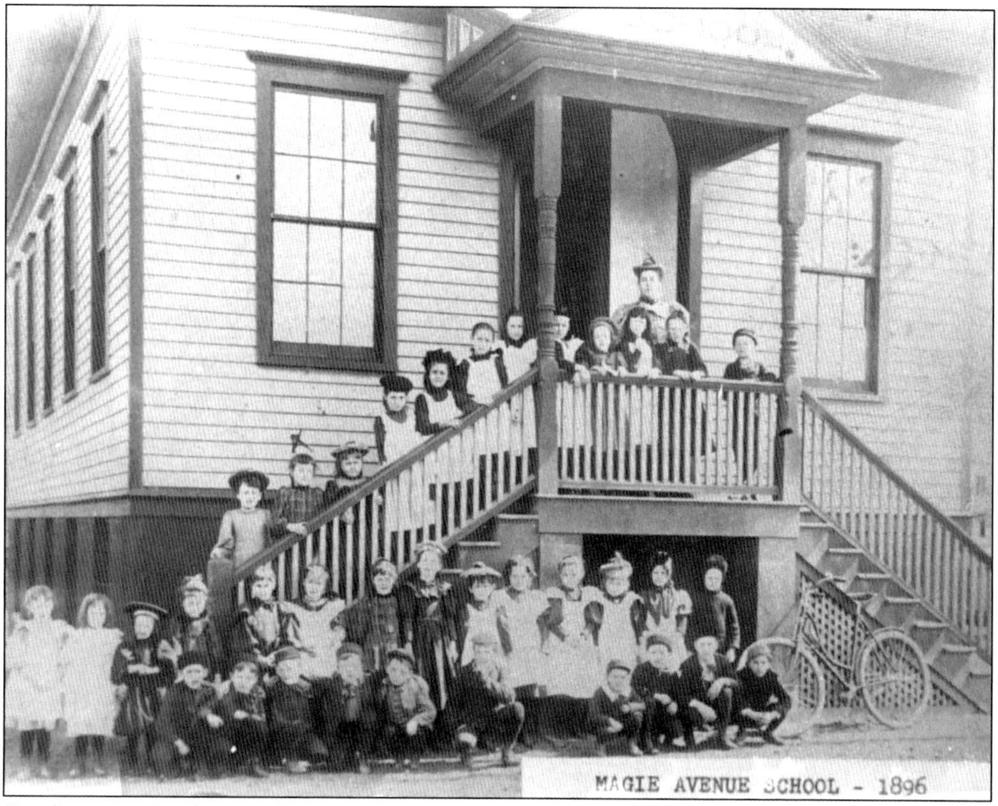

On the east side of town, the Magie Avenue School taught the three Rs to local children before Sherman School was built in 1912. The small, two-room building at 225–227 Magie Avenue was later separated into two residences. This photograph is dated 1896.

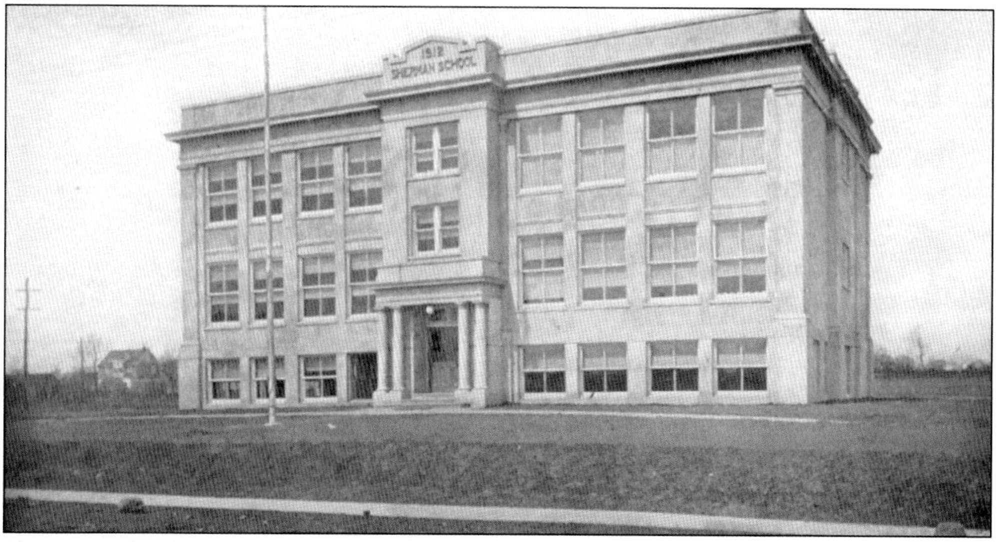

Sherman School, which replaced the Magie Avenue School, was built on East Grant Avenue between Sherman and Sheridan Avenues in 1912 and dedicated on November 1, 1913. Walter Elicker, the first principal, taught fourth grade. In 1927, six new classrooms and an auditorium were added. Part of the basement was later used for offices and the multipurpose "Green Room."

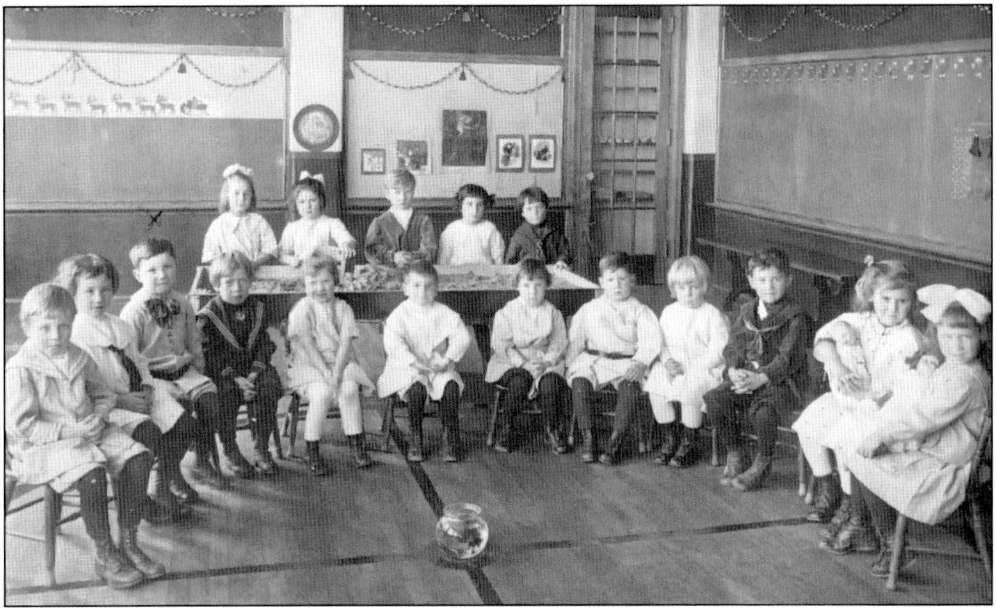

Ed Richards, the third pupil from the left, recalls that Sherman School's first kindergarten class of 1913–1914 started in a room over Bender's butcher shop: "When the new school was ready, they moved down Sheridan Avenue, each child carrying their little chair plus as much paper etc. that could be placed on it. No complaints from parents. They thought it was 'wonderful.'"

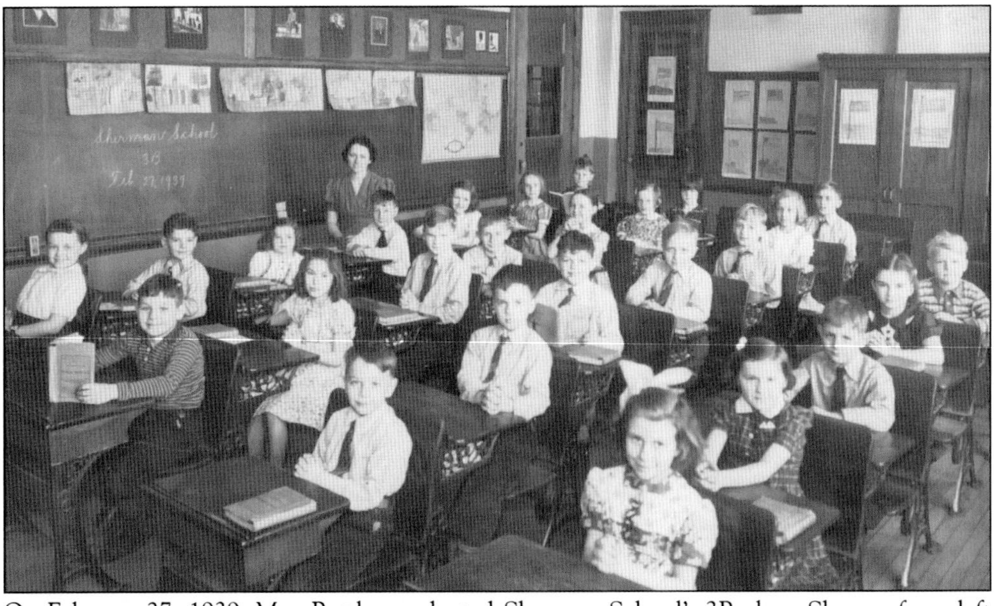

On February 27, 1939, Mrs. Bettle conducted Sherman School's 3B class. Shown, from left to right, are the following: (first row) Janet Gucker, unidentified, Edward Woodruff, Lucille Connors, and Alex Sheden; (second row) George Fischer, Fred Steffins, Chubby Birmingham, George Evans, Charles Rolff, Pat Murray, and Jack Torbush; (third row) Gordon Nobbs, Berta Imerman, Stewart ?, Robert Roth, Hazel Kay, Jean Schmidt, and Olive ?; (fourth row) Betty Finwall, Frank Schneider, ? Burdett, Edgar Mueller, Tessie Battell, Jane ?, and Mark Balanger.

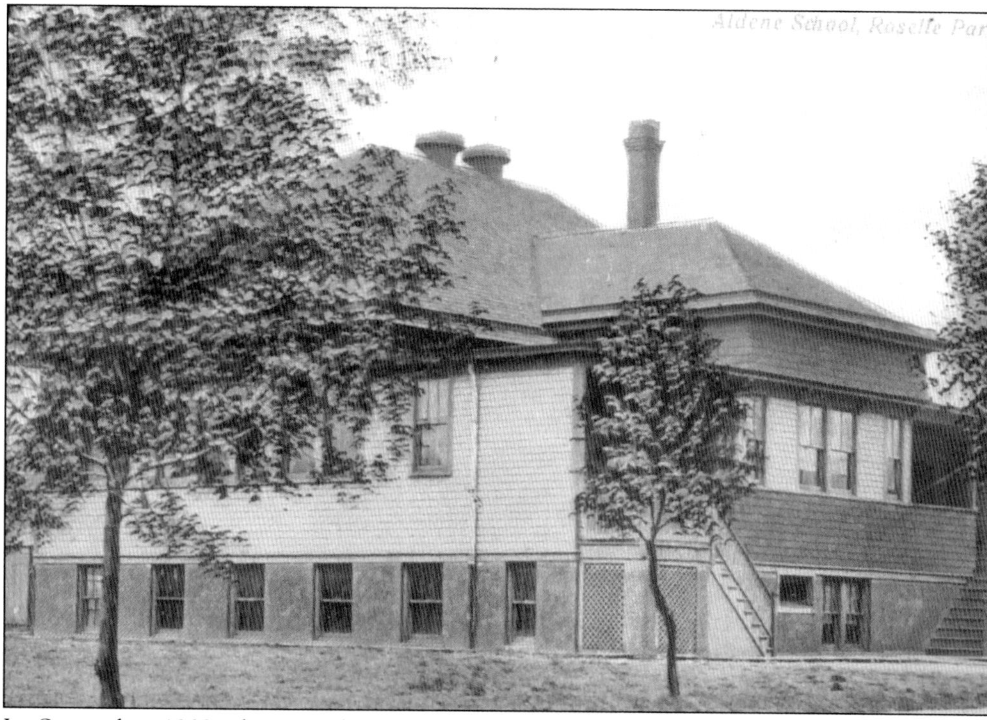

In September 1902, the Lincoln School on West Webster and Willow Avenues enrolled elementary students up to the fourth grade. Two classrooms were on the lower floor. On the upper floor was an assembly room, used for school parties, dances, and a basketball court. The board of education paid $350 for the land and $5,150 for the schoolhouse, furniture, and equipment. In 1912, the Lincoln School became a romper factory. It was replaced by three multiple-family houses.

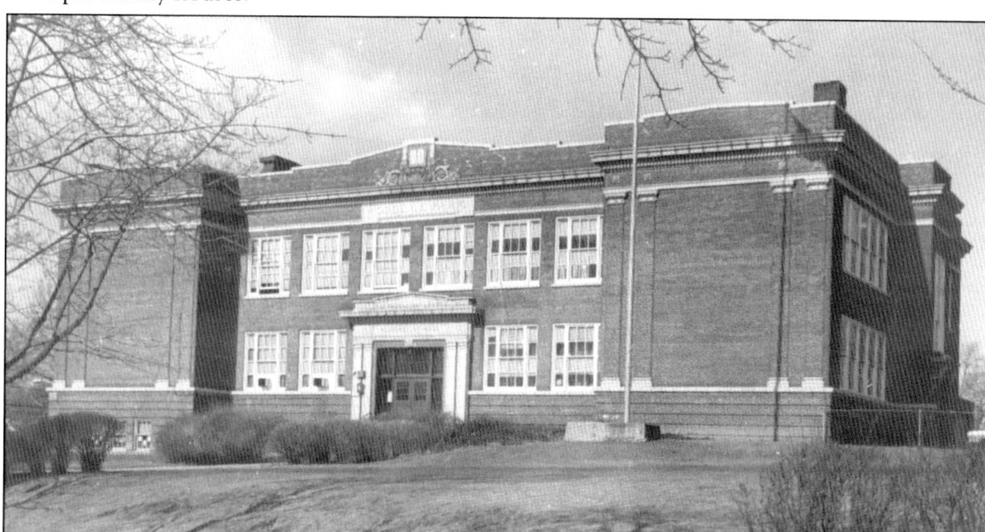

The Aldene School replaced the Lincoln School in 1921. The opening of school had to be delayed one week due to an outbreak of diphtheria. Six classrooms and an auditorium-gymnasium were added in 1952. It was renamed the Aldene-Ernest J. Finizio Elementary School in 1994.

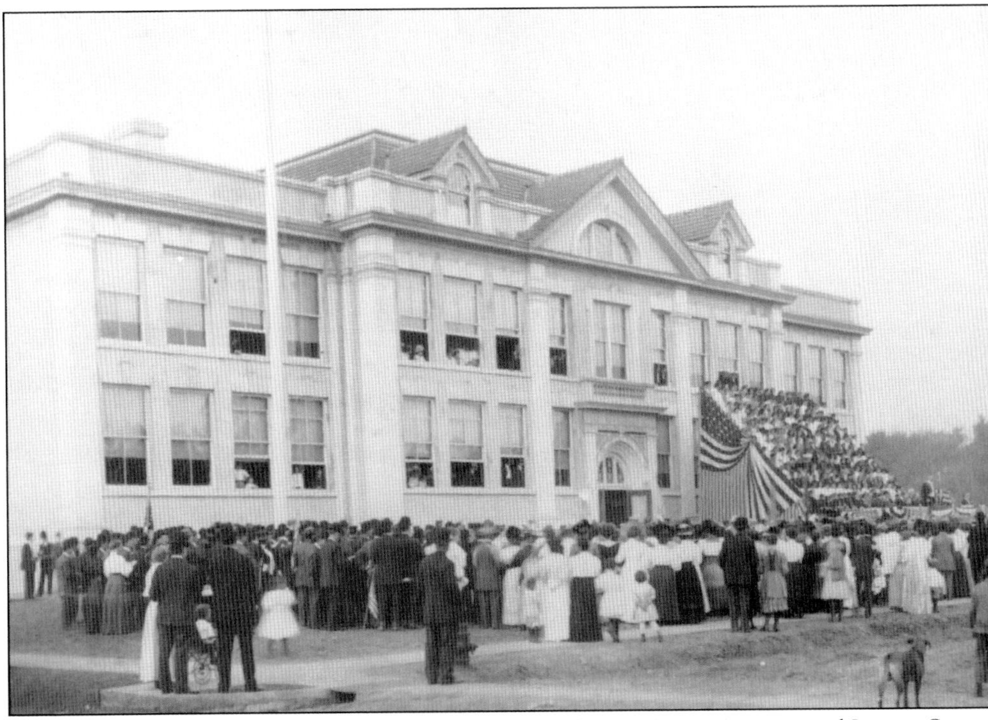

The Robert Gordon School was built on the corner of West Grant Avenue and Locust Street. It was dedicated in 1908 as a combined elementary and high school. It was one of the first buildings constructed of poured concrete, a process developed by Thomas A. Edison. In 1916, it was named after Robert Gordon, one of Roselle Park's first councilmen and president of the board of education. In 1968, the school received a Union County Historic Preservation award for 60 years of continuing use.

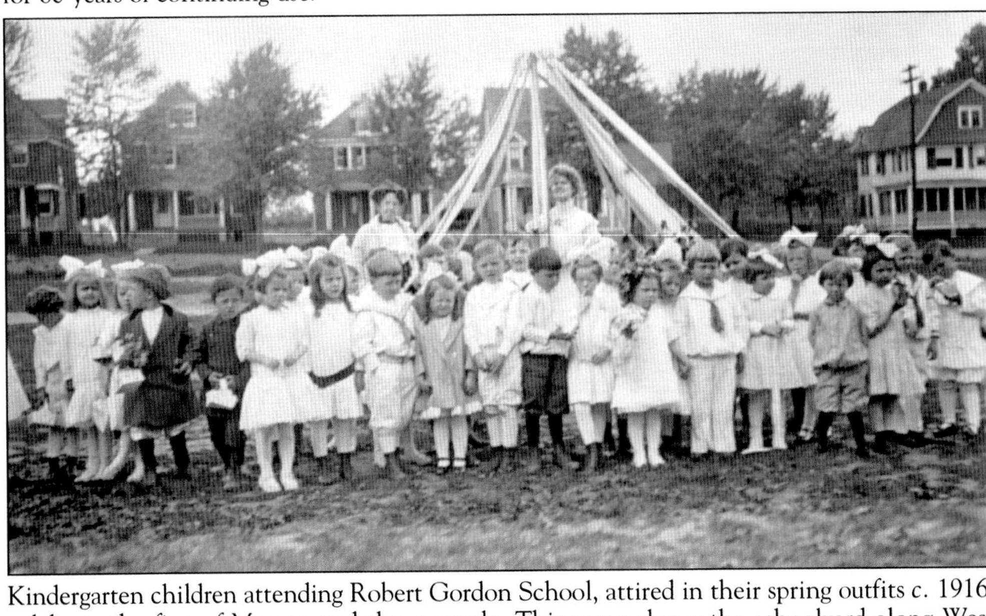

Kindergarten children attending Robert Gordon School, attired in their spring outfits c. 1916, celebrate the first of May around the maypole. This scene shows the schoolyard along West Clay Avenue where Woods School would be soon constructed.

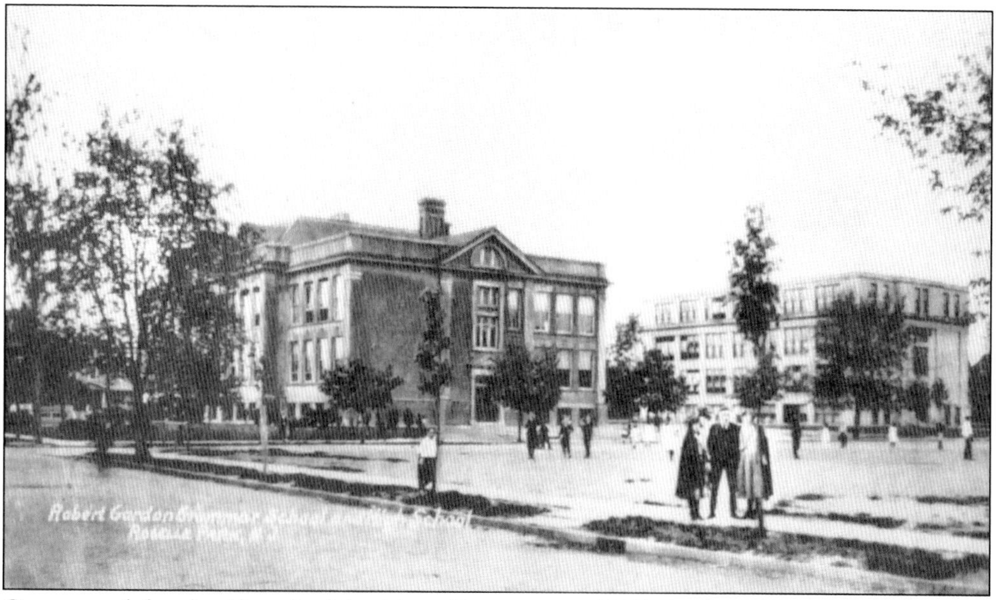

Constructed for the Hercules Munitions Company in 1917 on the corner of Locust Street and West Clay Avenue, the building on the right was dedicated as the high school in 1919. Enrollment included students from Springfield, Garwood, and Kenilworth. Laboratories, commercial classes, and a library were included, but students had to use the adjacent Robert Gordon School for gym, mechanical drawing, and industrial shop. In 1974, it was named for James P. Woods, a distinguished Roselle Park High School graduate.

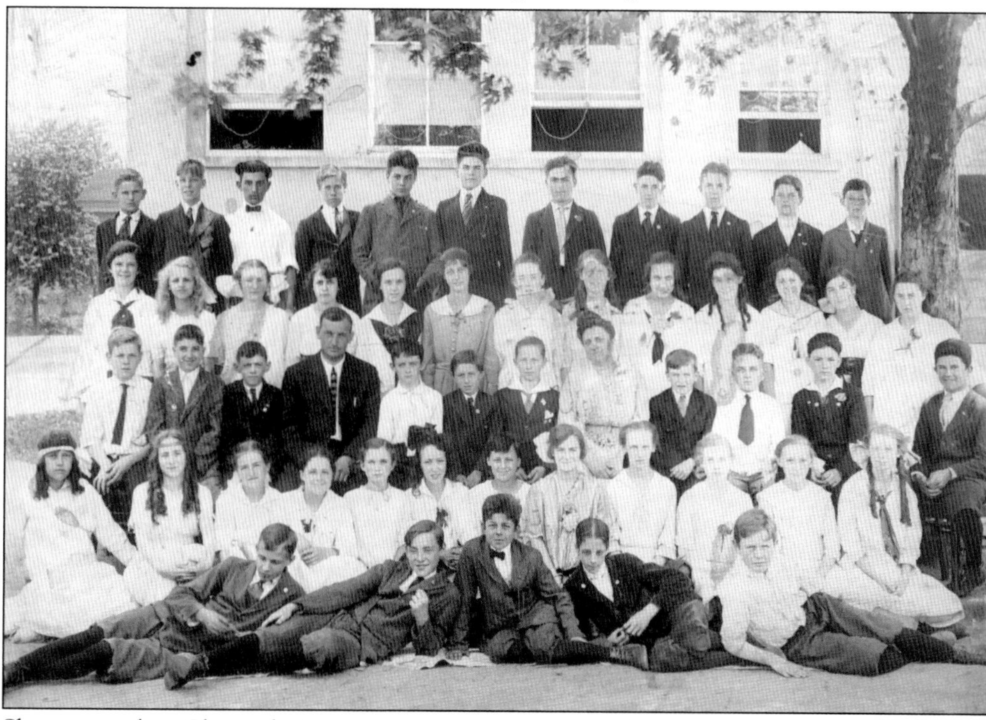

Shown in this Class of 1917 group portrait are eighth grade students of the Robert Gordon School.

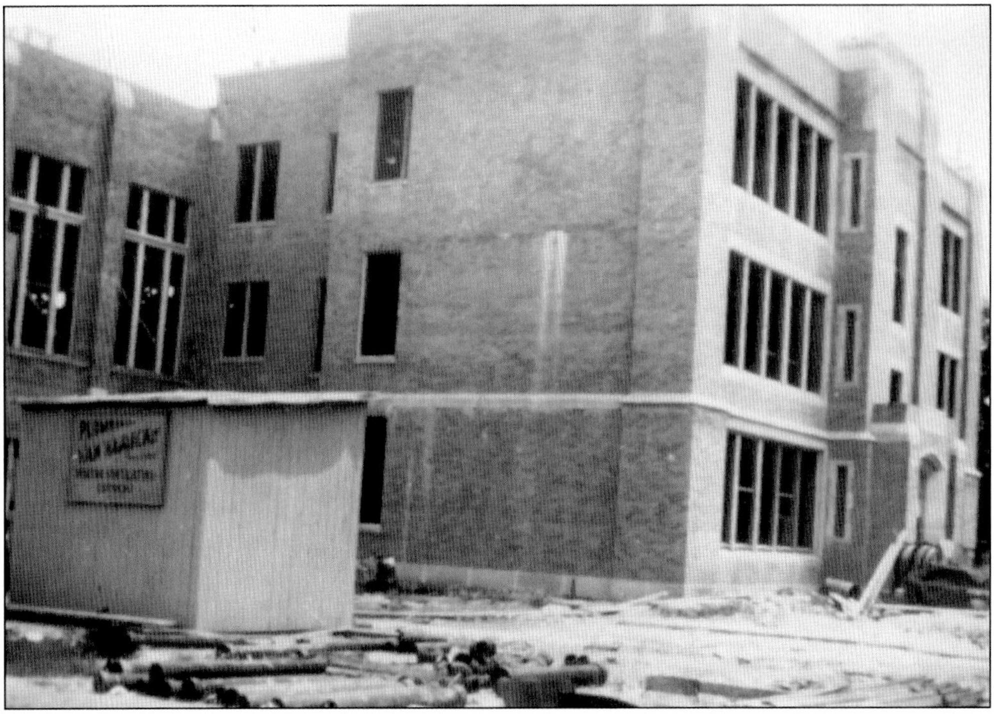

The Roselle Park school system had again grown to a point where additional space was needed. On April 30, 1931, a cornerstone laying ceremony for the new building on West Grant Avenue took place. This photograph, dated July 12, 1931, shows construction under way. Dedication was on December 7, 1931.

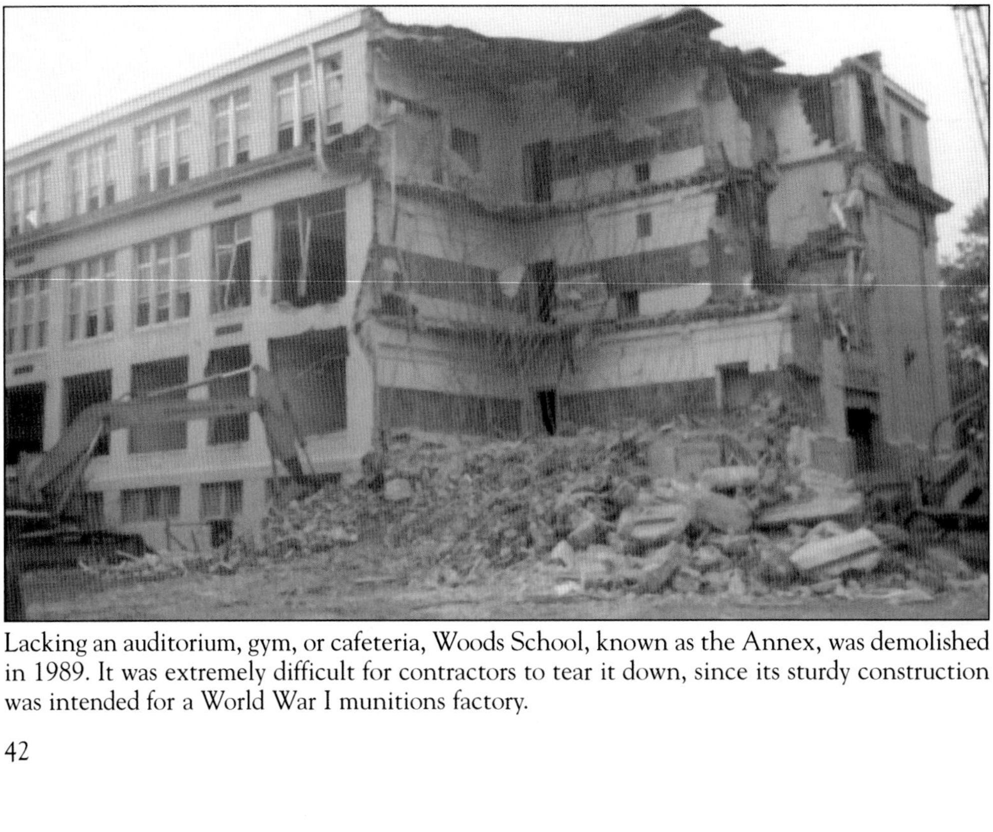

Lacking an auditorium, gym, or cafeteria, Woods School, known as the Annex, was demolished in 1989. It was extremely difficult for contractors to tear it down, since its sturdy construction was intended for a World War I munitions factory.

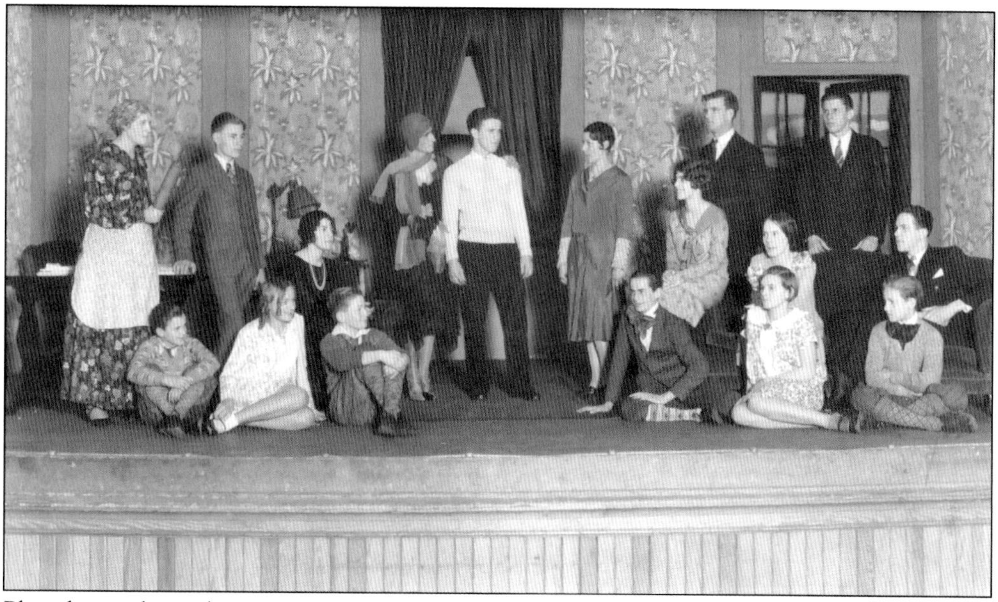

Plays have always been a part of the high school program. Members of the Class of 1930 produced *Fixing it for Father.* It starred Helen Lord as Fauchon La Voude, Marian Brittain as Aunt Lize, William H. Johnston as Harold, Harry Sayer as Elinor, and Thomas Quinn as Billie Merton.

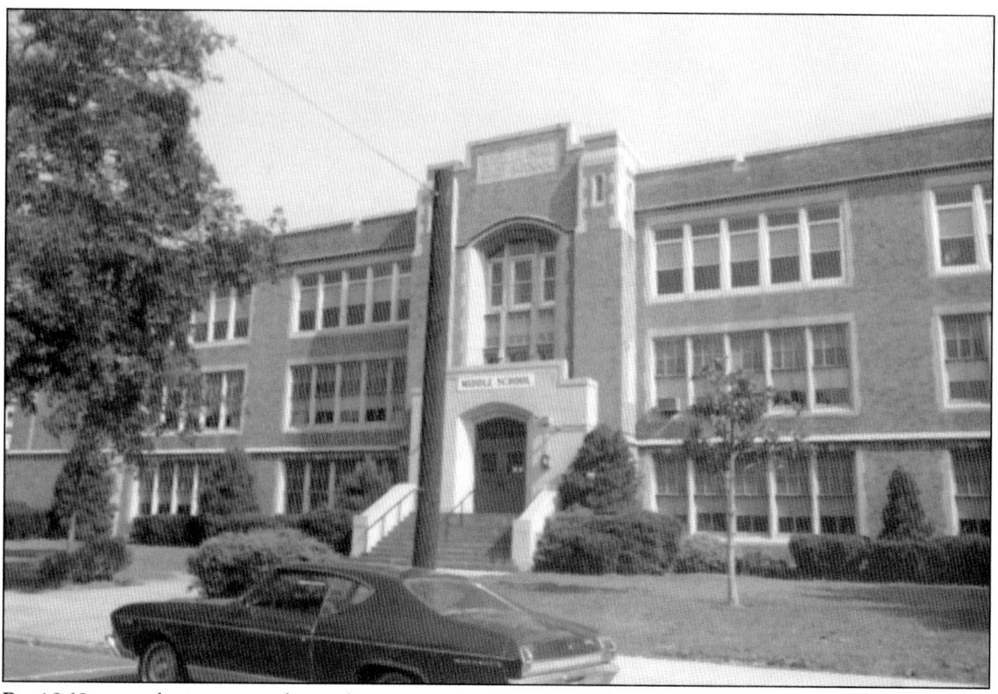

By 1969, population growth made it necessary to move the sixth, seventh, and eighth grades into this building, which became the middle school. Roy Dragon became the principal, with Anthony Basto as vice principal. Although the middle school sign has been added above the entrance, the words carved in cement near the roof, "Roselle Park High School," are still visible decades later.

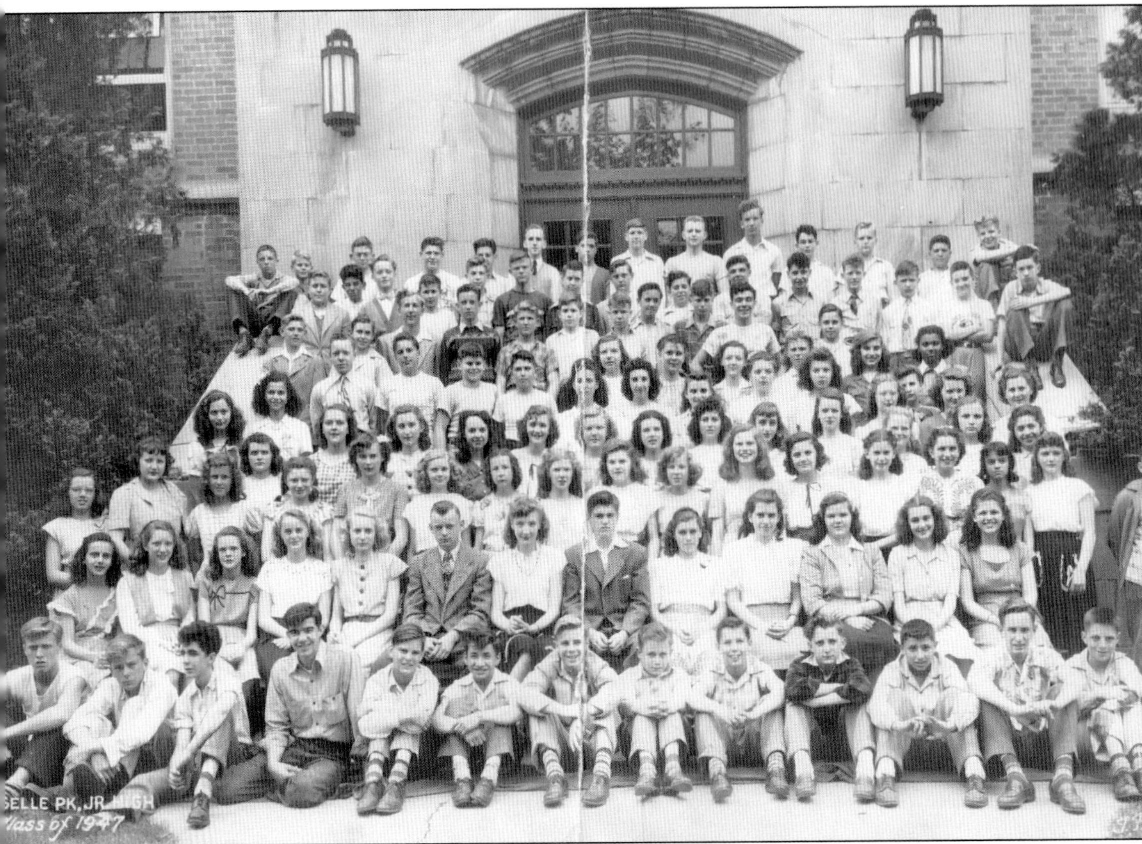

Roselle Park Junior High School Class of 1947 gathers on the steps of Middle School for their picture. Names written on back of this photograph are Joan Yarnall, Barbara Styln, Anne Bennett, Paula Saxer, Margaret Bain, Evelyn Kay, and Carolyn Bates. A generation too young for engagement in World War II, many would go on to become the parents of "Baby Boomers."

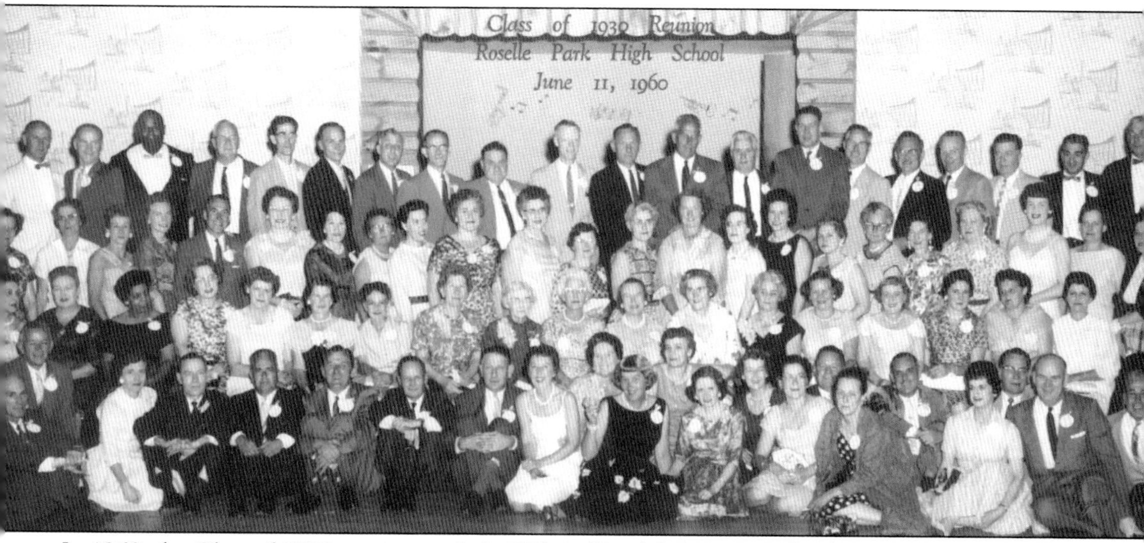

In 1960, the Class of 1930 reunion included Edith (Pete) Johnston, Bill Johnston, Therese Cere Matthews, Elmer Klein, Anne Scheuerman Klein, Thomas Quinn, Norma Quinn, Florence Buck, Mrs. Tom Conrad, Miss Thompson, Lois Fletcher, Elizabeth Wood, Maud Austin, Miss Chapin, Miss Hedley, Ione Stork Woods, Dorothy Shaw, Mrs. Young, Cerinele Vasta, Kathryn Lorcheim, William Brown, James Woods, Tom Conrad, Herm Shaw, George Lorcheim, and Mr. Geehr. Former students of all classes of Roselle Park High School meet annually. Although many still reside within a few miles of their alma mater, others who gather come from all over the world.

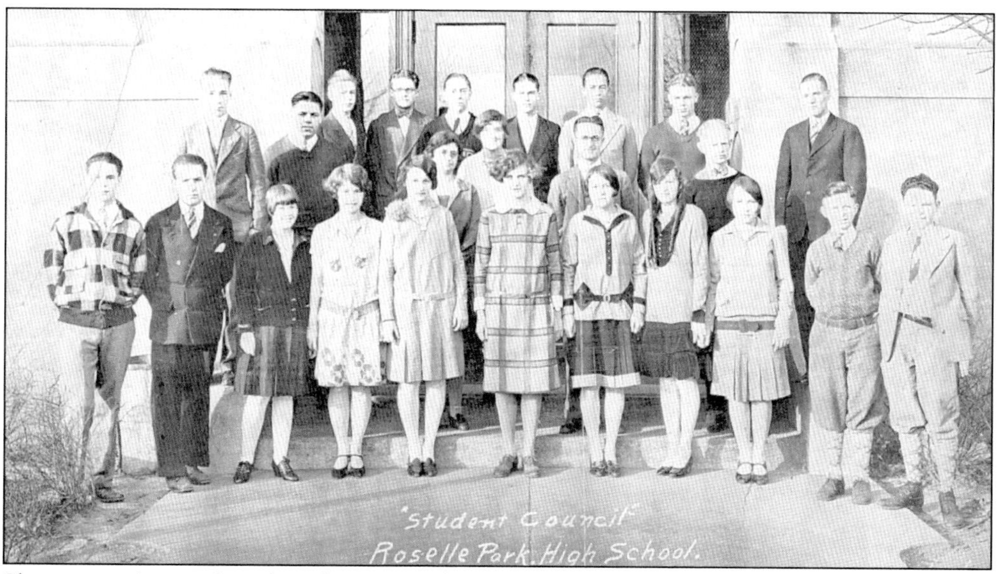

Shown are the combined student councils at the Roselle Park High School in 1928. Those identified are as follows: (first row, center) president Evelyn Gillings; (second row) faculty advisor Liela Chapin and principal G. Hobart Brown.

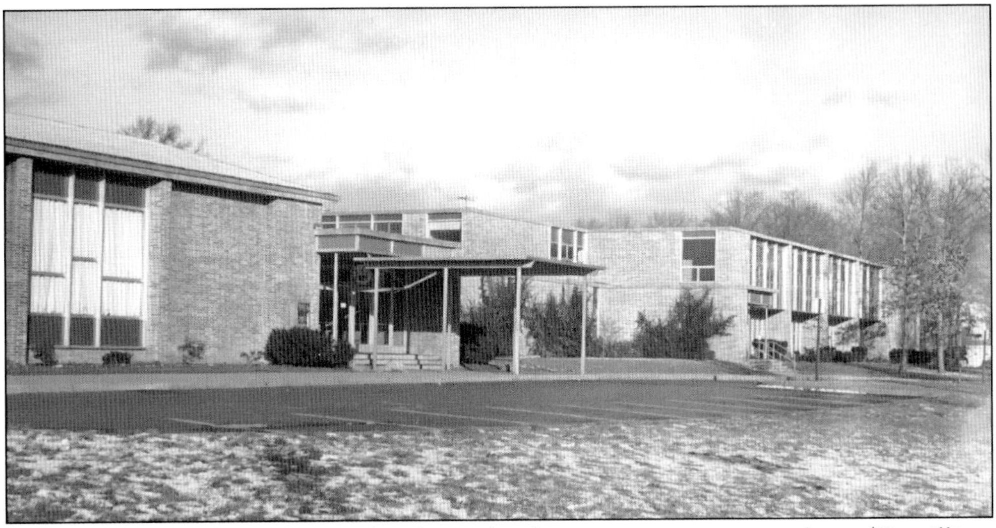

Eight hundred students began the first school term, enjoying a modern, $2 million, 34-classroom Roselle Park High School by September 9, 1963. The West Webster Avenue campus boasted a foreign language department; a library; gymnasiums; guidance, student activity, and visual aid centers; a 500-seat auditorium; a 450-seat cafeteria; and competitive sports fields.

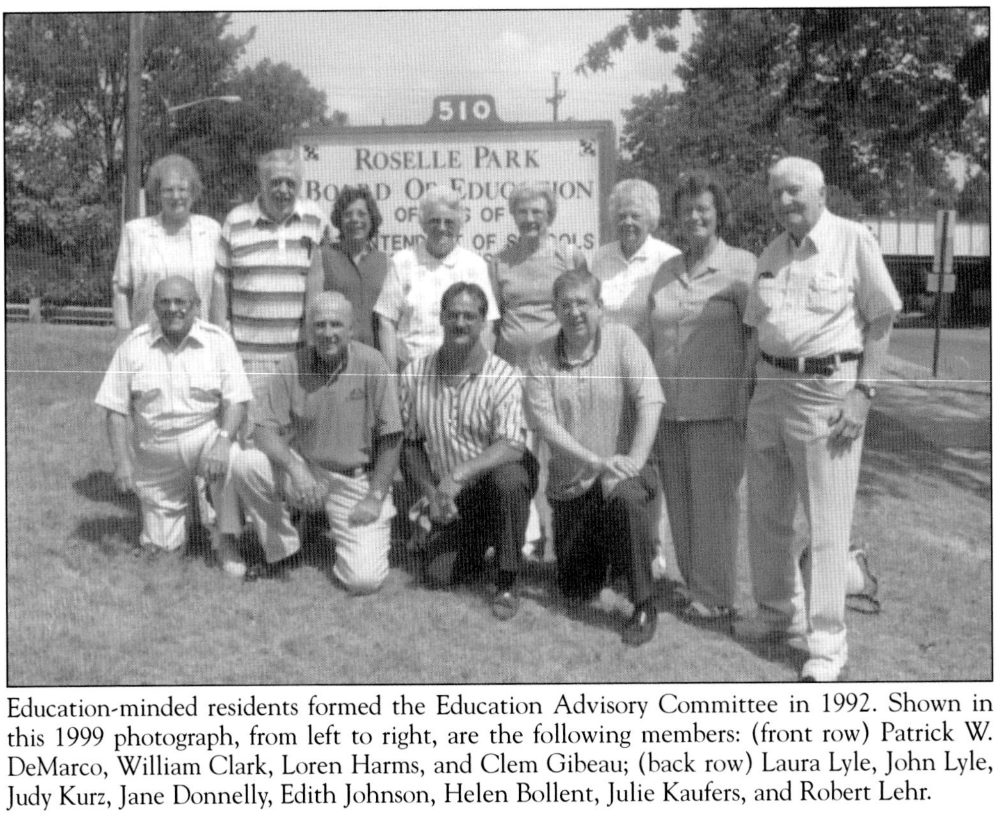

Education-minded residents formed the Education Advisory Committee in 1992. Shown in this 1999 photograph, from left to right, are the following members: (front row) Patrick W. DeMarco, William Clark, Loren Harms, and Clem Gibeau; (back row) Laura Lyle, John Lyle, Judy Kurz, Jane Donnelly, Edith Johnson, Helen Bollent, Julie Kaufers, and Robert Lehr.

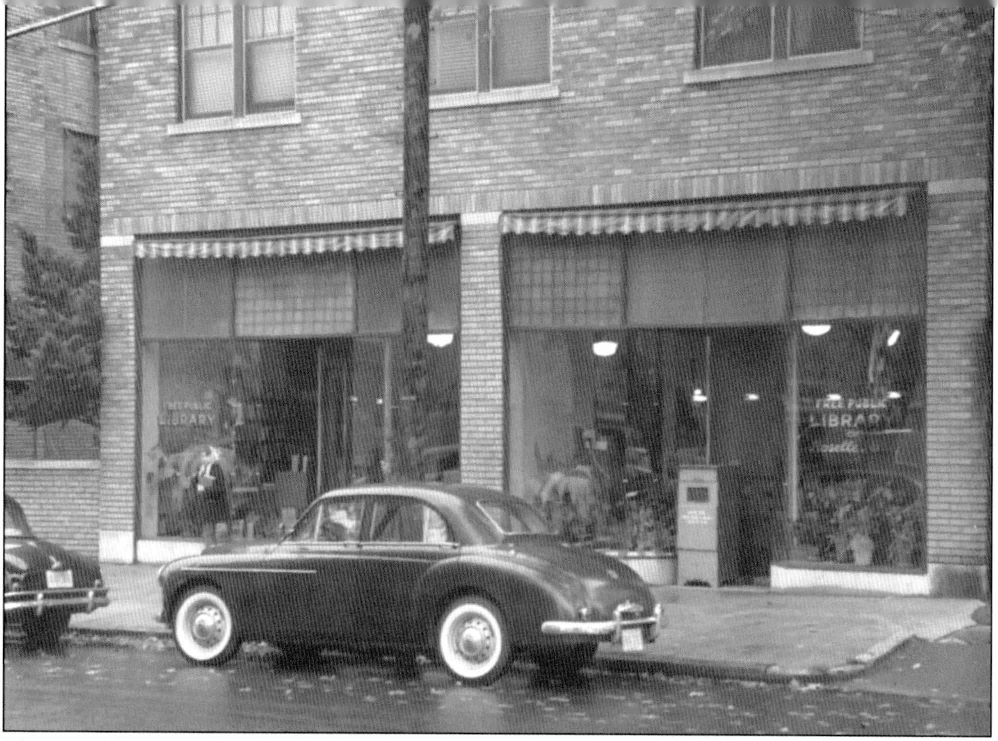

This storefront in the Washington Apartments on Chestnut Street was used as the first free public library. Opened to the public on April 1, 1930, with the help of a few volunteers and donated books, it became a popular meeting place during the Depression. Years later, Dr. Lester Burman had a dental practice there.

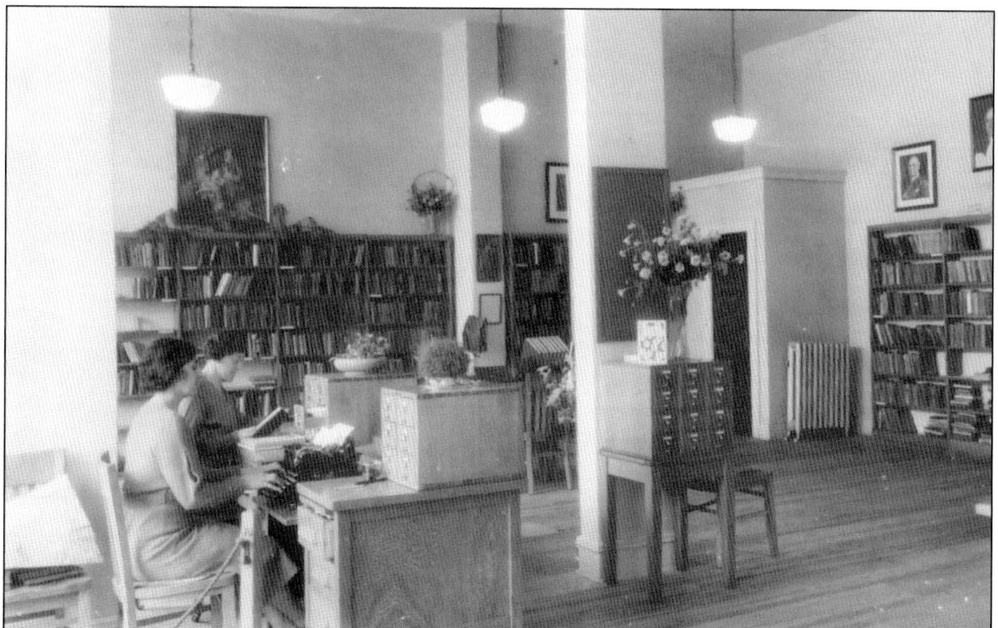

Librarians type on manual typewriters and sort books inside the library. The first board of trustees included Stuart Duffield, Frederick Nichols, Charles Ahrenfield, Mrs. George Irving, and Sue Housten. When the first librarian, A. Edith Kingsland, retired in 1955, the collection had grown to more than 15,000 books.

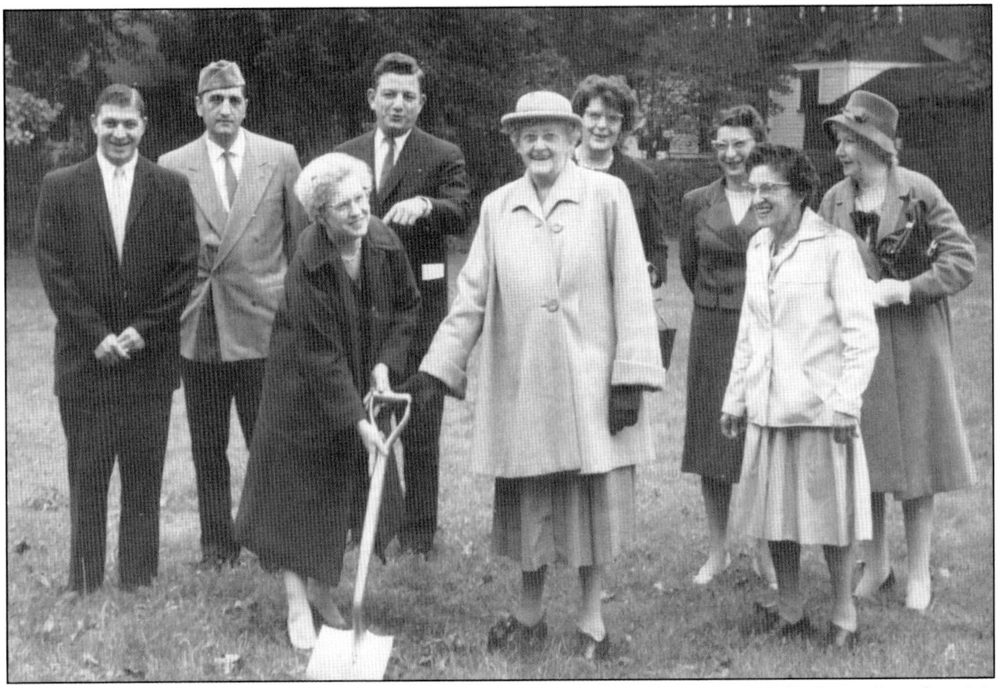

Groundbreaking for the Veterans Memorial Library at Veterans Memorial Park on October 14, 1961, was a joyous occasion for the Friends of the Library after years of financial negotiations. Shown, from left to right, are the following: William Boffa, Salvatore Tucci, Mrs. Flanagan (with shovel), mayor Arthur Dorfner, A. Edith Kingsland, librarian Ruth DeHoff, Rose Cardonsky, Ester Krauss, and Florence Buck.

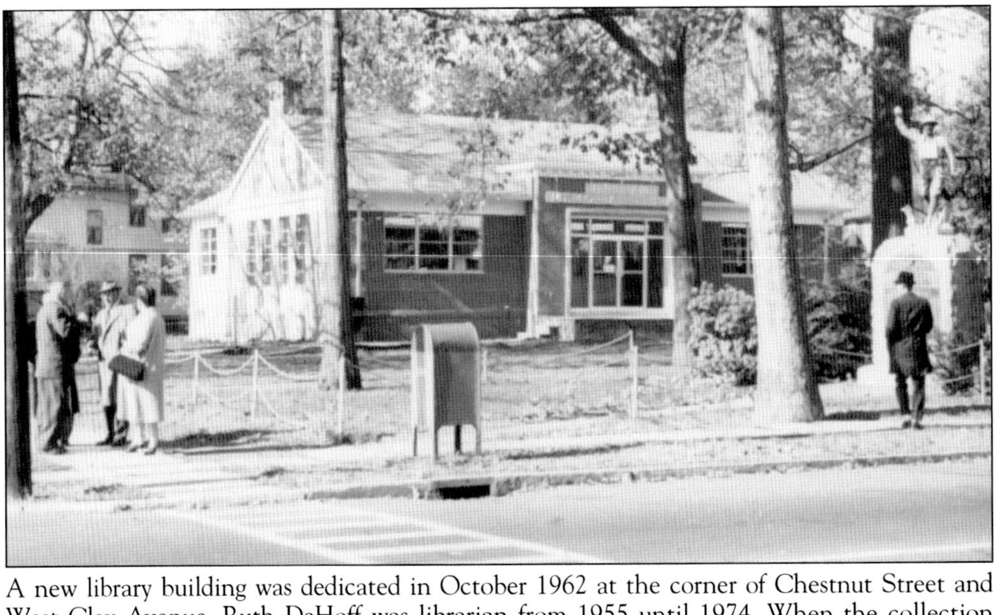

A new library building was dedicated in October 1962 at the corner of Chestnut Street and West Clay Avenue. Ruth DeHoff was librarian from 1955 until 1974. When the collection reached 25,000 volumes in 1974, an extension was added. Barbara Shallit became the children's librarian in 1981 and director in 1995. A new addition opened in October 1996.

Four

TRANSPORTATION

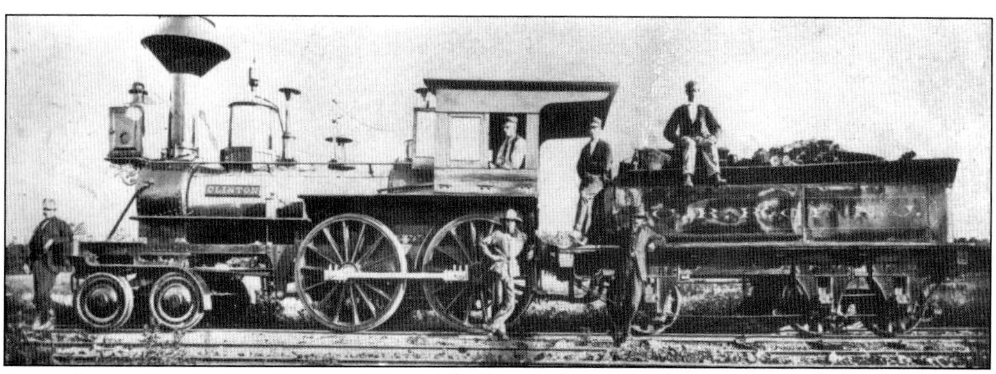

According to local railroad expert Warren B. Crater, this is the first engine built for the Central Railroad of New Jersey after it was formed by combining the Elizabeth and Somerville Railroad with the Somerville and Easton Railroad. It was built by Taunton Locomotive Works.

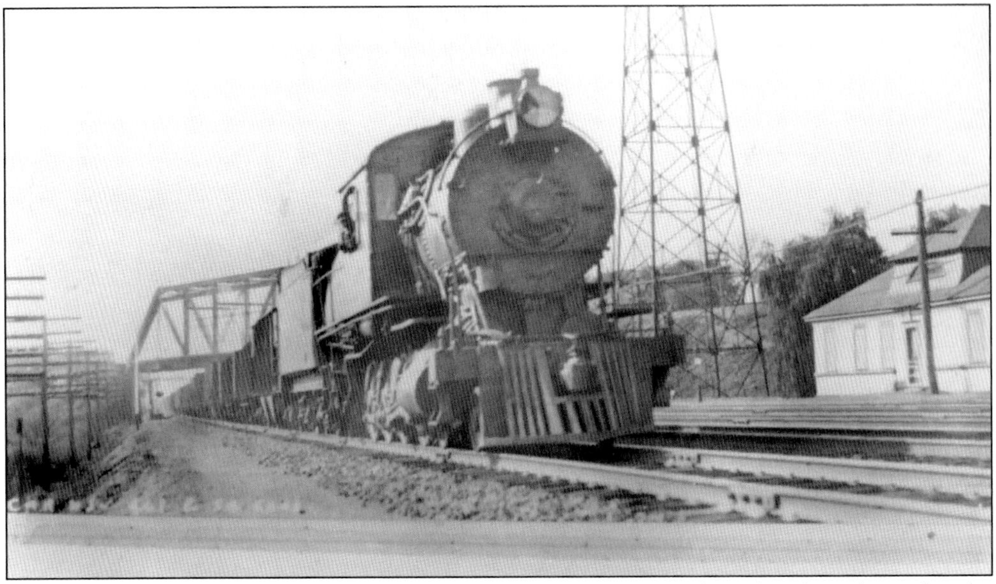

This camelback locomotive, *c.* 1902, treks eastbound on Central Railroad tracks under the Lehigh Valley trestle (left rear). The engineer hangs out the side window as he passes the Marconi transatlantic transmission tower and the early Aldene waiting room (right).

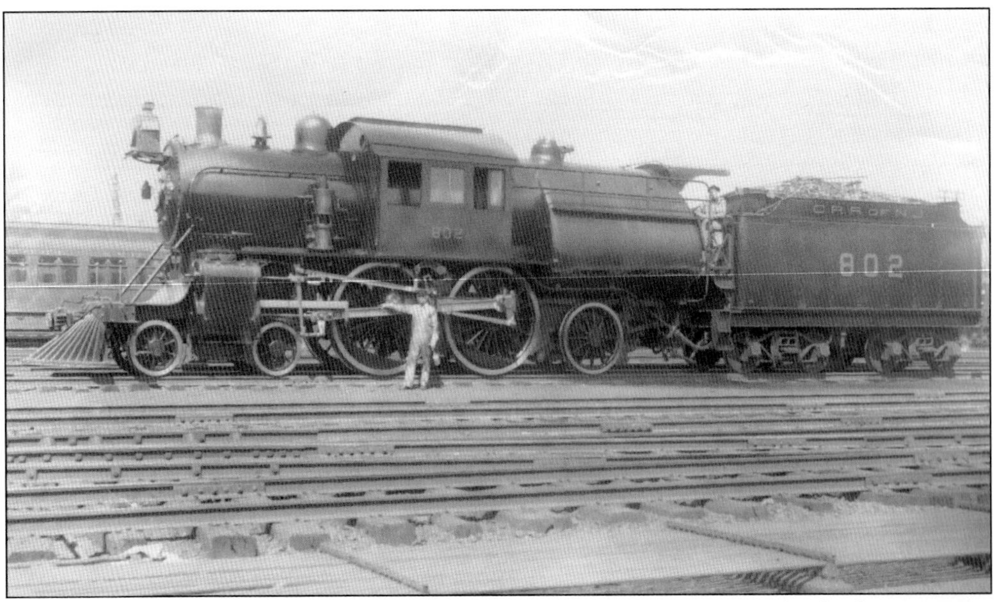

Handsome Atlantic-type engines were built by the Reading Shops in 1912 for the fast passenger trains. Engineer John V. Waite of Roselle Park poses in this 1913 photograph. At that time, Waite ran the B&O Interstate, which later became the National Limited. (CNJ photograph and text supplied by Warren B. Crater.)

This Central Railroad of New Jersey timetable of April 26, 1931, shows that the Blue Comet took visitors to Atlantic City by De Luxe Coach Train in 3 hours flat. Daily commuters could leave Aldene at 6:12 a.m., arriving at West Eighth Street 30 minutes later after 6 stops.

Central Railroad of New Jersey

Cranford, Aldene, Roselle, Lorraine, El Mora Avenue, Elizabeth, Elizabethport and West 8th Street

New Jersey Central

IN EFFECT APRIL 26, 1931
(Subject to Change)
EASTERN STANDARD TIME

LEAVE—WEEKDAYS

Cranford	Aldene	Roselle	Lorraine	El Mora Ave.	Elizabeth	Elizabethport	Arrive West 8th St.
2 29		2 34	2 36	2 38	2 42	2 47	2 53
3 28	f3 30	3 34	3 36	3 38	3 42	3 48	3 54
4 25	4 28	4 31	4 33	4 35	4 38	4 42	4 47
	4 51	4 55	4 57	4 59	5 03	5 08	5 14
5 02	5 05	5 09			5 15		5 25
	5 09	5 14	f5 17	5 19	5 22	5 28	5 36
	5 44	5 49	5 50	5 53	5 57	6 04	6 11
6 00	6 03	6 07		6 11	6 15		6 25
	6 12	6 17	6 20	6 24	6 28	6 35	6 42
	6 25	6 30	6 34	6 38	6 42	6 47	6 55
7 10		7 17		7 21	7 25		7 30
7 21		7 26		7 30	7 33	7 38	7 44
8 01	8 04	8 07		8 10	8 14	8 19	8 25
	8 34	8 37	8 39	8 41	8 44	8 49	8 55
9 03		9 08		9 11	9 15	9 20	9 27
10 01		10 06			10 13	10 18	10 23
10 42		10 47			10 52	10 57	11 03
11 48		11 53		11 56	11 59	**12 04**	**12 09**
	k11 51	k11 55	k11 57	k11 59	k**12 03**	k**12 09**	k**12 17**
	12 29	**12 32**	f**12 34**	**12 37**	**12 40**	**12 45**	**12 51**
1 23	**1 25**	**1 29**		**1 33**	**1 36**	**1 41**	**1 47**
2 32		**2 38**		**2 43**	**2 46**	**2 50**	**2 56**
3 07		**3 12**			**3 17**	**3 21**	**3 27**
					3 19	**3 23**	**3 30**
	3 22	**3 26**		**3 30**	**3 33**	**3 43**	**3 49**
3 48	**3 51**	**3 54**		**3 58**	**4 01**	**4 05**	**4 12**
			4 15		**4 22**	**4 27**	**4 33**
	4 32	**4 36**	**4 38**	**4 40**	**4 43**	**4 48**	**4 55**
4 52	**4 55**	**4 58**		**5 02**	**5 05**	**5 11**	**5 17**
	5 36	**5 40**	f**5 43**	**5 46**	**5 50**	**5 56**	**6 02**
6 23	**6 26**	**6 30**		**6 34**	**6 37**	**6 42**	**6 48**
7 17		**7 22**		**7 25**	**7 28**	**7 33**	**7 39**
9 07		**9 12**		**9 16**	**9 19**	**9 25**	**9 34**
10 38		**10 44**		**10 48**	**10 51**	**10 56**	**11 02**

SUNDAYS

Cranford	Aldene	Roselle	Lorraine	El Mora Ave.	Elizabeth	Elizabethport	Arrive West 8th St.
2 29		2 34	2 36	2 38	2 42	2 47	2 53
4 48	4 51	4 55	4 57	5 00	5 04	5 10	5 17
6 55	6 57	7 01		7 05	7 08	7 13	7 19
8 06		8 11		8 15	8 18	8 22	8 29
8 21	8 23	8 27	8 29	8 31	8 35	8 40	8 46
9 12		9 17		9 21	9 25	9 30	9 36
9 51		9 56		10 00	10 03	10 07	10 15
	11 04	11 08	f11 10	11 12	11 16	11 21	11 28
11 48		11 53		11 57	**12 01**	**12 07**	**12 14**
1 15	**1 18**	**1 22**		**1 25**	**1 28**	**1 33**	**1 39**
3 03		**3 09**		**3 13**	**3 16**	**3 21**	**3 27**
	4 05	**4 09**	f**4 11**	**4 13**	**4 16**	**4 21**	**4 27**
4 56		**5 01**		**5 05**	**5 08**	**5 12**	**5 18**
	5 19	**5 23**	f**5 25**	**5 27**	**5 30**	**5 37**	**5 44**
6 16		**6 22**		**6 26**	**6 29**	**6 34**	**6 40**
6 56	**7 00**	**7 04**	**7 06**	**7 08**	**7 11**	**7 16**	**7 22**
7 19					**7 28**	**7 32**	**7 37**
8 16		**8 21**			**8 26**	**8 30**	**8 35**
8 37	**8 40**	**8 44**	**8 46**	**8 48**	**8 51**	**8 56**	**9 02**
9 45		**9 51**			**9 57**	**10 02**	**10 12**
					10 24		**10 34**

f-Stops on signal or notice to conductor. k-Saturdays only. A.M. light type. **P.M. heavy type.**

The Blue Comet to Atlantic City
De Luxe Coach Train—3 hours flat

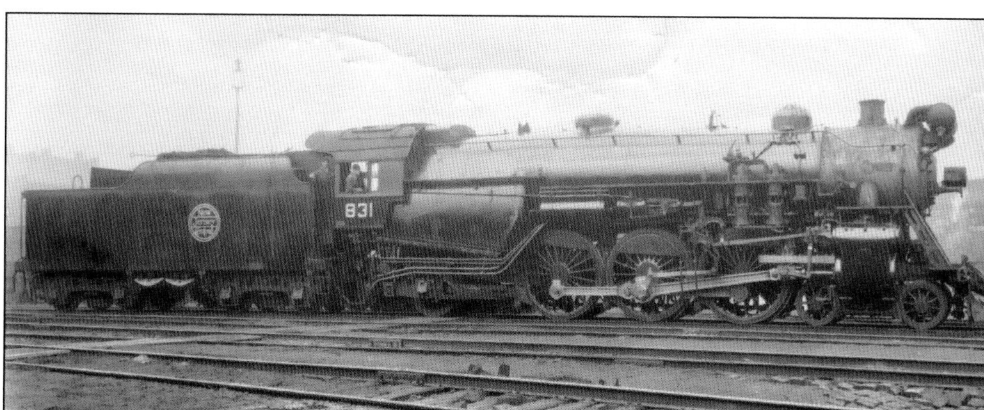

According to Warren B. Crater, this is one of the Blue Comet Pacifics that was built by Baldwin in 1928. (CNJ photograph.)

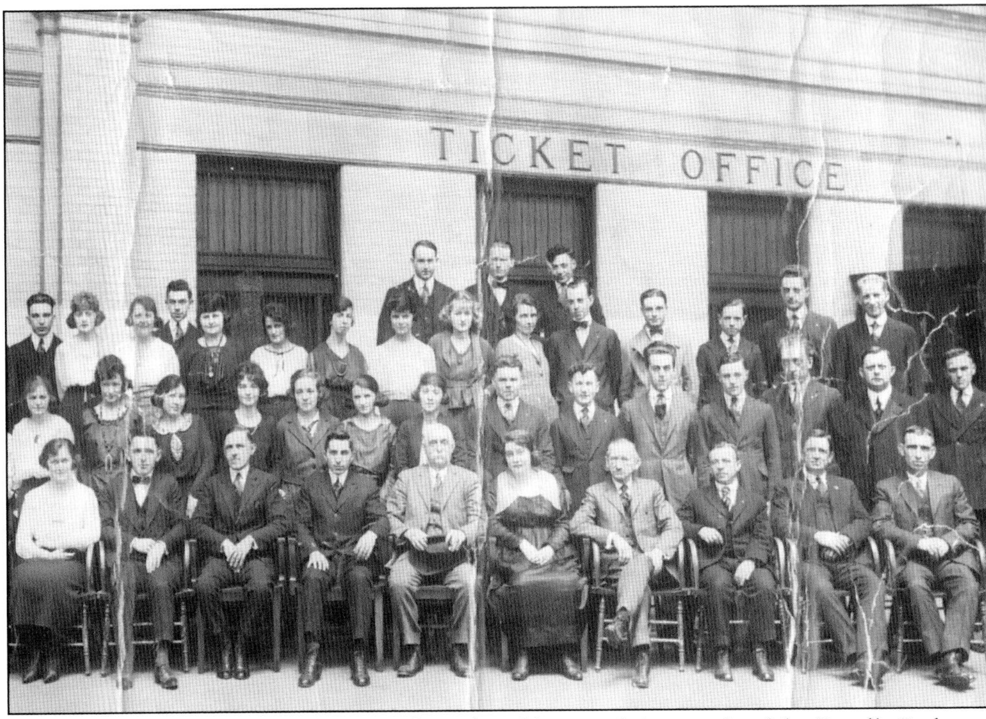

The convenient relationship between the railroad lines and the people of the Roselle Park area was a symbiotic one. Many railroad employees settled in Roselle Park before and during its most formative years. They enjoyed free transportation to their jobs along the line. In the photograph above, taken on May 10, 1920, some of the faces smiling in front of the Newark ticket office belong to borough residents that worked for the Central Railroad office force. Shown in the bottom photograph, taken on March 15, 1956, is the station at the foot of Chestnut Street, where commuters would climb off the train after their workday in Newark or New York City.

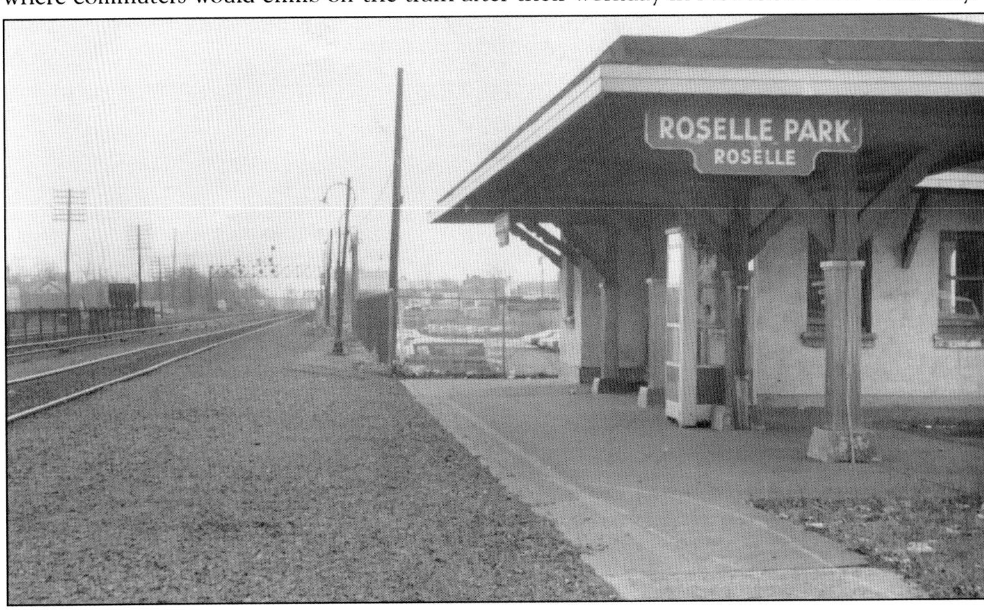

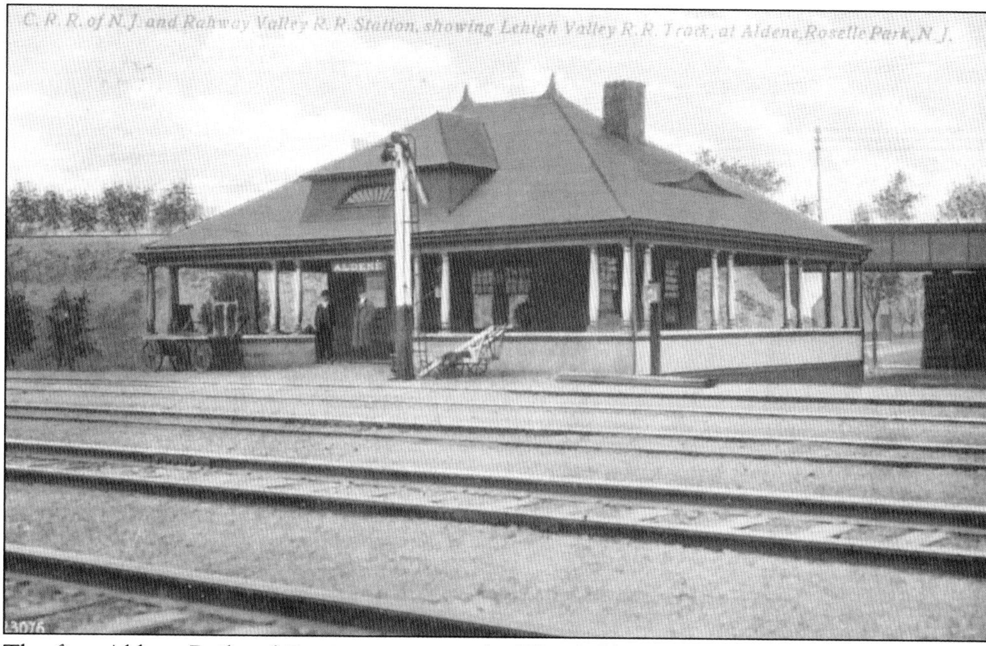

The first Aldene Railroad Station was near the Westfield Avenue overpass. It supported the traveling public between 1847 and 1911, serving the Central Railroad of New Jersey, the Rahway Valley, and the Lehigh Valley Railroads.

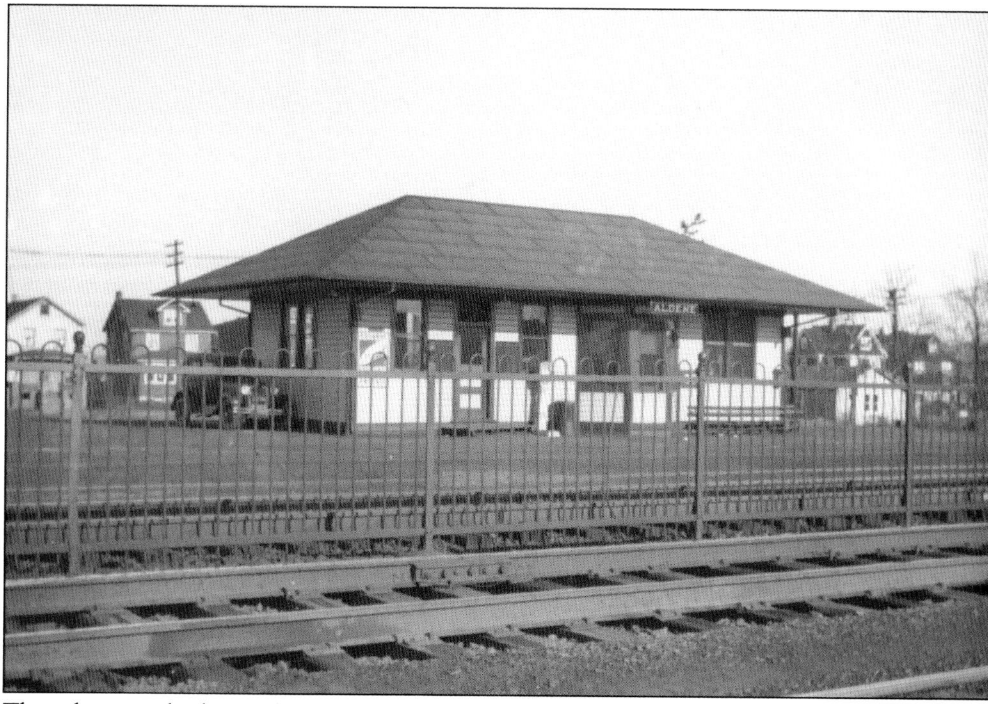

This photograph shows the second Aldene Railroad Station, which once stood where the parking lot of the Sun Tavern is now. The fence in the foreground is typical of the Central Railroad style, dividing north-south lines. Many years after this station had been razed, the Roselle Park Historical Society conducted an archeological dig on the site.

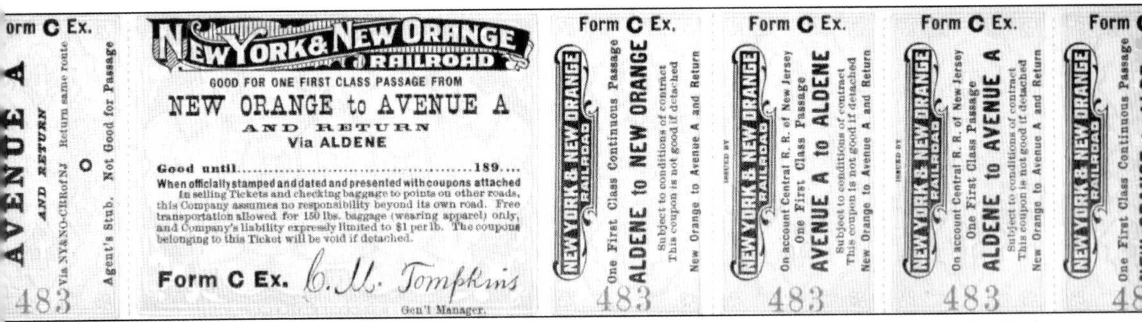

In 1895, a charter for the New York and New Orange Railroad, later known as the Rahway Valley Railroad, was issued. At the turn of the 20th century, it carried passengers about 4 miles from Roselle Park to New Orange, which later became Kenilworth, and connected with the Central Railroad at Aldene Station. This first-class passenger ticket No. 483, which was only "Good until 189–," traces the round trip from New Orange to Avenue A. Passenger service was discontinued in 1918.

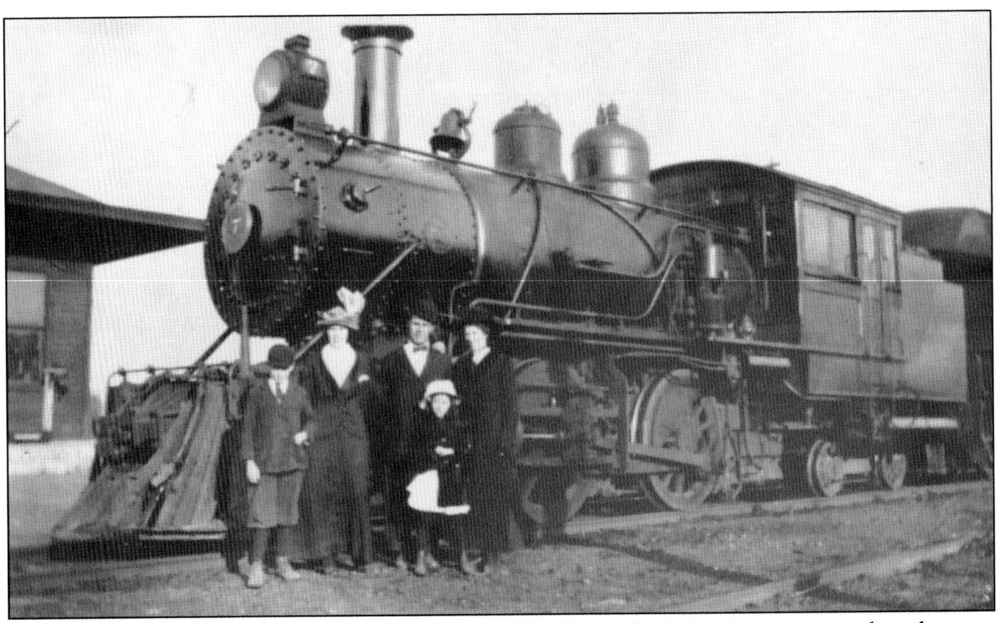

Rahway Valley Engine No. 7 pulled passenger cars in the early 1900s. It transported students to Upsala College, then in Kenilworth, as well as golfers from New York to the Baltisrol Golf Club in Summit. It also transported families such as this one, off for a picnic at Millers Grove.

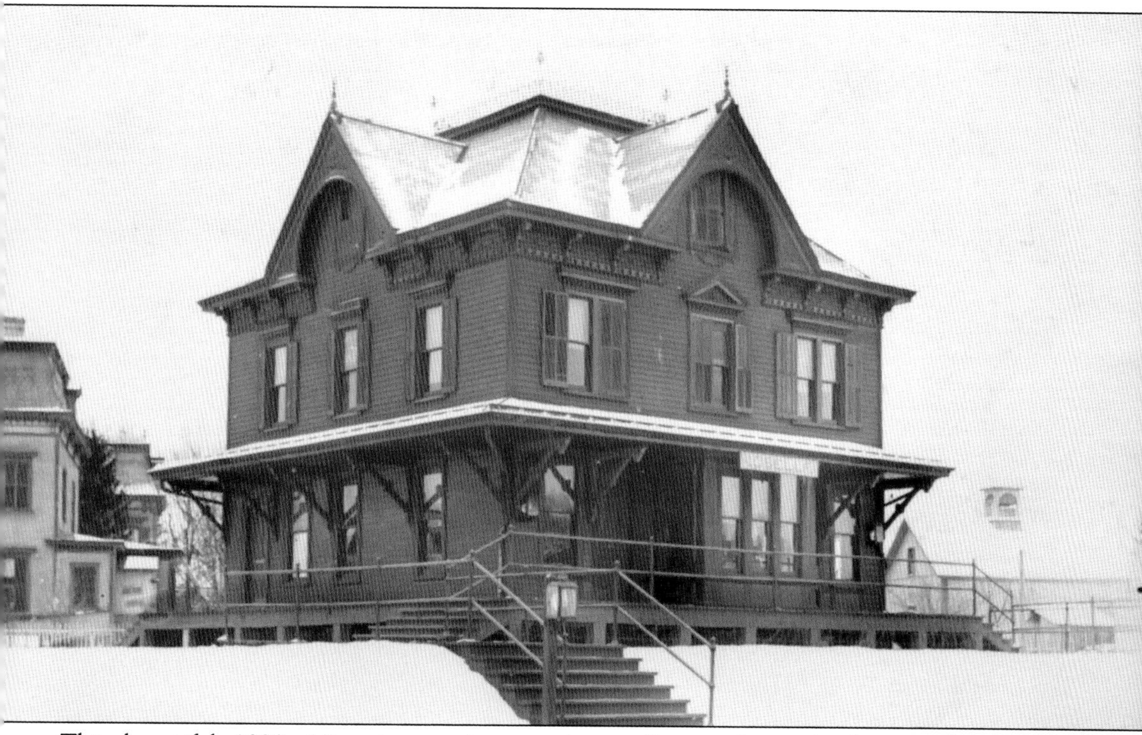

This beautiful 1890s Victorian station stood proudly on the embankment above the ground-level "Valley" tracks at West Lincoln Avenue near Chestnut Street. The "Roselle" sign was changed to "Roselle Park" after 1901. For more than 50 years, this shuttered, three-story shelter welcomed travelers waiting to board such trains as the ASA Packer or the Maple Leaf, as well as those watching the famous Black Diamond Limited express rush through. Almost 100 years later, the residence at the left became the board of education building.

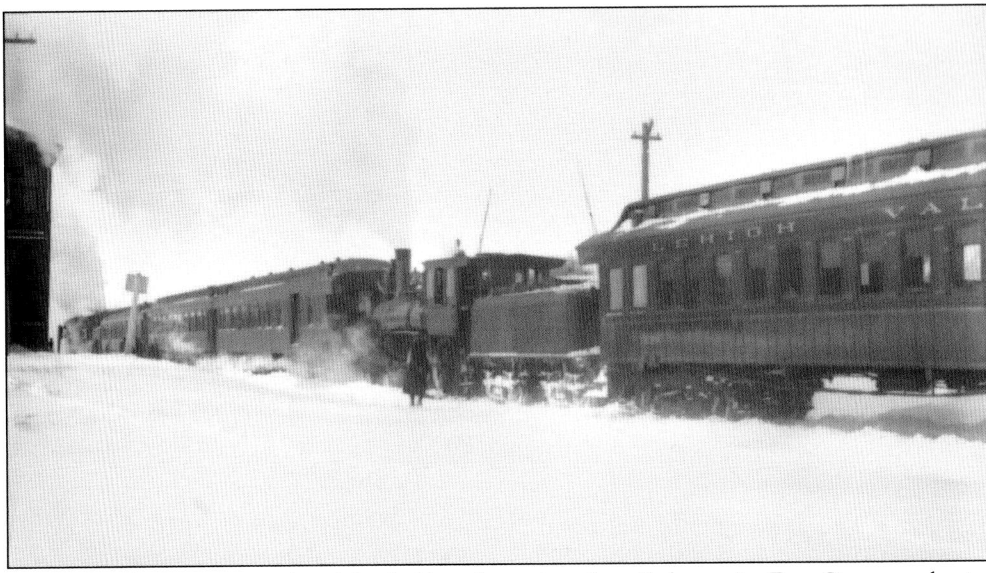

The Blizzard of 1888 started on March 11 and continued until the entire East Coast was buried in the most crippling snowstorm ever recorded in New York and New England. By March 14, transportation and communications had been brought to a standstill locally as well as in the big cities of North America, killing an estimated 400 people. This westbound Lehigh Valley passenger train is seen blocking the Chestnut Street crossing during another late 1890s winter storm. The American-type locomotive (center) is performing mid-train helper service, as it pushes the left train and pulls its own at right.

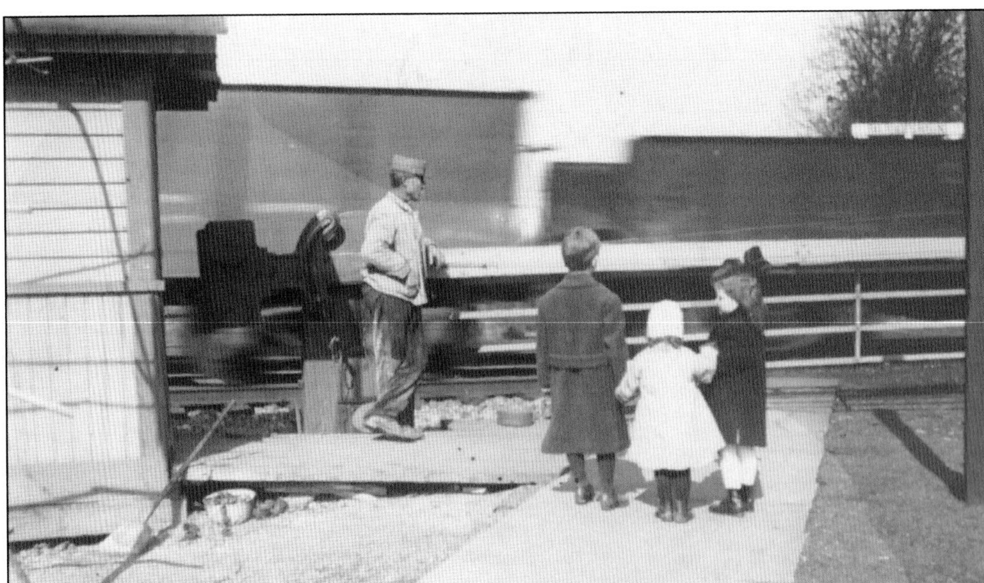

A big brother takes his little sisters on a boardwalk stroll that includes crossing the Lehigh Valley tracks when they were still at grade level in October 1913. The gateman ensures their safe passage near a shanty at Locust Street. For more than 50 years, the banshee cry of every train's whistle screamed as they approached every railroad street crossing. Drivers endured long waits as endless freight trains rolled past them, and children were often late for school.

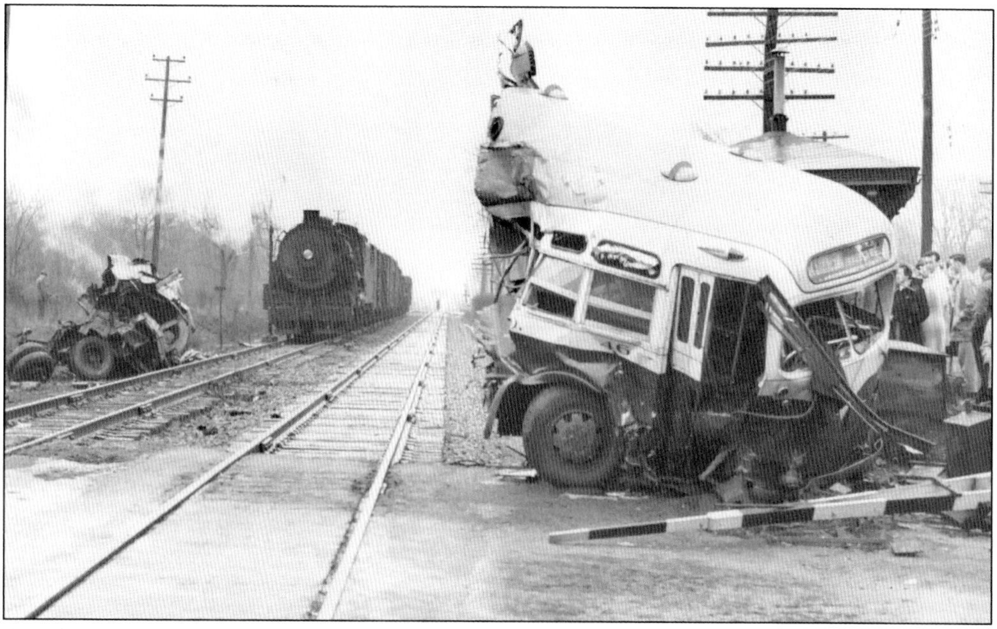

Another train-vehicle tragedy in a series of grade crossing accidents was reason enough to elevate the Lehigh Valley tracks that crossed Galloping Hill Road, Walnut Street, Chestnut Street, and Locust Street. On April 24, 1944, two people were killed and one seriously injured when this Stuyvesant Avenue bus was sliced in half by the streamlined nose of the Buffalo–New York Express. Although the gateman's shanty was demolished, the gate tender inside escaped with bruises.

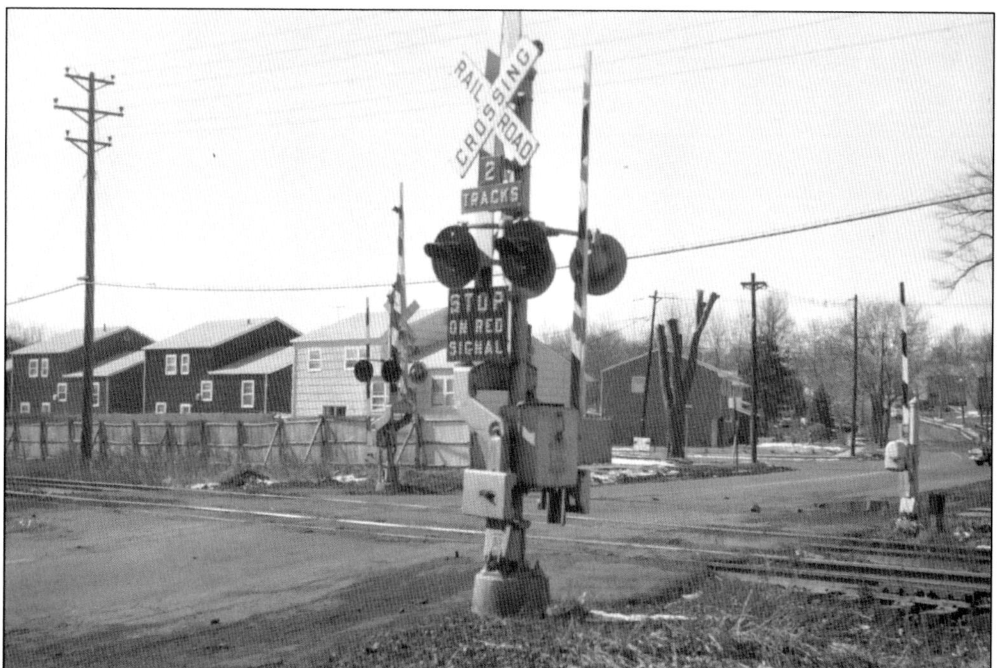

This was a once dangerous grade crossing on Galloping Hill Road and Lehigh Avenue at the Union border. In 1967, as population and vehicular traffic increased, the tracks were elevated.

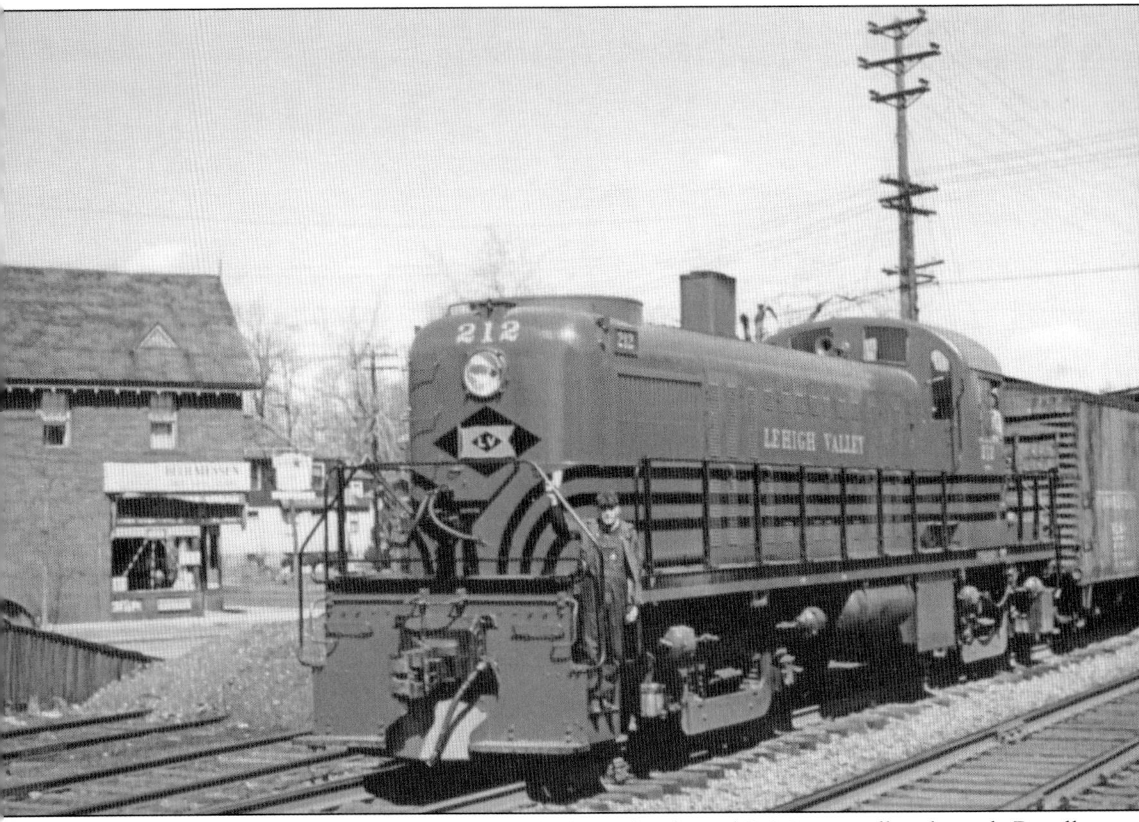

Lehigh Valley Engine No. 212—a sharp-looking, bright red RS-2—trundles through Roselle Park's Chestnut Street grade crossing in 1950. To the left is Mickey's Delicatessen, owned by Mickey and Muriel Salkeld.

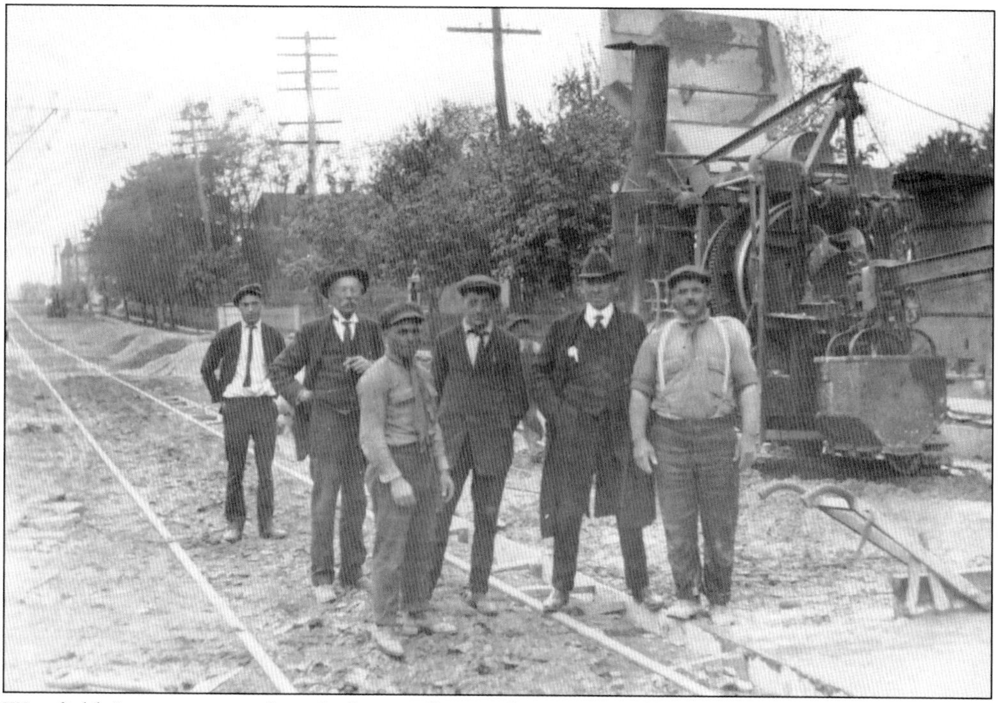

Westfield Avenue was widened when trolley tracks were installed in 1898. Local transportation changed dramatically from horse-drawn conveyances on dusty roads to comparatively smooth running cars on rails. The mechanical installation equipment shown is a crane with a vertical steam boiler that has a bucket up front used to move and pour concrete. In this photograph, several workers take a break to pose with the boss. The plow-type tool at the right was used to pull heavy track by hand.

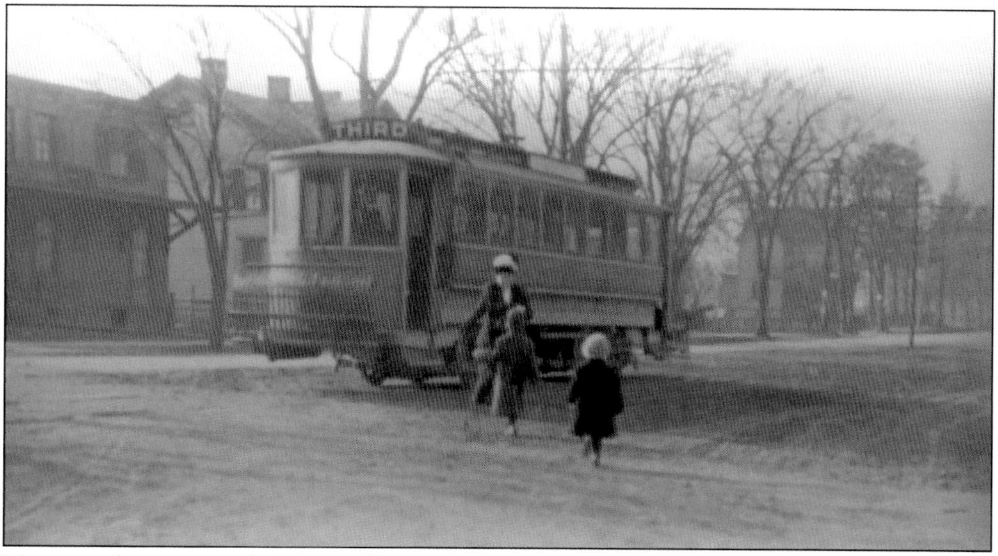

Many residents remember the trolley car ride to Elizabeth. Sadie Wilson recalls, "The fare was 5¢ and you got a transfer, and then you could come back on the transfer." In this 1919 photograph, Mrs. Waite Sr. is greeted by her children, Robert and Irma, as she exits the Public Service Railway (Trolley Car) at Westfield Avenue and Filbert Street.

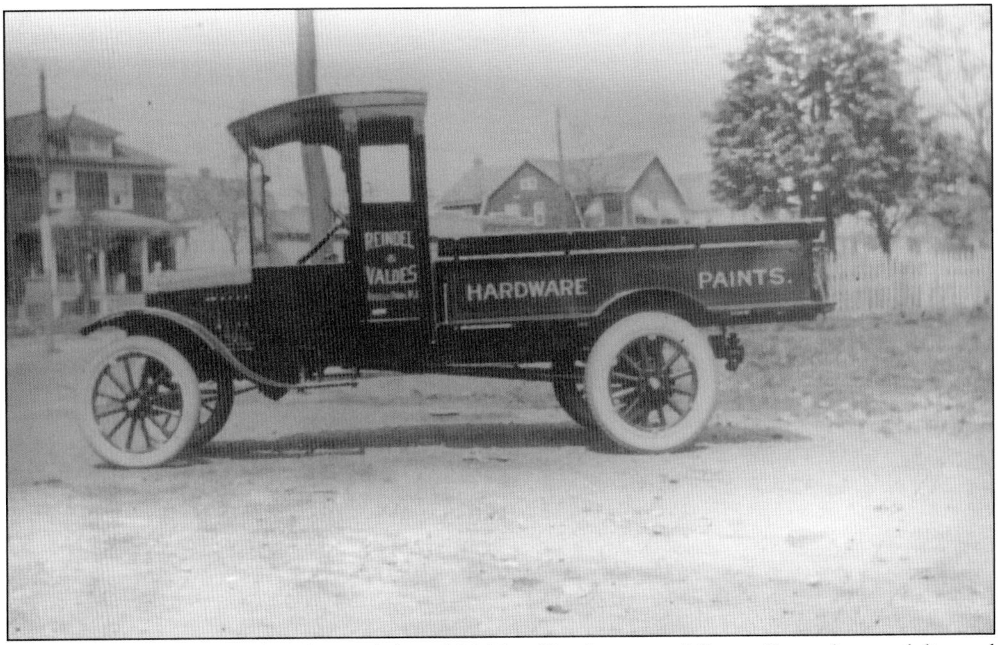

The first business vehicle of Reindel and Valdes Hardware and Paint Store home-delivered homeowners' materials. Note the spoke "artillery" wheels and new balloon (air-filled) tires in natural white rubber. Later tires were dyed black; those with a rim of white left showing came to be known as whitewall tires.

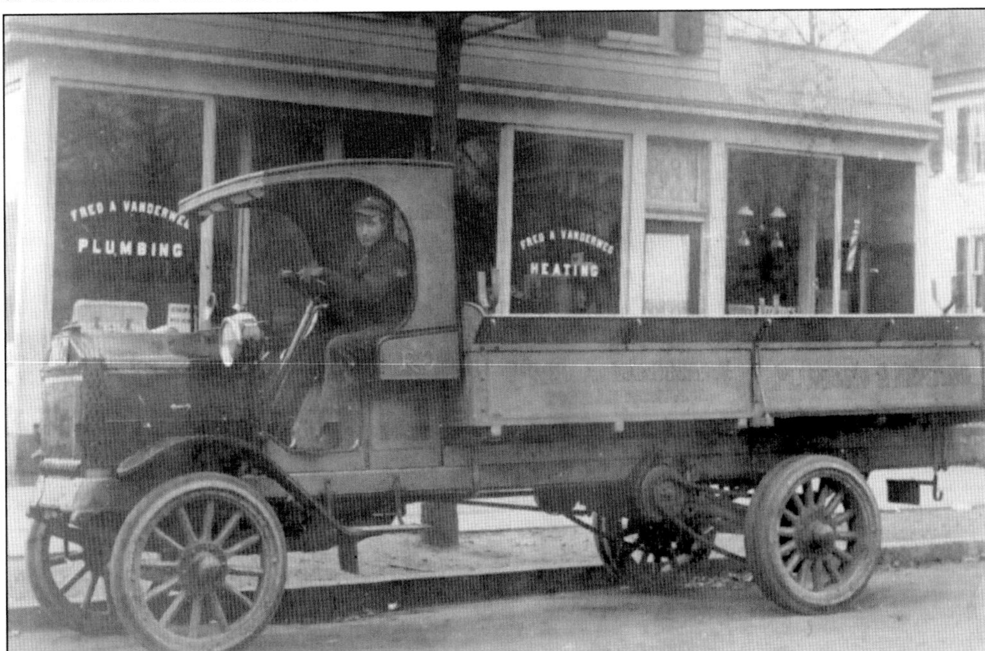

Fred Vanderweg, chairman of the board of the First National Bank of Roselle, owned a Heating and Plumbing establishment on Chestnut Street in the early 1900s. This 1915 photograph shows his Reo truck, a chain-driven rear wheeler, which predates the modern rear-end differential gears.

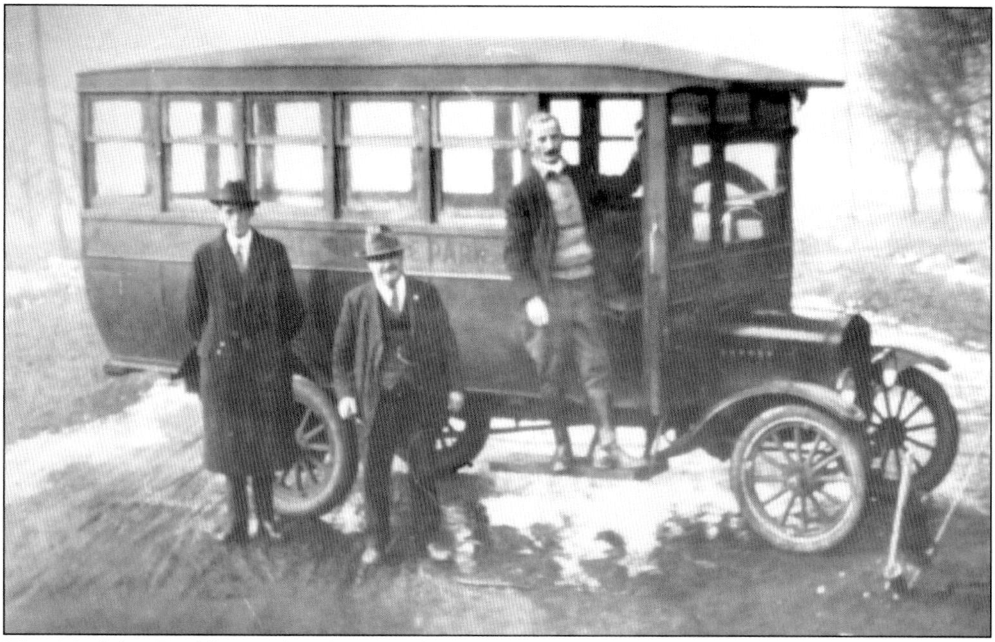

This Model T Ford bus makes the rounds between Roselle Park and Kenilworth along Faitoute Avenue in the 1920s. There is a story about a horse that dropped dead on Faitoute Avenue. The responding policeman, in writing the police report, did not know how to spell *Faitoute*, so he dragged the dead horse around the corner to Clay Avenue.

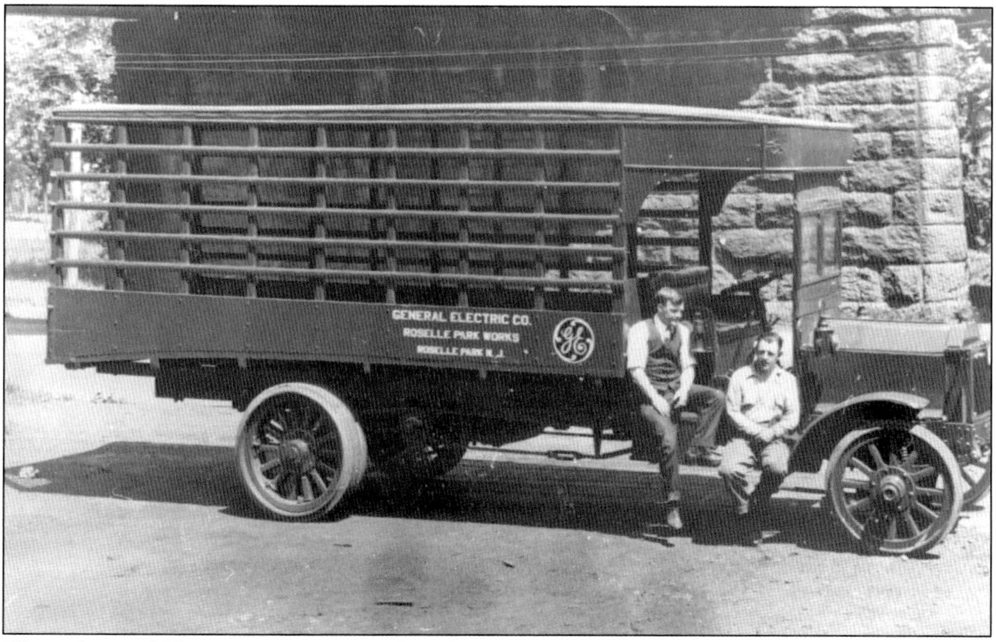

These General Electric Company truckers have picked a shady spot to park their delivery truck, under the Lehigh Valley overpass crossing West Westfield Avenue near Seaton Avenue. The solid rubber tires on their rack body truck predate balloon tires. These types of tires made for a terribly rough ride, but drivers never had a flat. General Electric took over the Marconi Plant in 1922, manufacturing and distributing for the emerging small electric appliance industry.

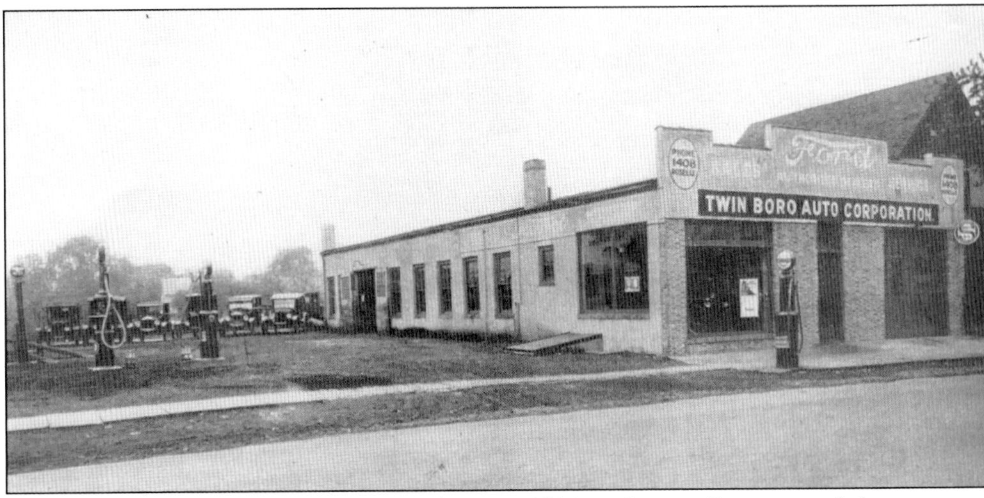

The Twin Boro Auto Corporation started out in 1921 in this small garage and showroom on Westfield Avenue. Note the vintage Fords, the round-head gas pumps, and the four-digit phone number on the building. By 1926, Fred Hebeler was president and treasurer, William J. Schmelz was vice president, and George Mercer was secretary. Mercer's son, George, became chairman of the board of directors for the Goodyear Tire Company.

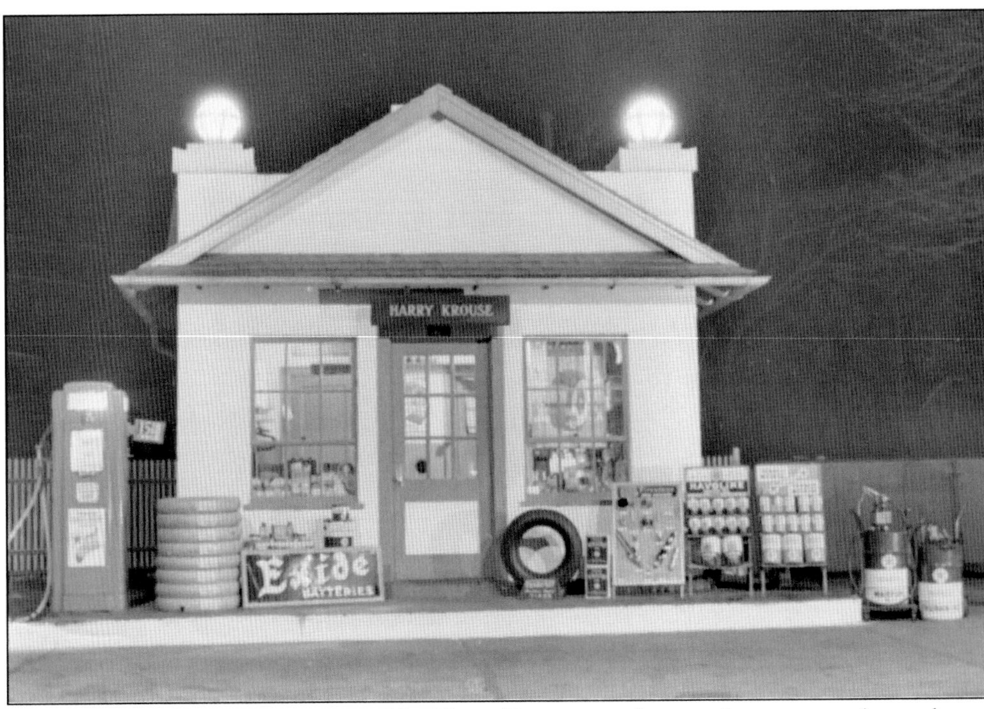

This 1920s gasoline station operated by Harry Krouse, a volunteer fireman, was located on a main artery at 413 East Westfield Avenue.

Five

Serving Their Community

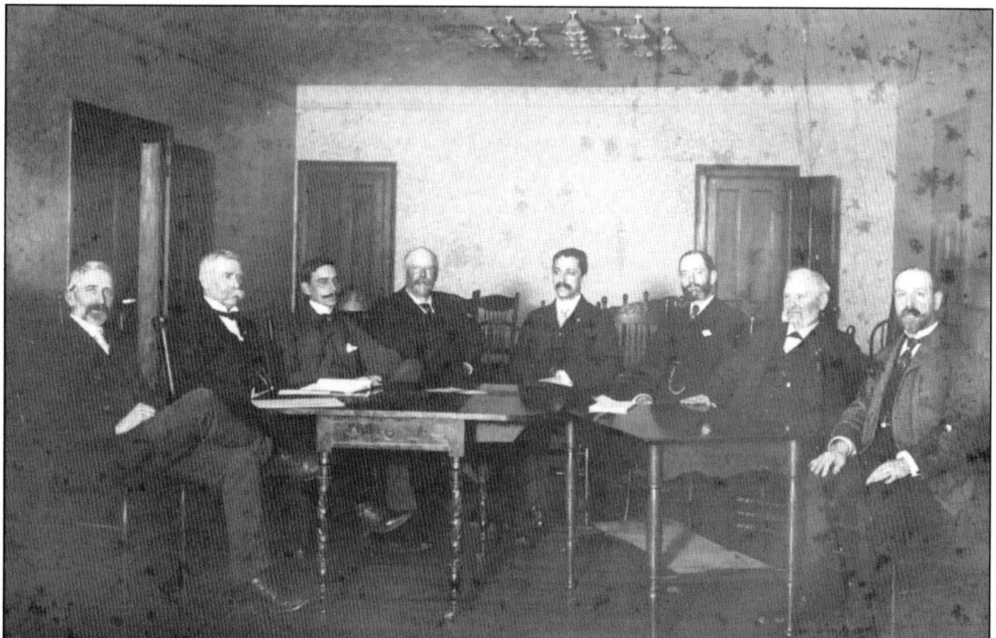

The founding fathers petitioned for separation from Union Township, and on March 22, 1901, an act of the legislature of the State of New Jersey authorized the incorporation of the borough of Roselle Park. An election to choose the first governing body was held on April 16, 1901. Roselle Park's first mayor and councilmen are shown in this photograph. From left to right, they are Abraham Woodruff, mayor John Cummins, Emery L. Lillibridge, Robert Gordon, Paul Hochart, John Herman, Alfred Atkins, and Charles A. Potter. The area consisted of 790 acres and a total population of 1,000 people residing in 225 homes.

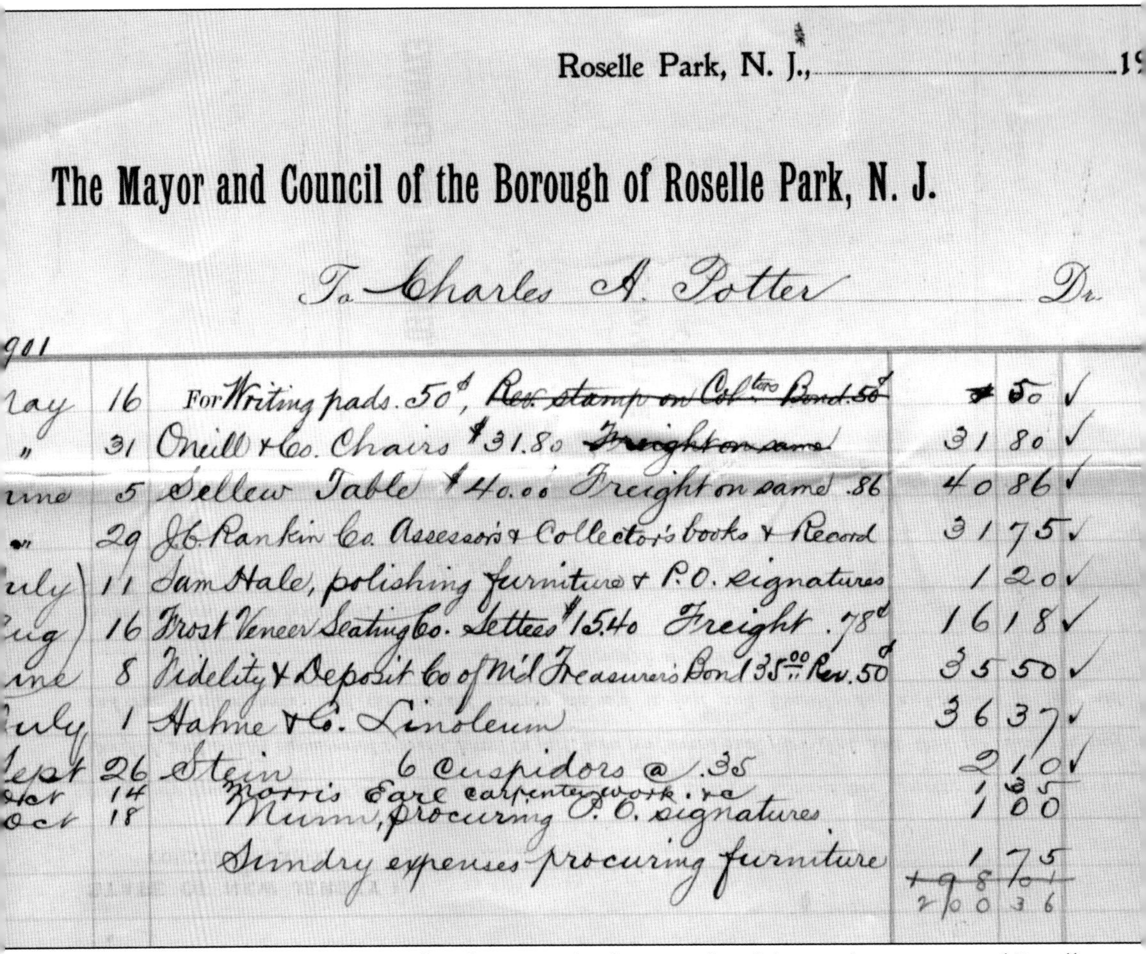
Roselle Park, N. J., ... 19

The Mayor and Council of the Borough of Roselle Park, N. J.

To Charles A. Potter Dr.

901				
ay	16	For Writing pads. 50¢, ~~Rev. stamp on Col^tors Bond .50¢~~		50 ✓
"	31	Oneill & Co. Chairs $31.80 ~~Freight on same~~	31	80 ✓
une	5	Sellew Table $40.00 Freight on same .86	40	86 ✓
"	29	J.B. Rankin Co. Assessor's & Collector's books & Record	31	75 ✓
uly	11	Sam Hale, polishing furniture & P.O. signatures	1	20 ✓
ug	16	Frost Veneer Seating Co. Settees $15.40 Freight .78¢	16	18 ✓
ine	8	Fidelity & Deposit Co of Md Treasurer's Bond 35.00 Rev. .50¢	35	50 ✓
uly	1	Hahne & Co. Linoleum	36	37 ✓
ept	26	Stein 6 cuspidors @ .35	2	10 ✓
Oct	14	Morris Earl carpenter work. re	1	35
Oct	18	Munn, procuring P.O. signatures	1	00
		Sundry expenses procuring furniture	1	75
			~~198~~	~~01~~
			200	36

Budget time is always tense and no less so in the first months of the newly incorporated Roselle Park. The first mayor was presented with this hand-written bill for start-up expenditures. Operating costs were $200.36 from May through October 1901. Try obtaining cuspidors at 35¢ today.

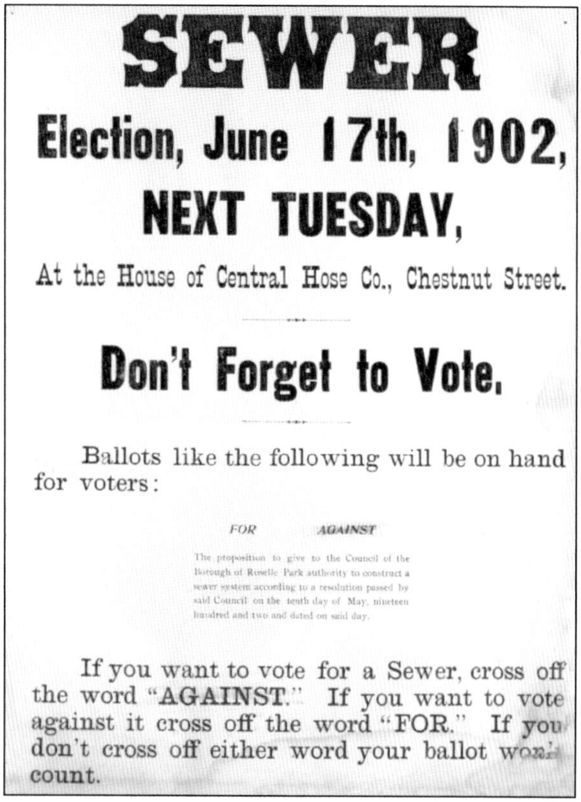

SEWER

Election, June 17th, 1902,

NEXT TUESDAY,

At the House of Central Hose Co., Chestnut Street.

Don't Forget to Vote.

Ballots like the following will be on hand for voters:

FOR *AGAINST*

The proposition to give to the Council of the Borough of Roselle Park authority to construct a sewer system according to a resolution passed by said Council on the tenth day of May, nineteen hundred and two and dated on said day.

If you want to vote for a Sewer, cross off the word "**AGAINST**." If you want to vote against it cross off the word "**FOR**." If you don't cross off either word your ballot won't count.

This handbill instigates voters in the newborn borough to rush off to the polls and to bring their community into the 20th century with in-ground sewer lines. The sewerage system specifications were put out for bid in 1902 and constructed in 1903 by Higginson & Shannon Contractors at a cost of $46,783, which was paid for by assessing homeowners.

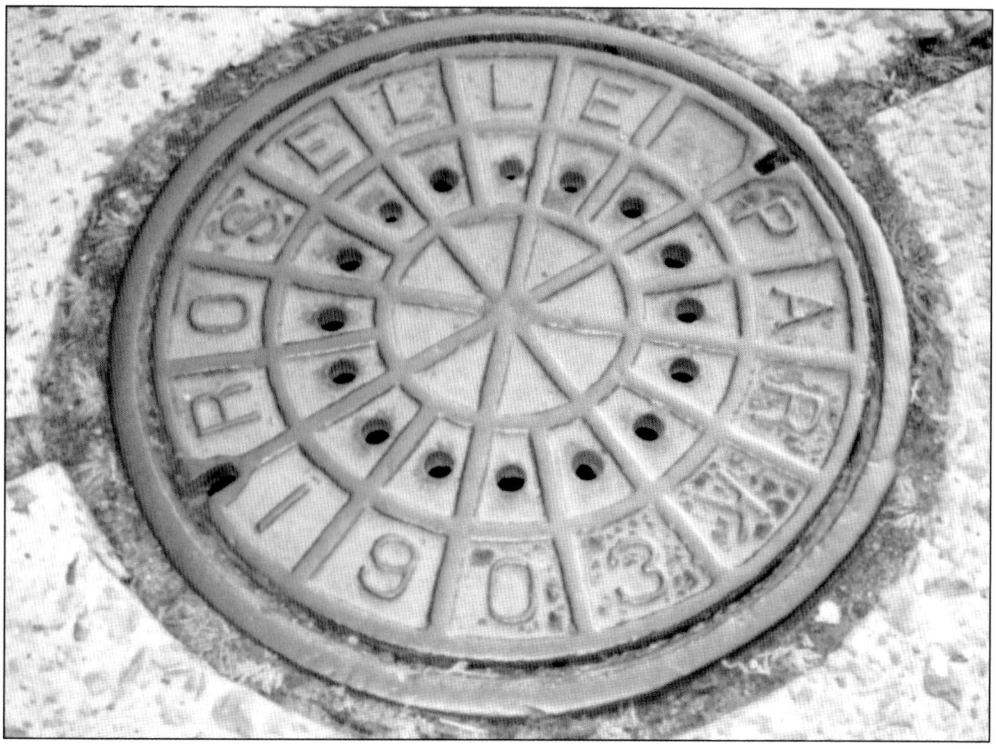

Ninety-seven years later, this original sewer plate is a relic representing several that are still in service on busy borough streets. With the installation of the sewerage system, outdoor plumbing would soon become a thing of the past.

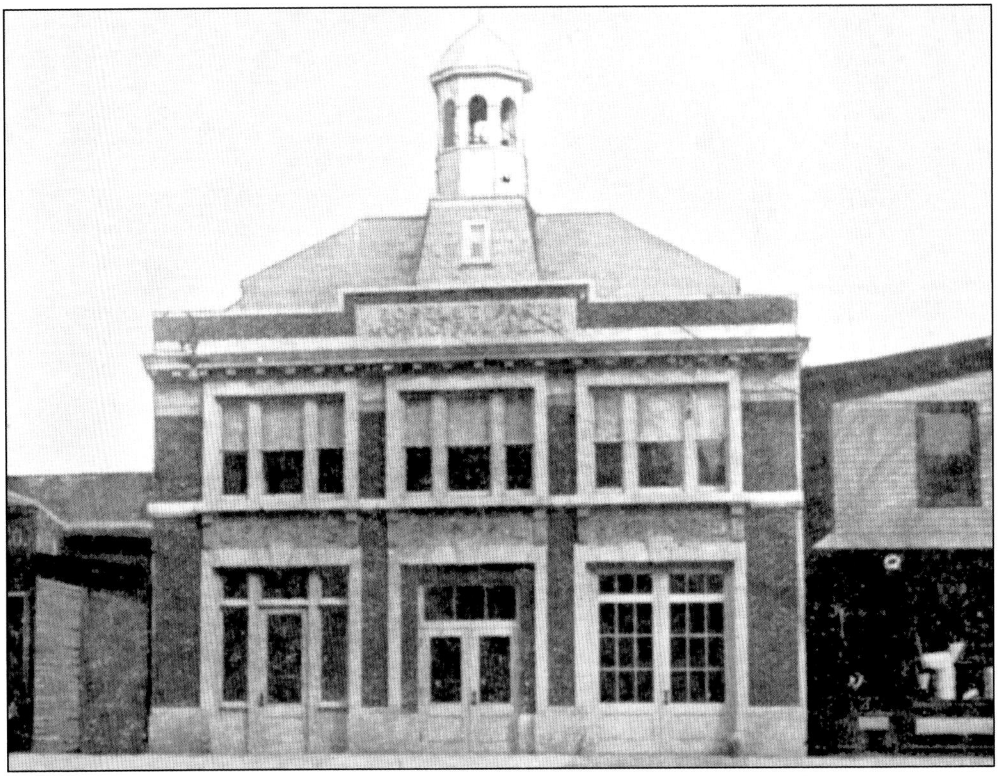

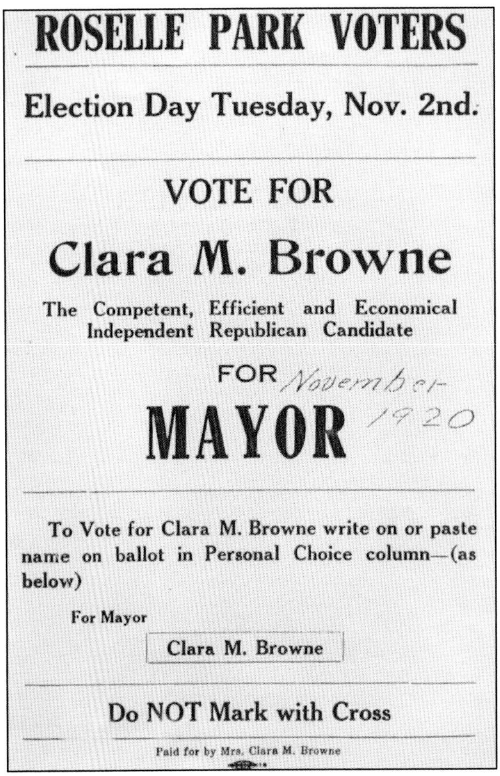

Built in 1915 and demolished in 1992, the borough hall at 317 Chestnut Street was the center for borough administration offices, police and fire headquarters, council chambers, and a courtroom. During its early years, the council chambers were used as a movie theater or rented privately for parties and wedding receptions. The cupola held a bell and later a horn that was used to summon volunteers to fires or emergencies.

Clara M. Browne of Warren Avenue filed a petition to run as an Independent Republican candidate for the office of mayor in the 1920 election. Browne was the first woman to run for mayor in any municipality in the country, according to Roselle Park's *25th Anniversary Souvenir Book* of 1926. She was defeated by George E. Moore, who became the ninth mayor of Roselle Park and introduced a zoning ordinance.

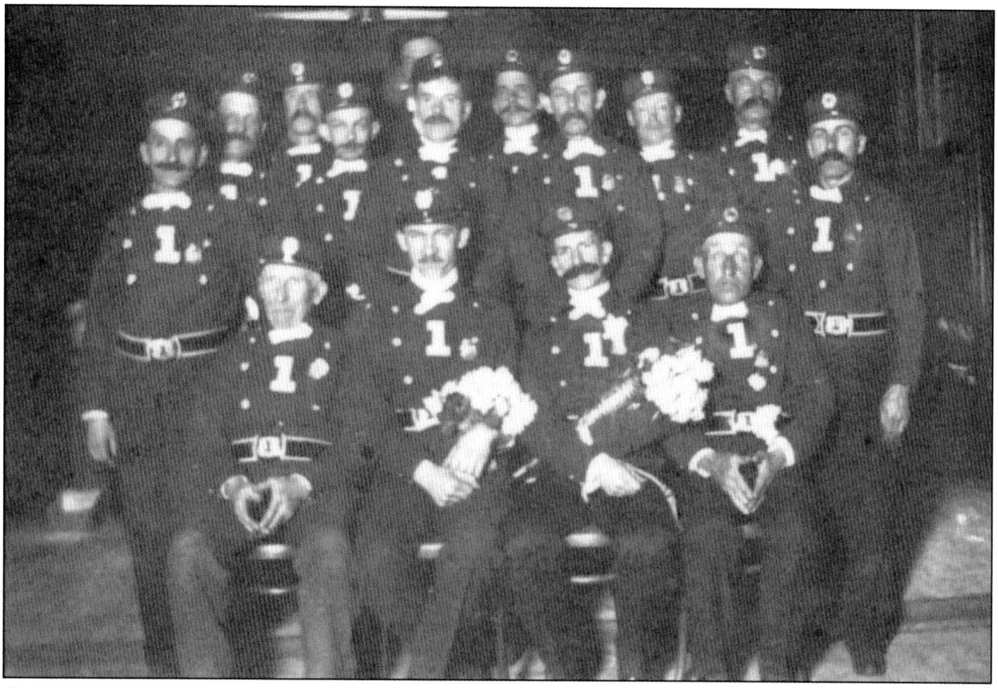

On May 10, 1902, Lorraine Hose Company No. 1 firemen pose for a group portrait. The members shown, from left to right, are as follows: J.W. Shreve, foreman; Charles Farley, assistant foreman; Thomas Anderson; R.A. Bellis; W.A. Bembridge; Thomas Benjamin; William Bodine; Paul Cavanaugh; B. Doremus: P. Hochart; F.S. Lewis; L. Markthaler; P. Quinn; and L. Shuster.

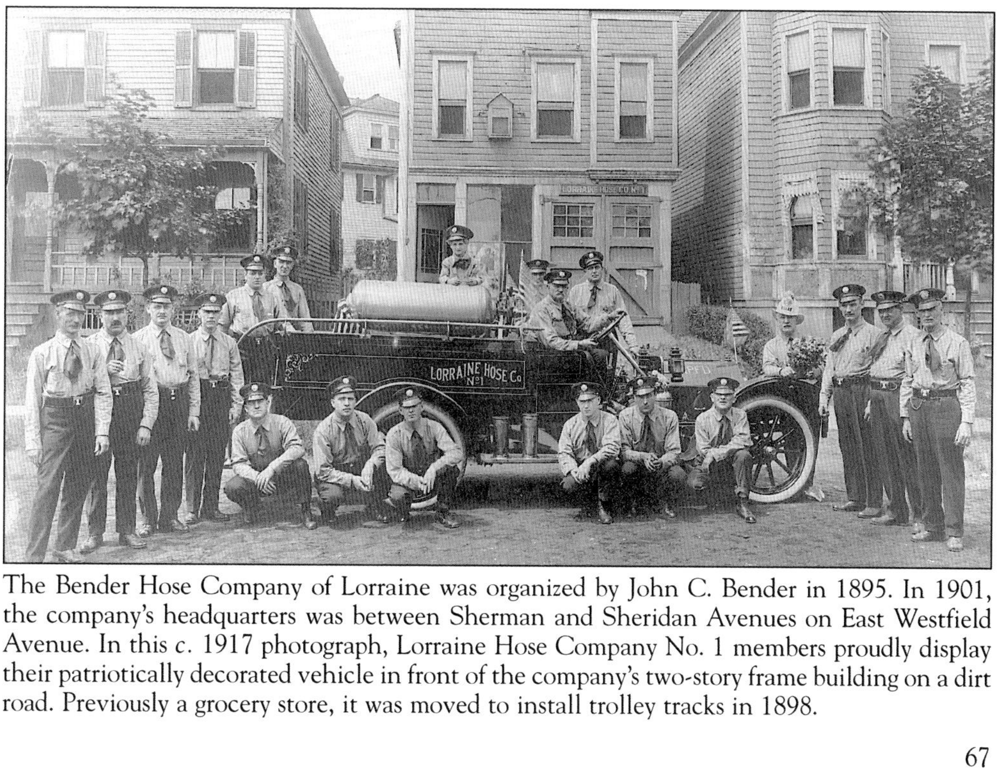

The Bender Hose Company of Lorraine was organized by John C. Bender in 1895. In 1901, the company's headquarters was between Sherman and Sheridan Avenues on East Westfield Avenue. In this c. 1917 photograph, Lorraine Hose Company No. 1 members proudly display their patriotically decorated vehicle in front of the company's two-story frame building on a dirt road. Previously a grocery store, it was moved to install trolley tracks in 1898.

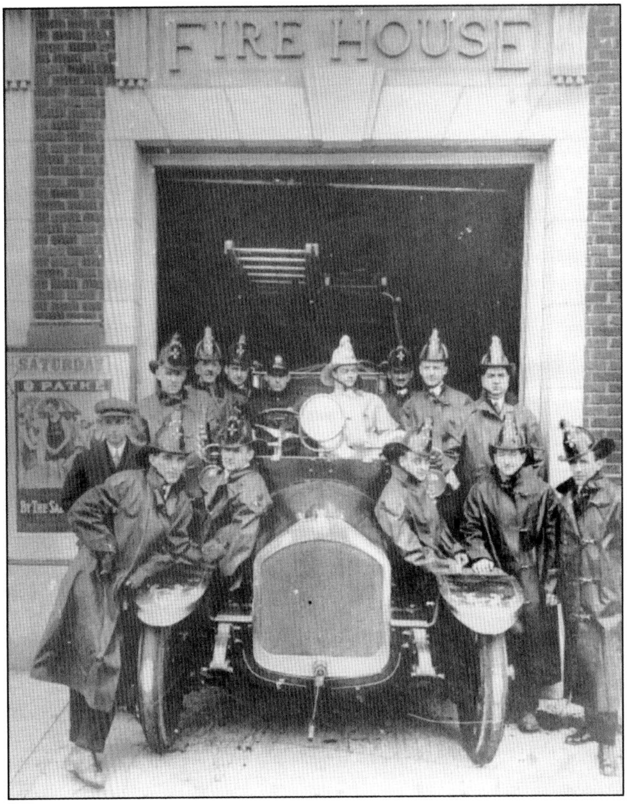

Firemen of the Central Hose Company pose in firefighting gear and surround their truck with obvious pride at their headquarters in the old town hall. The billboard to the left testifies to the movies that were shown upstairs in the council chambers.

Central Engine Company No. 2 volunteers and Dalmatian mascot pose astride their Sauer fire pumper (left) and their American La France ladder truck in the mid-1920s. The Sauer, manufactured in Switzerland, was one of only three imported into the United States. The banner across Chestnut Street reads, "Hear the call of God, go to church Sunday October 18th." The third civilian in front is Henry Berringer, councilman.

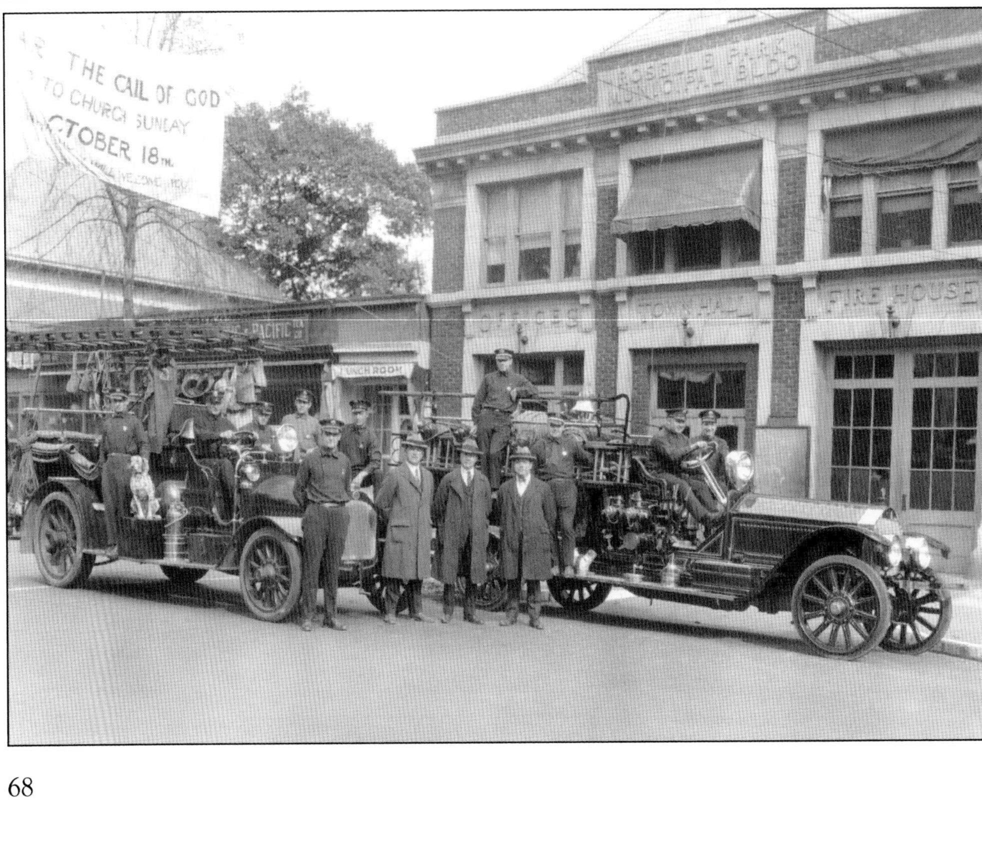

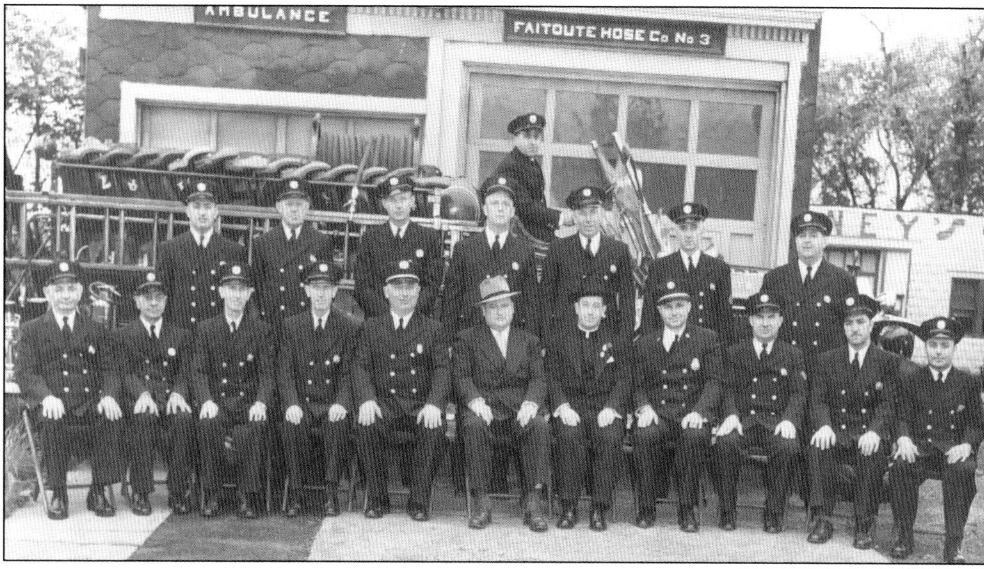

Faitoute Hose Company No. 3 occupied this two-story frame building on West Westfield Avenue. Shown in this c. 1948 photograph, from left to right, are the following: (front row) Nick Manfredo, Alex Mulford, Tom Kelly, Tim Kelly, Joseph Stefanic, Rev. Elsworth G. Schabert (chaplain), Rev. S.J. Chiego (chaplain), Anthony Stefanic, John Carney, Joe Chiaravallo, and Anthony "Farmer" Cere; (back row) Joe Vancio, Herman Gathman, Carl Anderson, Charles Rose, Runyon Doss, Robert Capaldo, and Rocky Chiaravallo. On the GMC 750-gallon pumper is Charlie Florio.

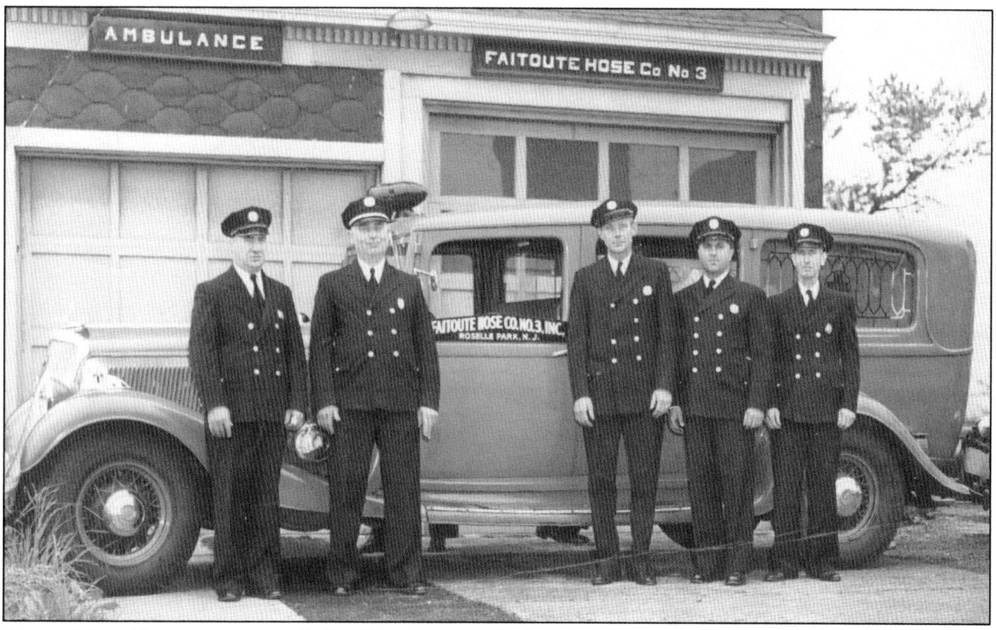

Capt. John Carney organized the Faitoute Ambulance Squad out of Hose Company No. 3 in 1941. Pictured with their 1934 Studebaker ambulance are John Carney, Joe Stefanic, Carl Anderson, Charlie Florio, and Tim Kelly. The Studebaker, originally owned by Christ Hospital in Jersey City, then Rahway First Aid Squad, was purchased for $100 by 20 squadsmen who chipped in $5 apiece.

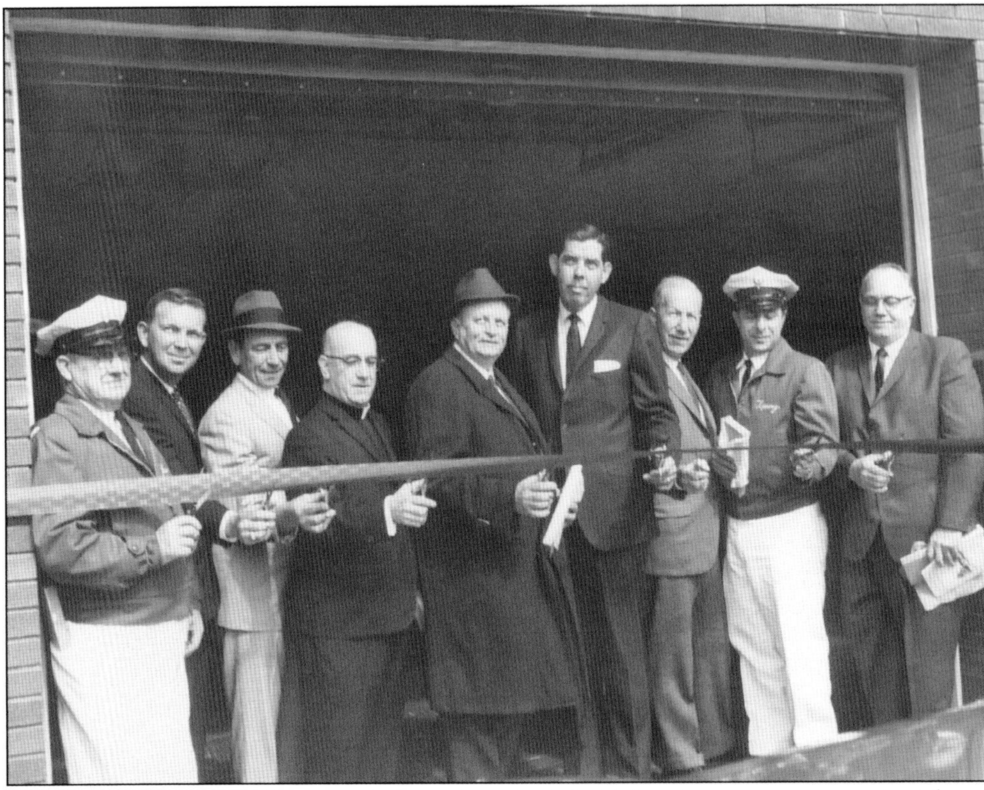

The First Aid Squad Building was dedicated on April 9, 1967, with proper ceremonies. Shown cutting the ribbon, from left to right, are the following: John Carney, First Aid Squad captain; Eugene Carmody, councilman; Edward Miciek, councilman; Rev. Sebastian Chiego, chaplain; Henry Decker, mayor; Rev. Roger Smith, pastor of the Community United Methodist Church; John Harder, councilman; Leonard Genova, councilman; and Peter Demas, councilman. The photograph below shows the completed building on Laurel Avenue.

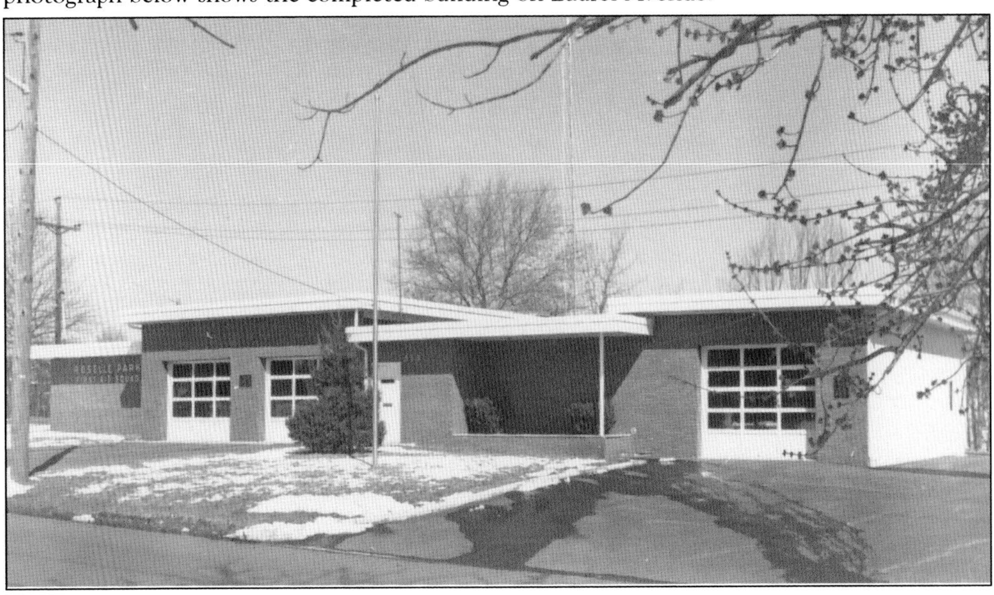

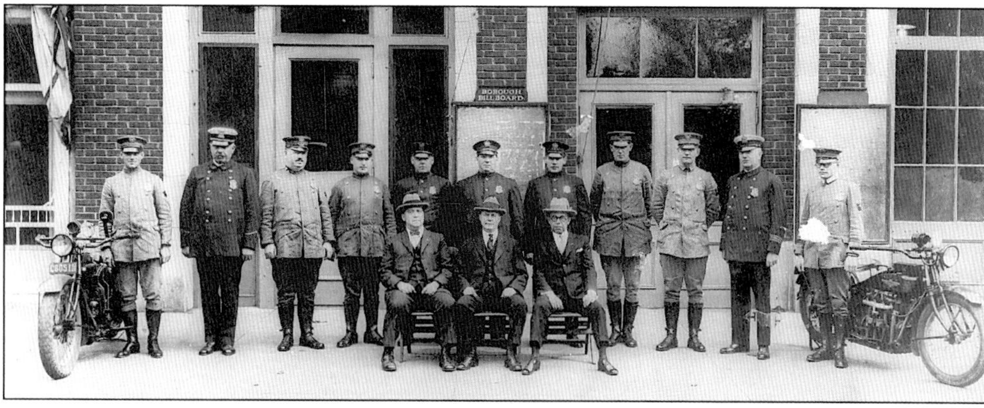

The police force shows off its new motorcycles on October 18, 1925, at the town hall. From left to right are the following: (standing) Walter Day, Roselle Park's first police chief; Simon Bermingham; Sgt. John Shugrue; Frank Schmidt; Simon Bermingham Jr.; Sgt. Charles Kraus; Frank Behring; Roy Duychimick; Norman Olsen; Capt. James Ratchford; and Edward Stevens; (seated) commissioner Henry Biringer, mayor Alfred N. Bagley, and commissioner Edwin T. McNaughton.

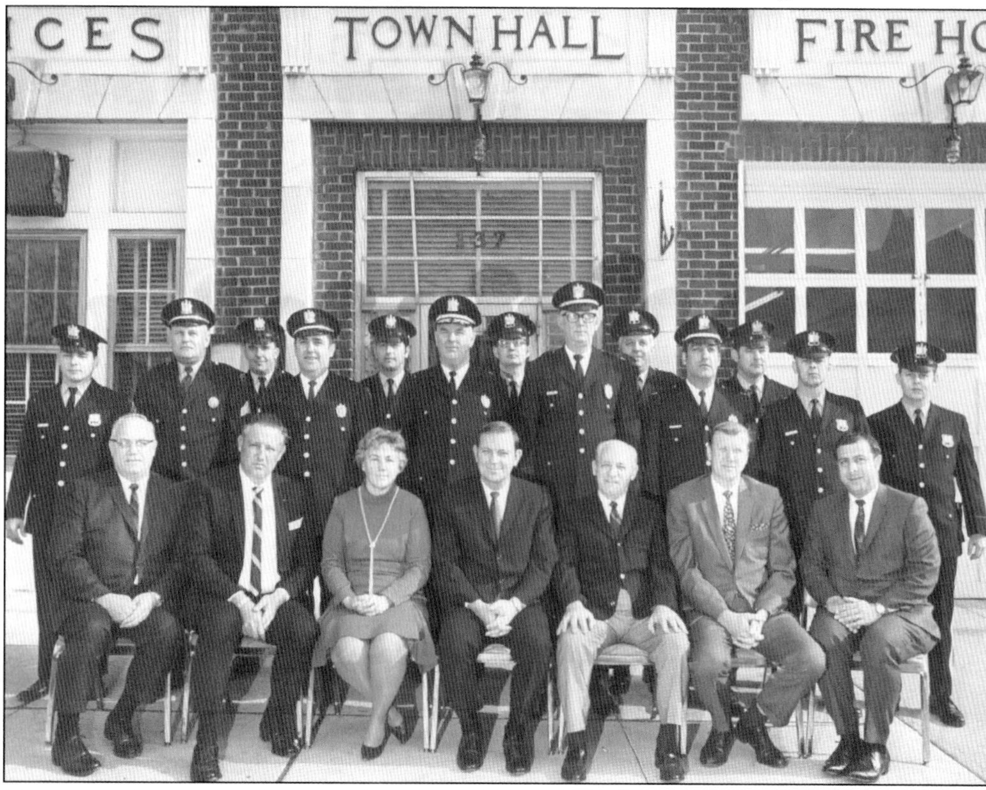

Shown are the mayor, the council, and the 1969 police department. From left to right, they are as follows: (first row) Peter Demas, councilman; Robert Morgan, councilman; Penny Hahn, councilwoman; Eugene Carmody, mayor; Salvatore Cacosa, councilman; James Sykes, councilman; and Leonard Genova, councilman; (second row) Off. Ronald Scull; Sgt. Anthony Kranick; Capt. Walter Terbecky; Chief Thomas Quinn; Dep. Chief Thomas Maher; Sgt. Ben Malaspina; Off. Ronald Bebert; and Off. William Jenkins; (third row) Off. Joseph Salinardo; Off. James Kompany; Off. Jack Murphy, Off. Raymond Parenteau; and Off. Dominick Vecchio.

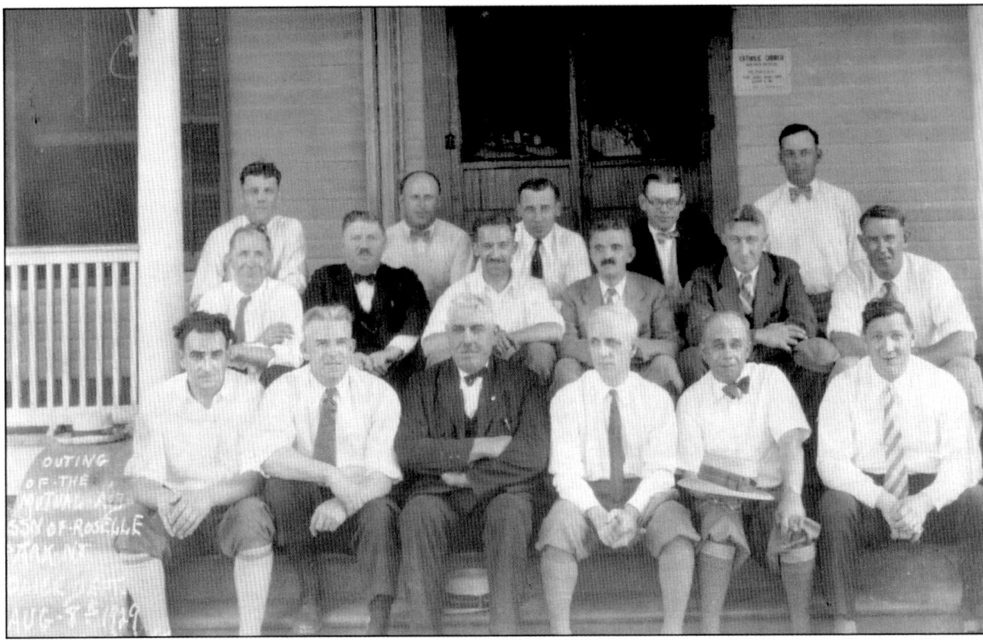

On August 8, 1929, the Mutual Aid Association of the Roselle Park Police Department met at Highlands, New Jersey. Shown, from left to right, are the following: (first row) Casimer Valdes, unidentified, Cy Birmingham, Elliot Dill, Edwin McNaughton, and unidentified; (second row) unidentified, John Shugrue, Otto Paulson, Charley Renton, unidentified, and Roy Duychimick; (third row) John Ahle, unidentified, unidentified, Ed Stevens, and Walter Day.

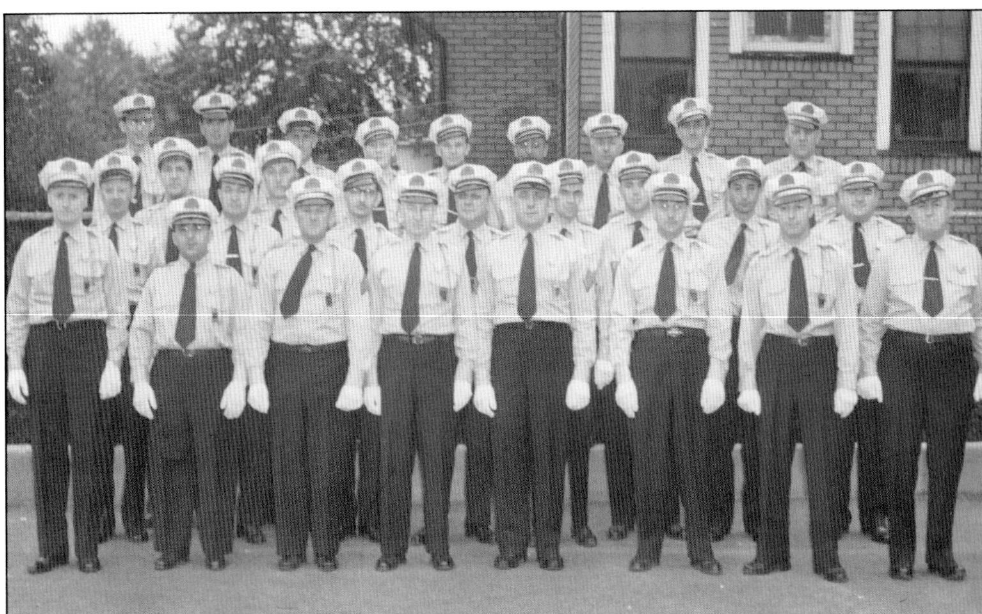

Among the members of the 1952 Auxiliary Police are Dave Keenan (first row, first on left) and Fred Wolf (first row, last). Keenan was the founder and first president of the Roselle Park Historical Society. Wolf was the organizer of Roselle Park's little league baseball; Wolf Field is named after him.

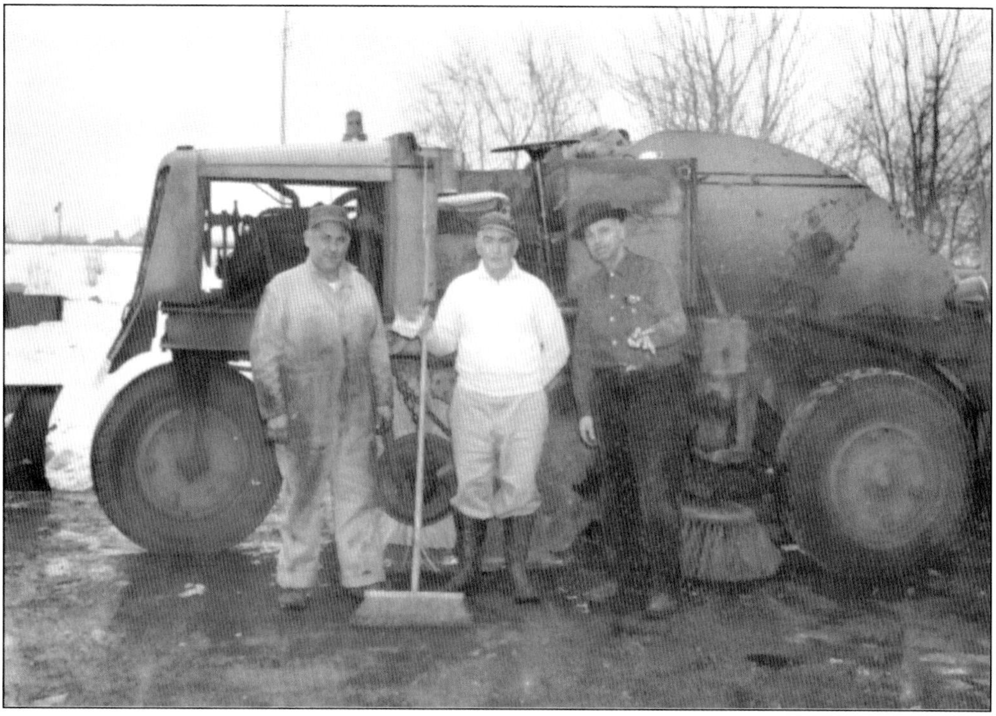

Department of Public Works employees Pat "Bobo" Vecchio and Nick Florio (with the broom) were supervised by Pat Adase as they cleaned up during the 1960s with their open-top Elgin sweeper, which was "brutal to drive," according to Frank Iscaro. He and Vecchio, who were drivers, eventually became DPW supervisors. Charlie Florio voluntarily cleaned town streets on Sundays.

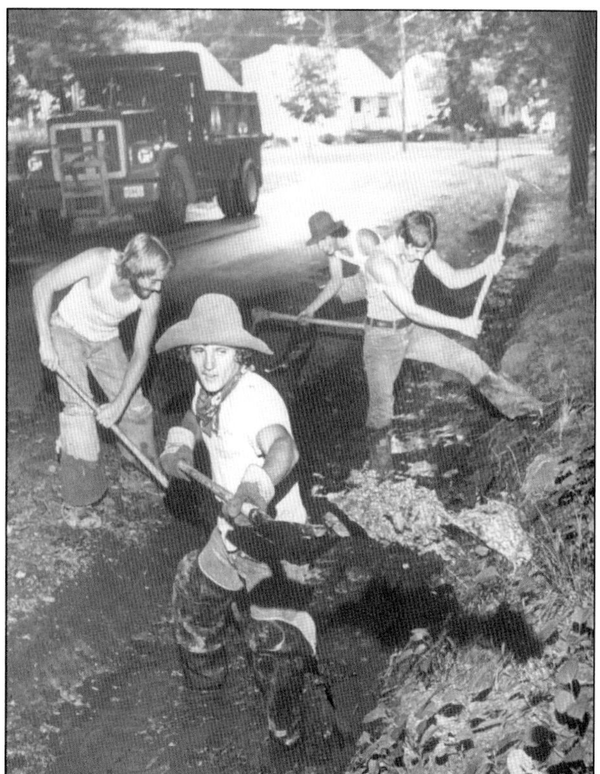

Four young men, members of the 1971 seasonal work force with the Roselle Park Public Works Department, clean the brook along Lehigh Avenue. In the foreground, under the campaign-type hat, is Todd Morgan, with Kevin Carroll at the left. In the background are Frank Iscaro and Glenn Gallo.

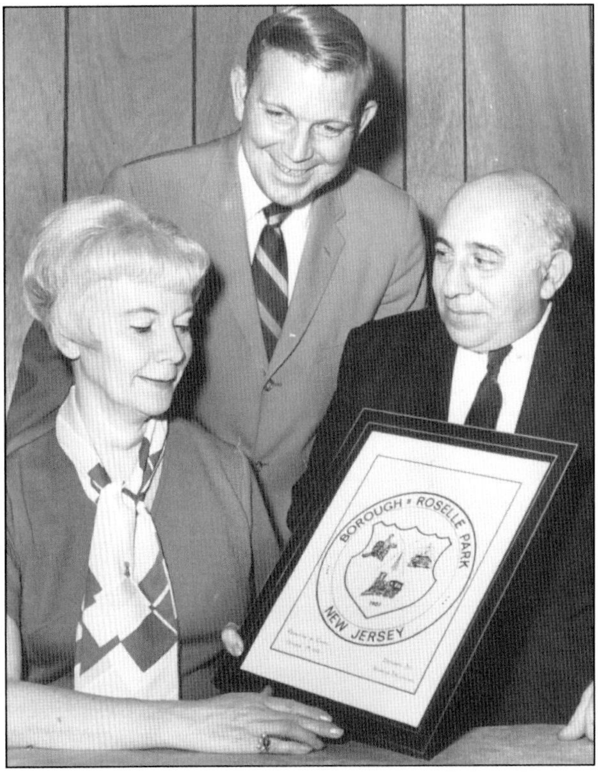

On October 9, 1969, a resolution was adopted to recognize the official borough seal, designed by Nicholas J. Delloiacono. He won the design contest initiated by Ginnie McKenney. Mayor Eugene Carmody is at center.

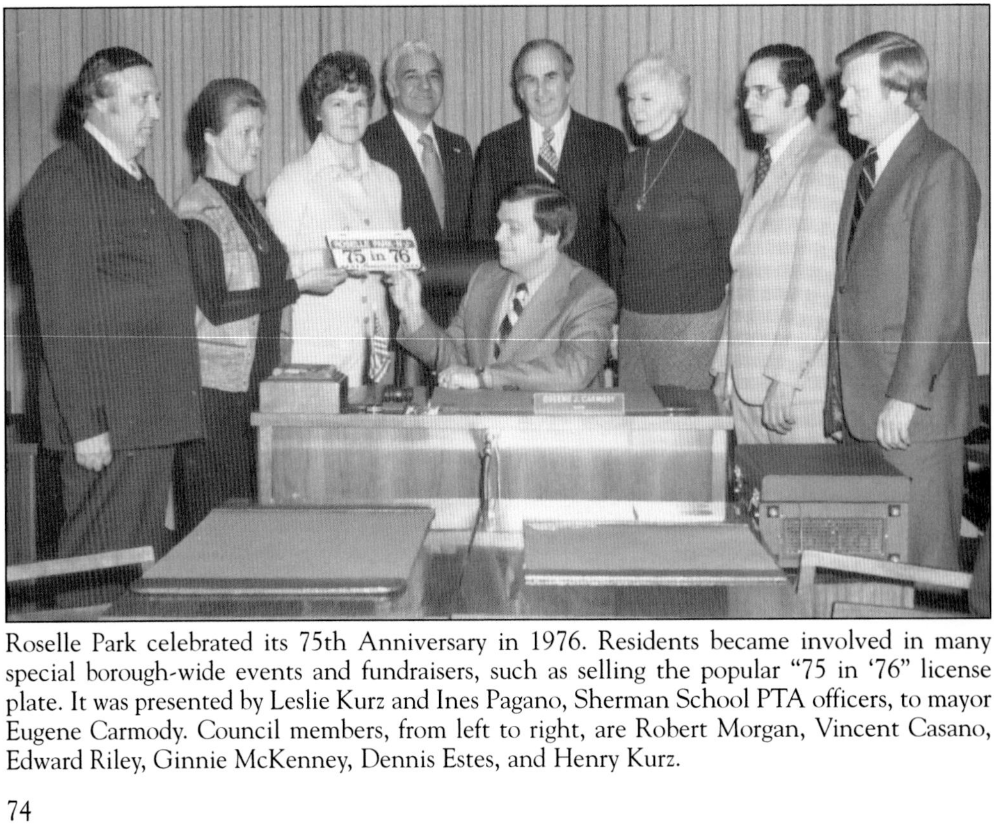

Roselle Park celebrated its 75th Anniversary in 1976. Residents became involved in many special borough-wide events and fundraisers, such as selling the popular "75 in '76" license plate. It was presented by Leslie Kurz and Ines Pagano, Sherman School PTA officers, to mayor Eugene Carmody. Council members, from left to right, are Robert Morgan, Vincent Casano, Edward Riley, Ginnie McKenney, Dennis Estes, and Henry Kurz.

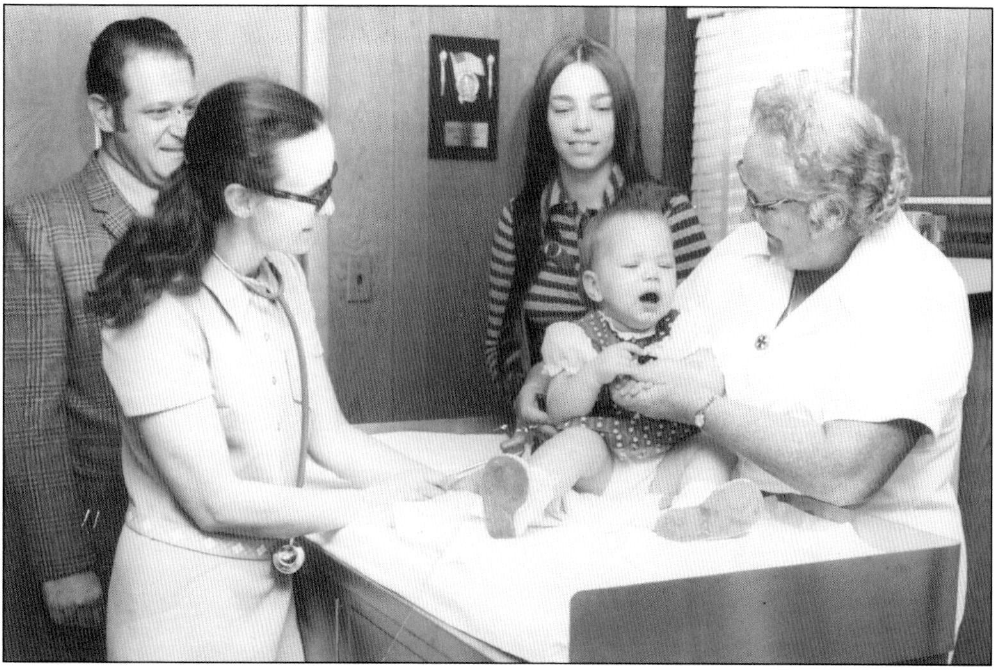

The board of health was created by Ordinance No. 1 on May 4, 1901. The Child Health Station opened in a clinic room at the First Aid Squad Building in 1968. During its first year of operation, it served 81 families. In the foreground, Dr. Carol Kay Lissenden, pediatrician, and Veronica Harvey, RN, examine baby Wendy Reddington, as Fred Colucci and Patty Reddington look on.

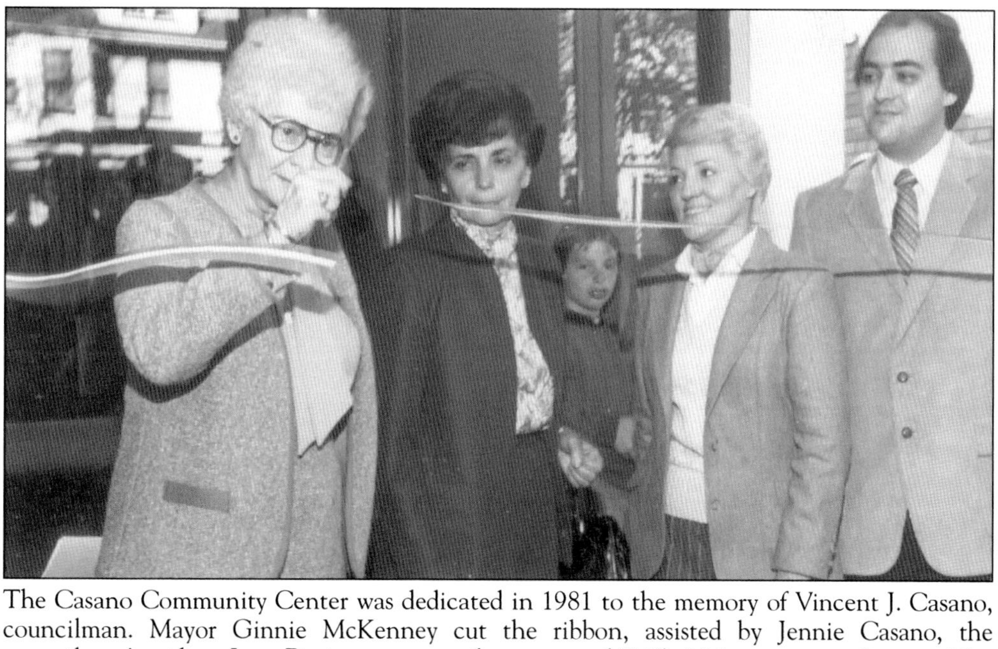

The Casano Community Center was dedicated in 1981 to the memory of Vincent J. Casano, councilman. Mayor Ginnie McKenney cut the ribbon, assisted by Jennie Casano, the councilman's widow; Joan Desimone, councilwoman; and "Mike" Maury, center director. The center is used for scout meetings, teen dances, aerobics, senior citizens' card games, movies, nutrition programs, and exercise classes.

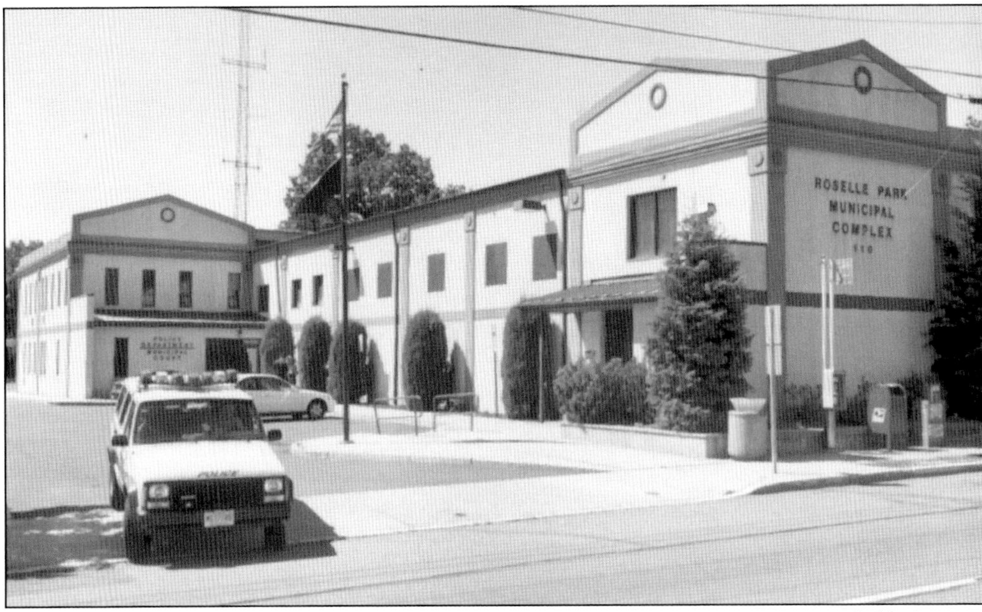

The Roselle Park Municipal Complex was dedicated in 1989 at 110 East Westfield Avenue, replacing the aging 1915 structure at 137 Chestnut Street. Administrative offices, the police department, and council chambers upgraded to the modern facility.

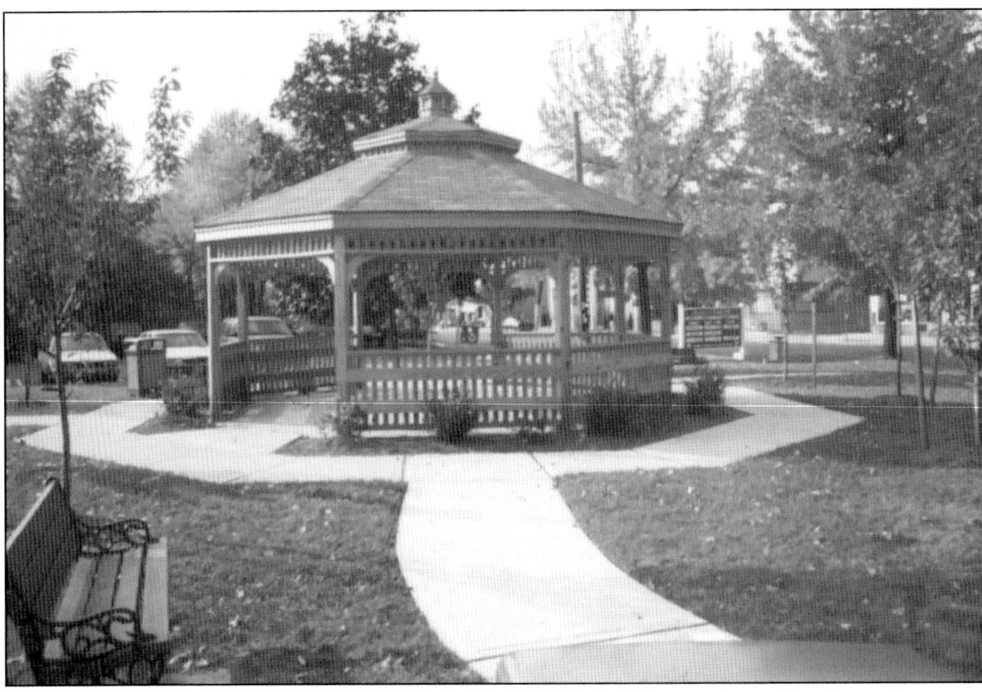

Dedicated to the memory of the first Casano Center director, the gazebo and park on the corner of Grant Avenue and Chestnut Street was named for Michael J. Mauri on June 20, 1992. This focal point serves as a meeting place for many activities, including parade reviews, antique car shows, a farmers' market, and as a bandstand. It is popular for wedding portraits and Easter sunrise services.

Six

All around Town

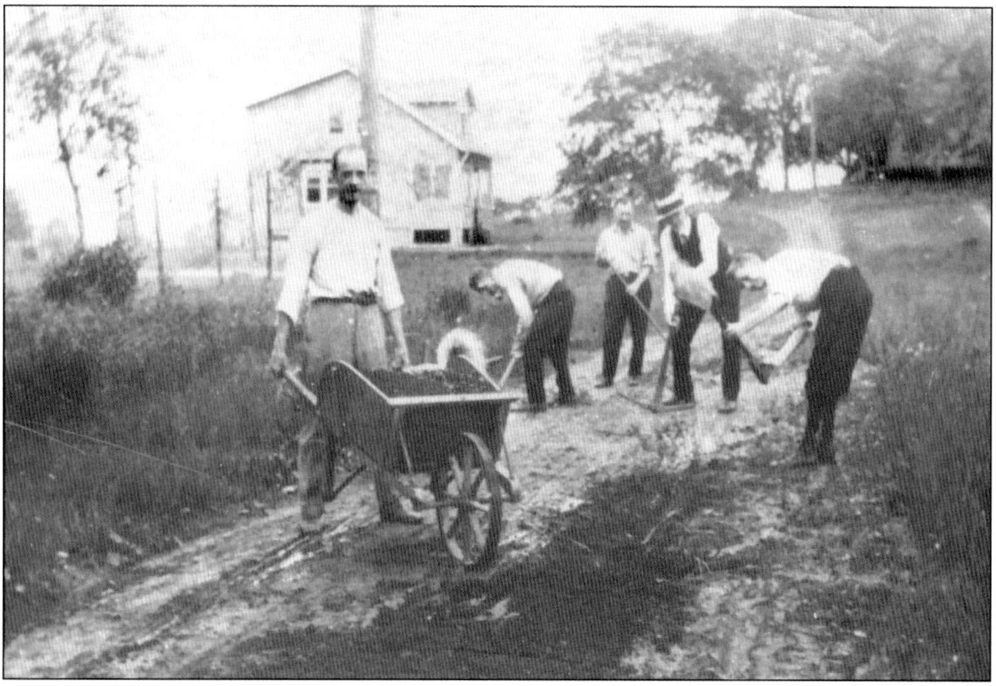

Side streets by the 1900s were little more than unnamed pathways leading from home to home. These neighbors roll up their sleeves and use picks, shovels, wheelbarrows, and hard work to widen a trail that would one day be called Roselle Avenue. Street names in most communities offer insight into the history and character of a town. Approximately 25 streets are named for trees or bushes. Other streets are named after prominent people, both local and national. Local family names include John C. Bender, Charlotte R. Charlier, Fr. Sebastian Chiego, Peter Donald, J.T. Faitoute, Ellen F. Gordon, David Magie, M. Markthaler, the Ragland brothers, John Seaton, E.I. Tucker, M.J. Warren, and the Williams family. Galloping Hill Road brings back the memory of Revolutionary War messengers on horseback galloping to bring important news to George Washington at Morristown.

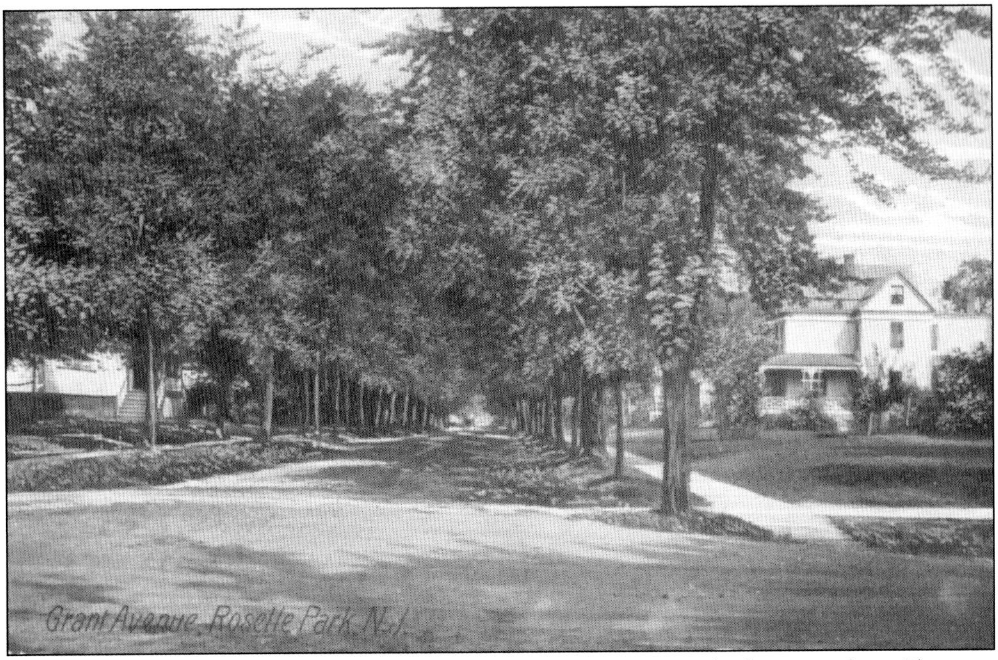

This lovely tree-shaded lane in the late 1800s is East Grant Avenue, looking east from Chestnut Street. The steps of the Methodist Church are visible on the left.

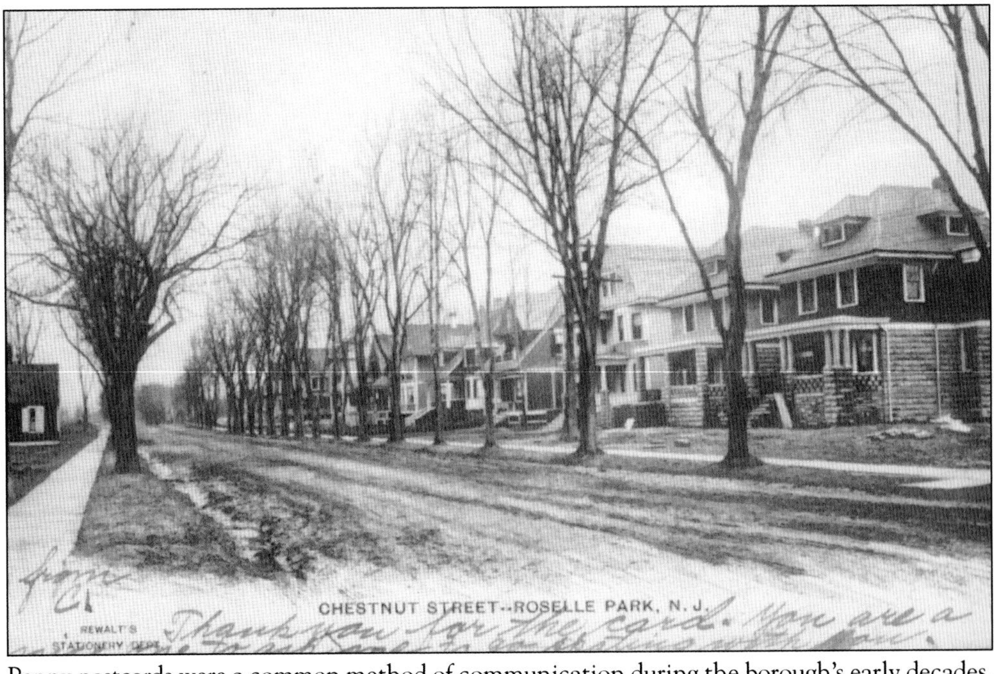

Penny postcards were a common method of communication during the borough's early decades. This one shows sturdy homes on the east side of Chestnut Street north of Clay Avenue. Although sidewalks existed, the road was uncurbed and unpaved. A message addressed to W.T. West Jr. of the Alpha Delta Phi House in Amherst, Massachusetts, reads, "Thank you for the card. You are a nice one to ask one to go skating with you. From C."

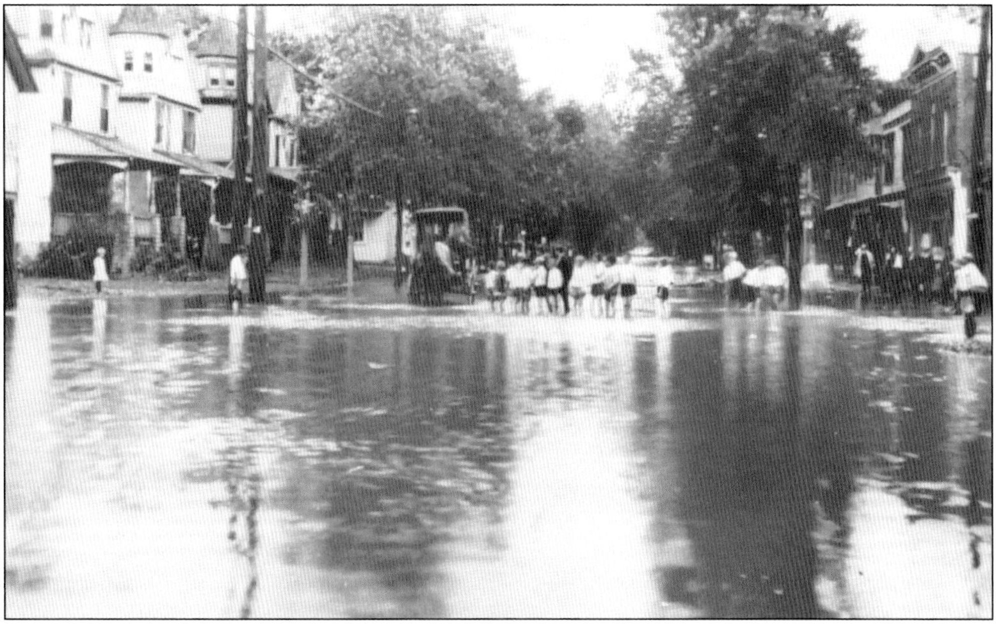

Few remember a Chestnut Street that looked like this. Children take advantage of slow draining rainwater as they cavort in the middle of what is the center of town today. Houses lined the main street before storefronts replaced open porches.

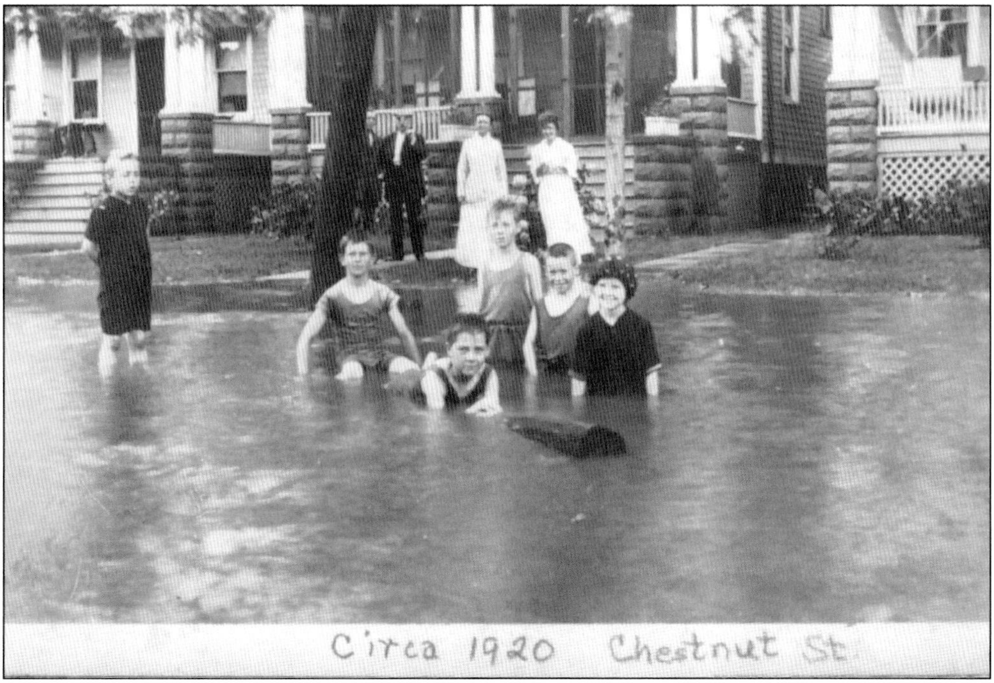

Children enjoy an impromptu swim after a summer rainstorm while watchful parents observe. Street flooding was a major problem in the borough's early years, until proper drainage systems were completed. This scene in front of 163, 165, and 169 East Grant Avenue hints of a leisurely pace, with comfortable furniture on the porches.

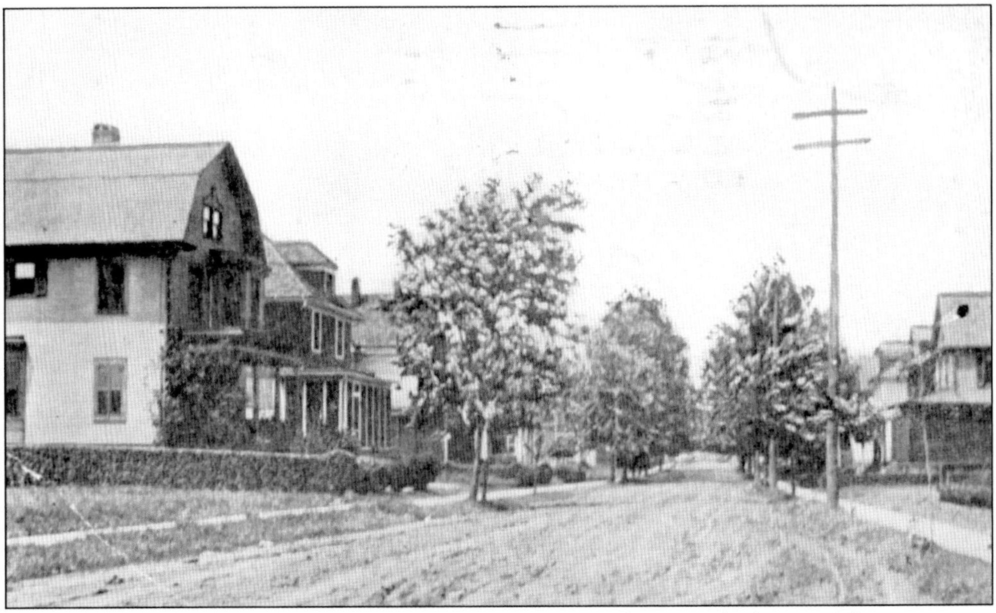

Camden Street homes are featured on this penny postcard postmarked 1919. The streets are still unpaved in this view. Many older residents remember that when it rained, the horse drawn wagons would get stuck in the mud. The message reads, "Hope you are having a fine time." The postcard is addressed to "Edward Richards . . . c/o D.H. Winters" from "Uncle John and Aunt Mattie."

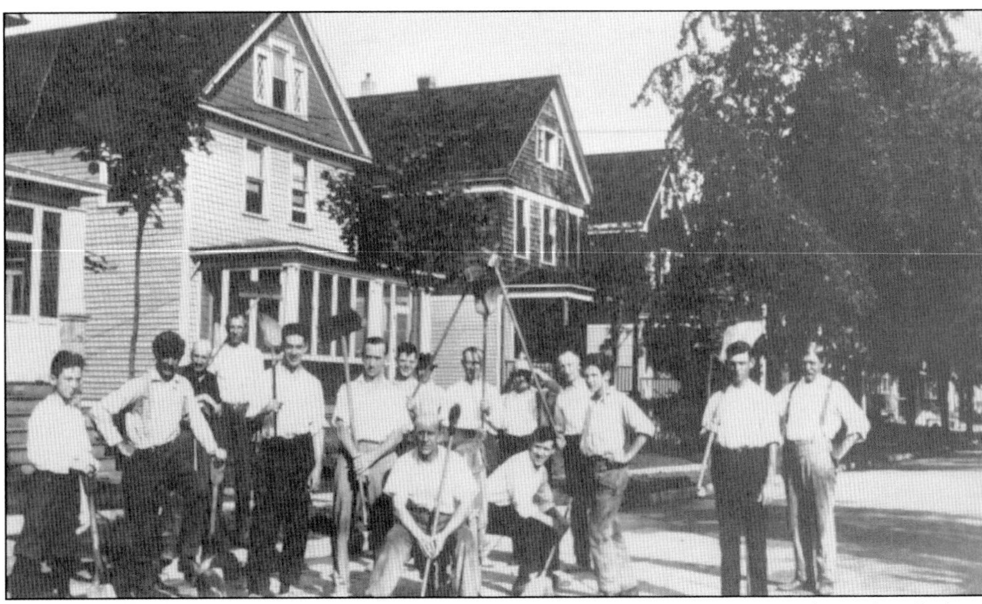

With shovels, brooms, and rolled sleeves, these men on Dalton Street take a break for a photograph after cleaning up the neighborhood, c. 1930s. This street is part of the block made up of the "A, B, C, and D" streets—Avon, Berwyn, Camden and Dalton Streets.

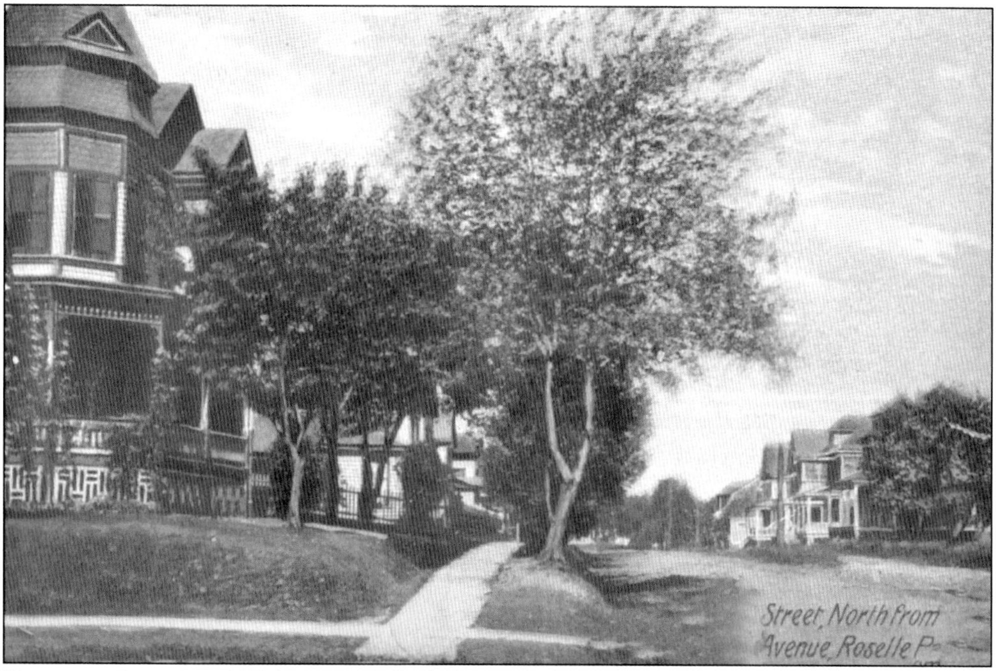

Homes in this view of Walnut Street looking north from Westfield Avenue reflect turn-of-the-century architecture. Once called St. Joseph's Place, this block was planned by G. Gott and opened in late 1800s with township aid. This postcard to Charles Potter, Grant Avenue, from Elsie Lewis, was an invitation to a Junior League Social at the Lewis's on Friday evening.

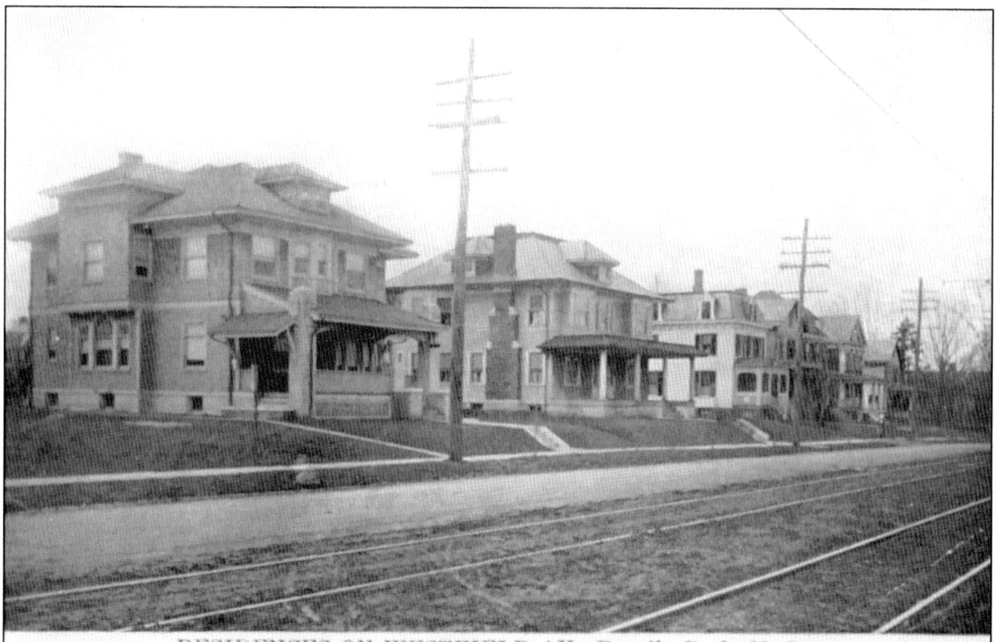

RESIDENCES ON WESTFIELD AV., Roselle Park, N. J.

Looking west from Walnut Street, early-20th-century homes like these line the south side of East Westfield Avenue. The trolley tracks in the foreground took the local trolley rider east into Elizabeth or west to Aldene, and then on to Kenilworth.

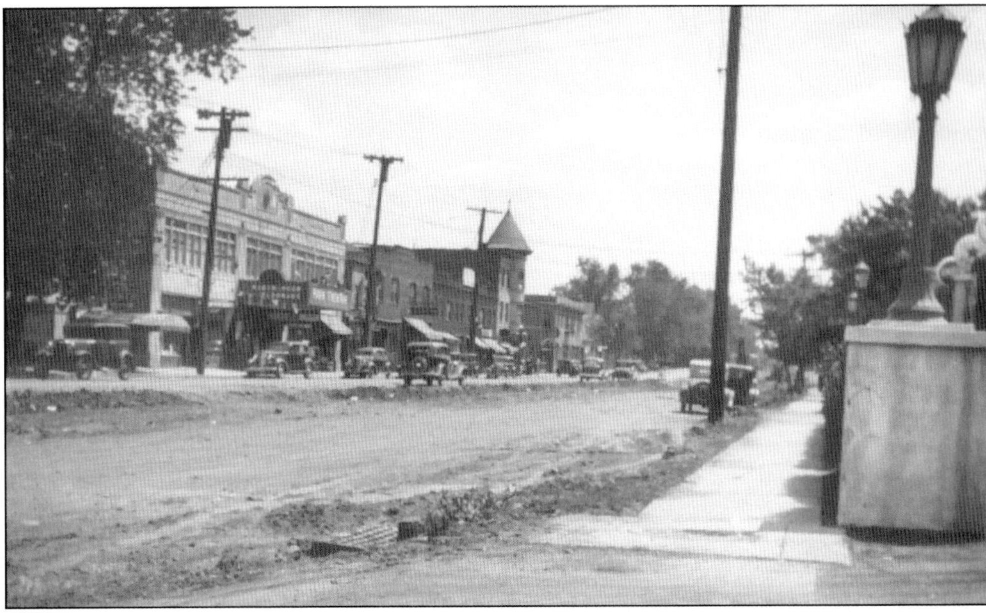

Weekends found the art-deco style Park Theater bustling with crowds over the decades. An elaborate interior was restored in the 1970s. The facade received a facelift and a new name, the New Park Cinema. Antique decor now hides behind partitions that divide the movie house into multiple viewing rooms. The work of road-widening is in progress in this view.

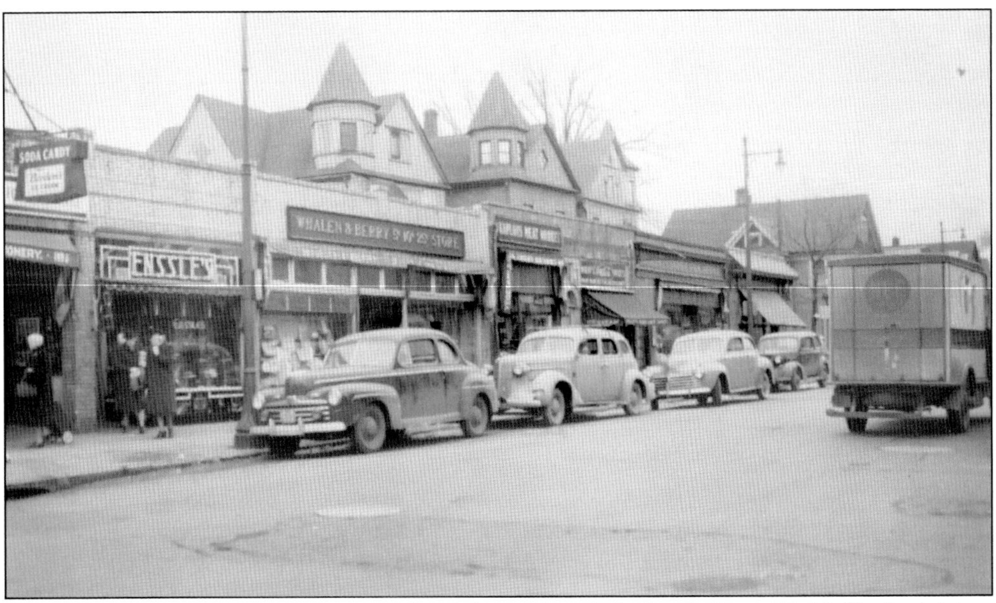

In a 1948 view of Chestnut Street, Enssle's Bakery Shop, Whalen & Berry 5&10, Kaplan's Meat Market, Wulff's Ice Cream and Candy, Rosenblat Variety Store, and the Superior Market entice customers. These stores are long gone, but houses behind the stores remain part of the skyline. Costa's Ristorante replaced several of these businesses.

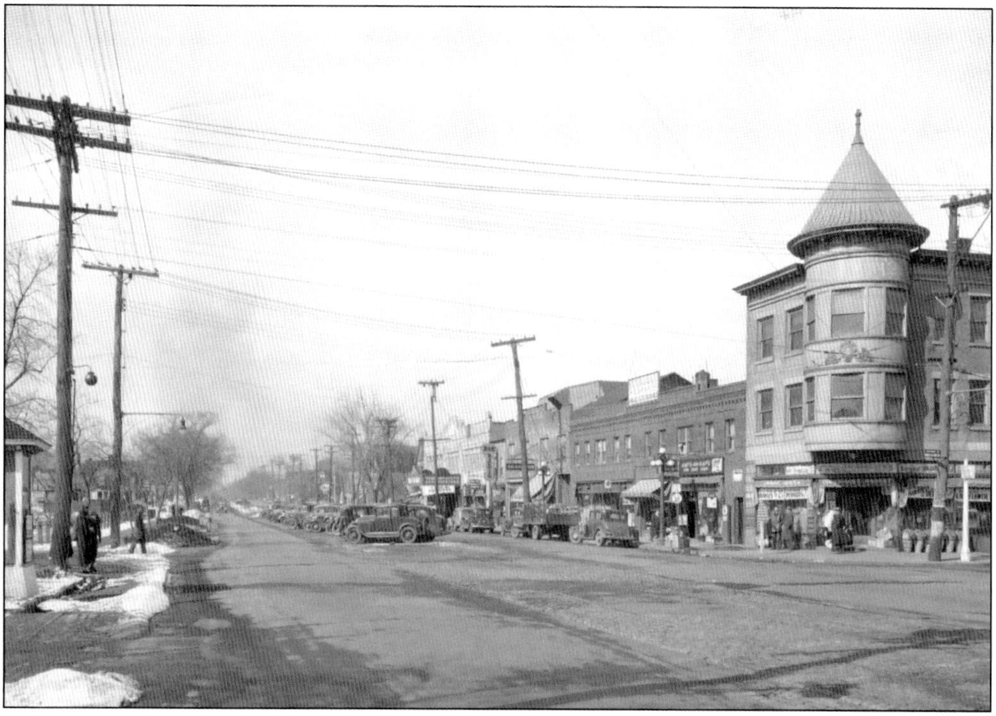

What a difference a year makes. Two views demonstrate the march of progress between March 6, 1936, and April 14, 1937. Before, motorists parked on a cobblestone center of the street, and overhead wires and poles brought electricity to five-ball streetlights (mid-right). After the center divider was installed and Westfield Avenue was resurfaced, shoppers angle-parked vehicles into curbsides.

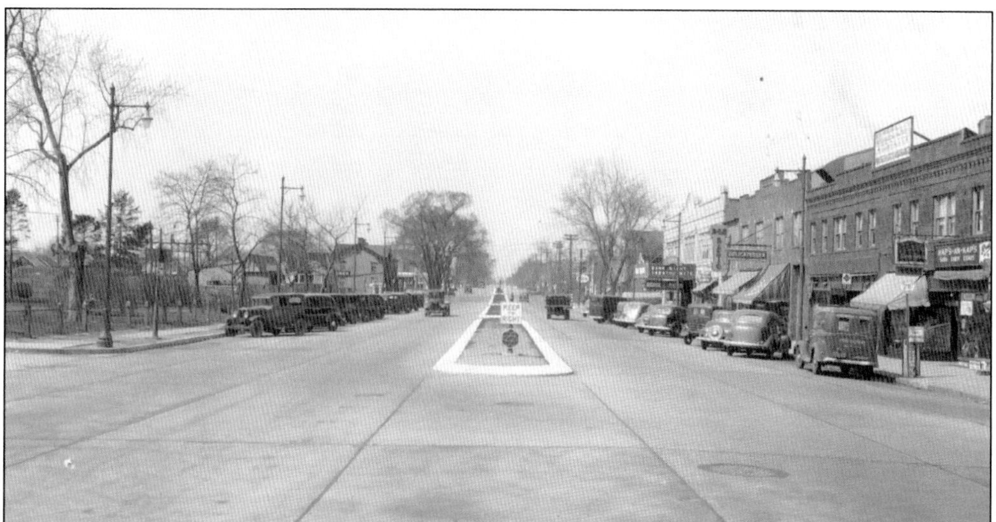

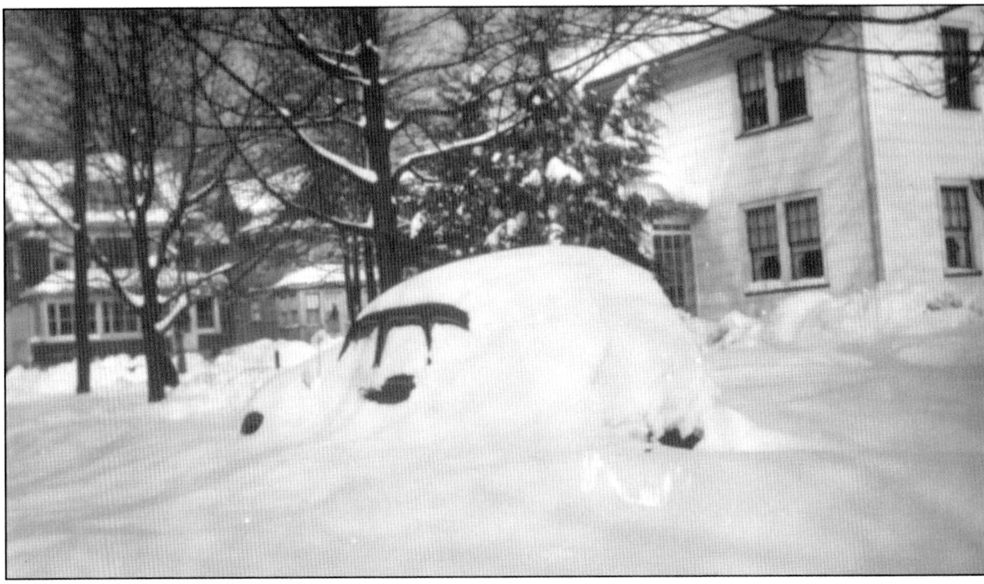

The blizzard that devastated the northeast on December 26, 1947, left the borough of Roselle Park buried under 3 feet of snow. This 1946 Ford stranded in front of 341 Pershing Avenue is not much more than a white bump in the road. The homes in the background are on East Clay Avenue.

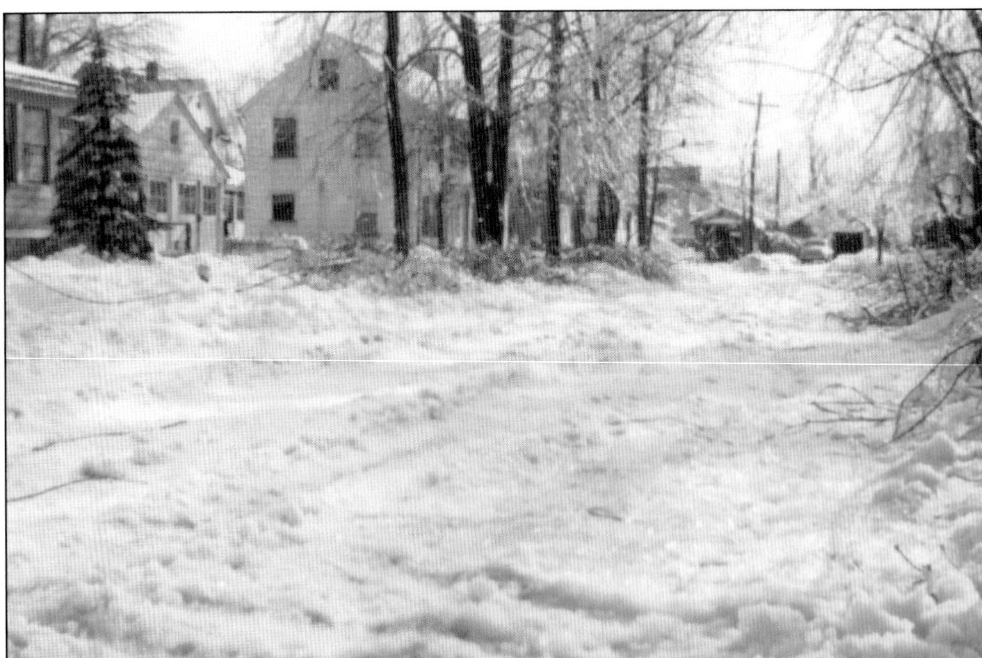

After a week of digging out, many streets were still impassable and sections of town were isolated. This January 2, 1948 view looks south on Hemlock Street toward East Grant Avenue. After years of normal winter weather, it was a wake-up call to public officials to make future snow removal a priority.

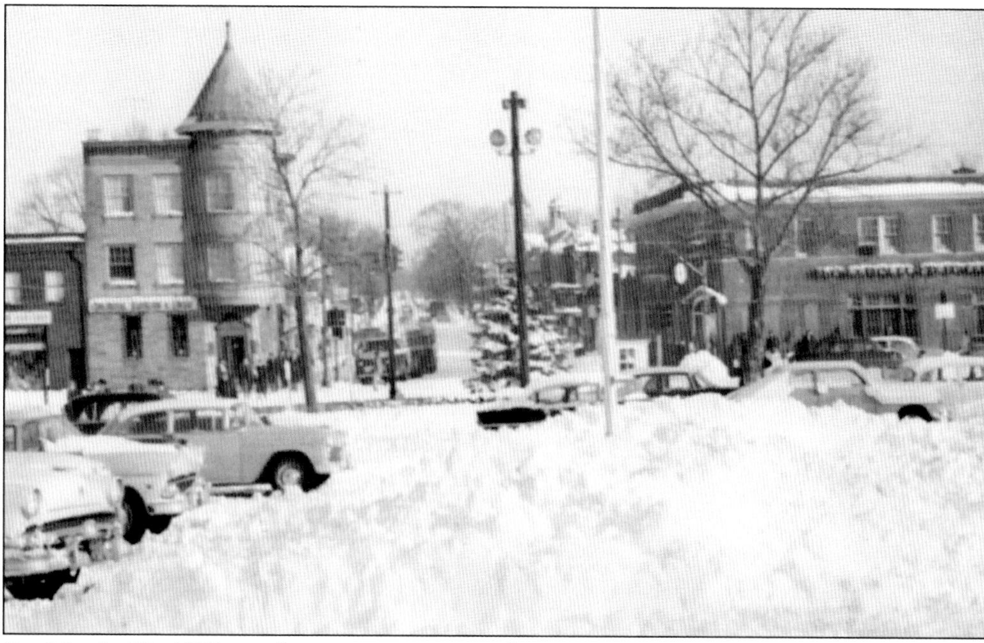

On March 18, 1956, residents were emerging from a picturesque winter storm. Looking up Chestnut Street from the Central Railroad Station, one can identify the landmark dome of the Colonial Savings Bank and the historic clock of the National State Bank. These 1950s vintage cars are parked free at "the Oval," once borough property.

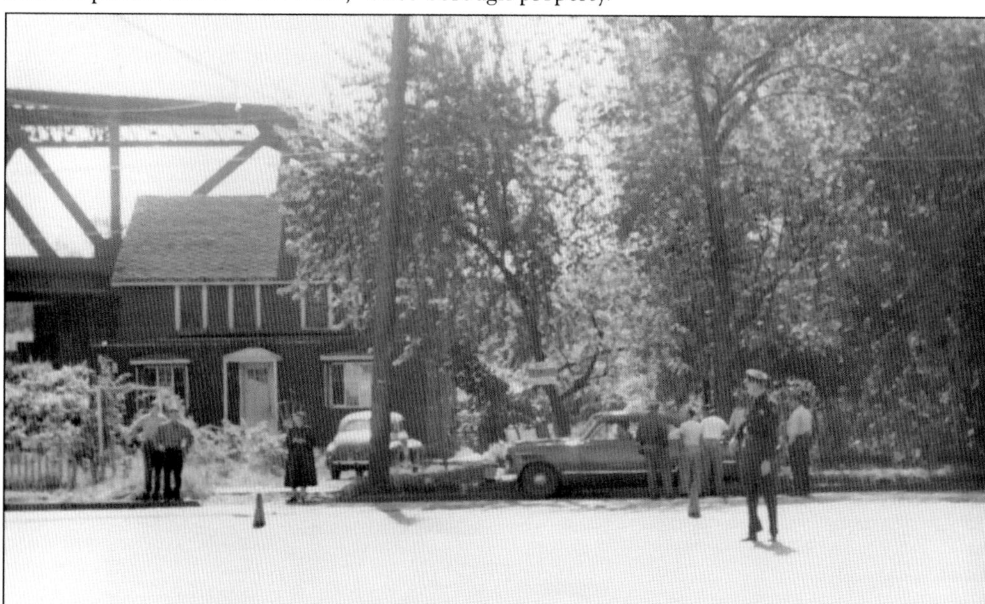

Police officer Martin Eldred directs traffic following a construction accident on West Westfield Avenue and Jerome Street on October 3, 1956, where three people were burned in a road-surfacing fire, and one later died. Well known as "Marty," the officer went on to become a captain. The trees and homes in the background were leveled to become the site of Quality Auto Center and Burger King. (Note the For Sale sign on middle tree.) The railroad trestle on the right belongs to Lehigh Valley.

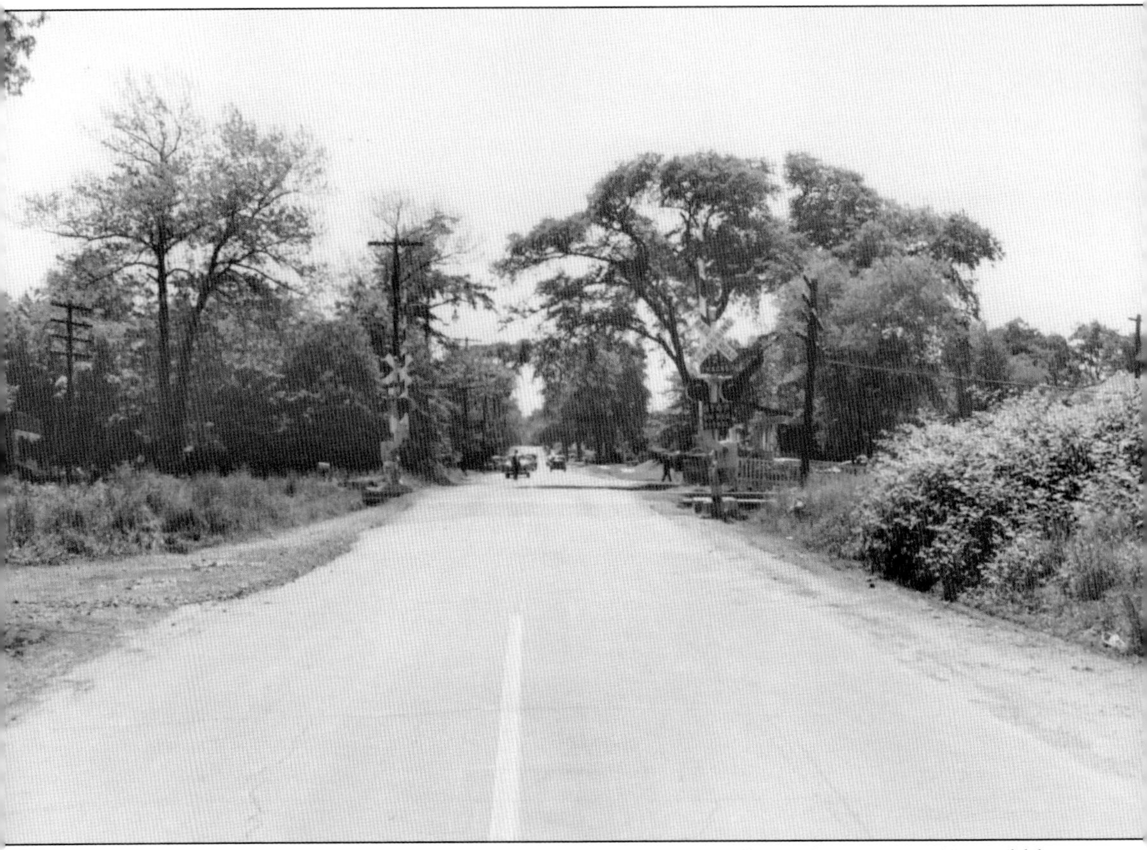

Motorists entering the borough southbound on Galloping Hill Road in May 1953 would have enjoyed this rural view, but would have to negotiate the Lehigh Valley street-level tracks. Roselle Park is on the right side of this narrow road. Union Township is on the left side.

Seven

BUSINESS AND INDUSTRY

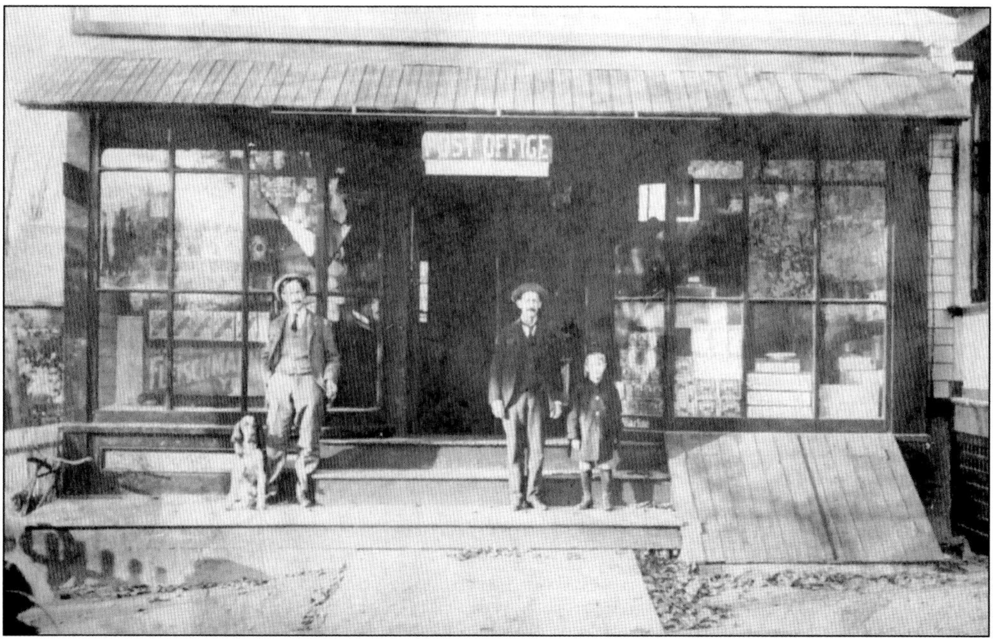

In 1883, the first store in the world to be lighted by electricity was Charles E. Stone's general store at 14 East Westfield Avenue. It was wired by Thomas A. Edison, whose Roselle laboratory was only blocks away. The solitary light fixture was made of a gas pipe with three arms, bearing a bulb at each end. Stone received three years of electricity free as reward for his courage in allowing this new invention in his store. Hearsay is that when the first bulb burned out, Stone held his hand over the socket to keep electricity "from escaping," while a helper went to get a new bulb from his friend, Edison. His store was also the first official U.S. post office, located inside what would soon become Roselle Park (note the sign).

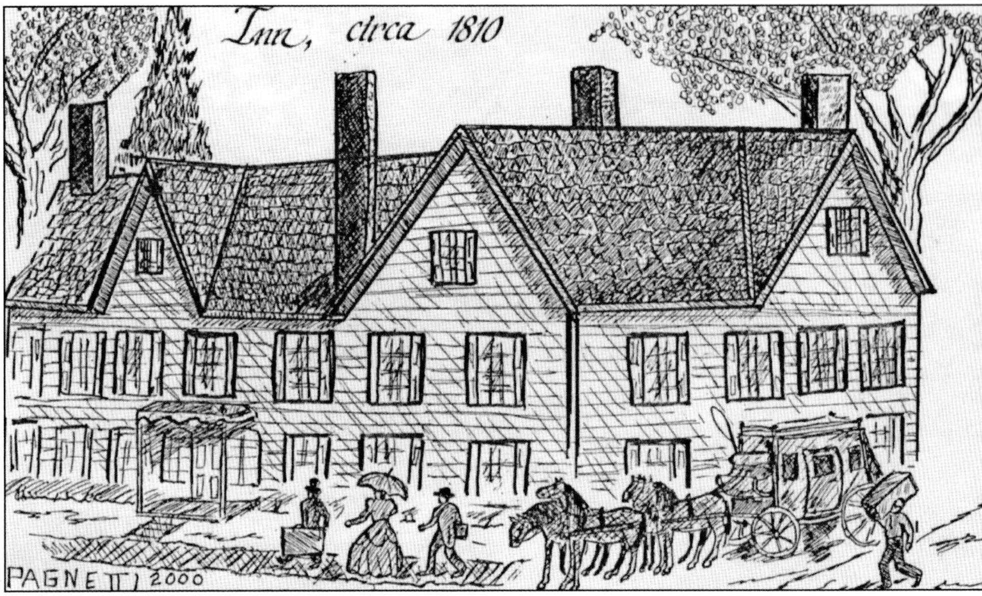

On the "Road to the Westfields," this c. 1810 building was once a stop on the stagecoach route between New York and Philadelphia. The drawing represents the original concept of the inn, and the 1999 photograph shows an extension to the front. It has been a lodging house, billiards parlor, tavern, and restaurant. Legend says the spirit of Etta Hatten, a previous owner who died in 1934, still protects the establishment, currently Domani's Restaurant. Employees and customers claim that strange apparitions and events only occur in the original structure, but not in the 1970s front annex.

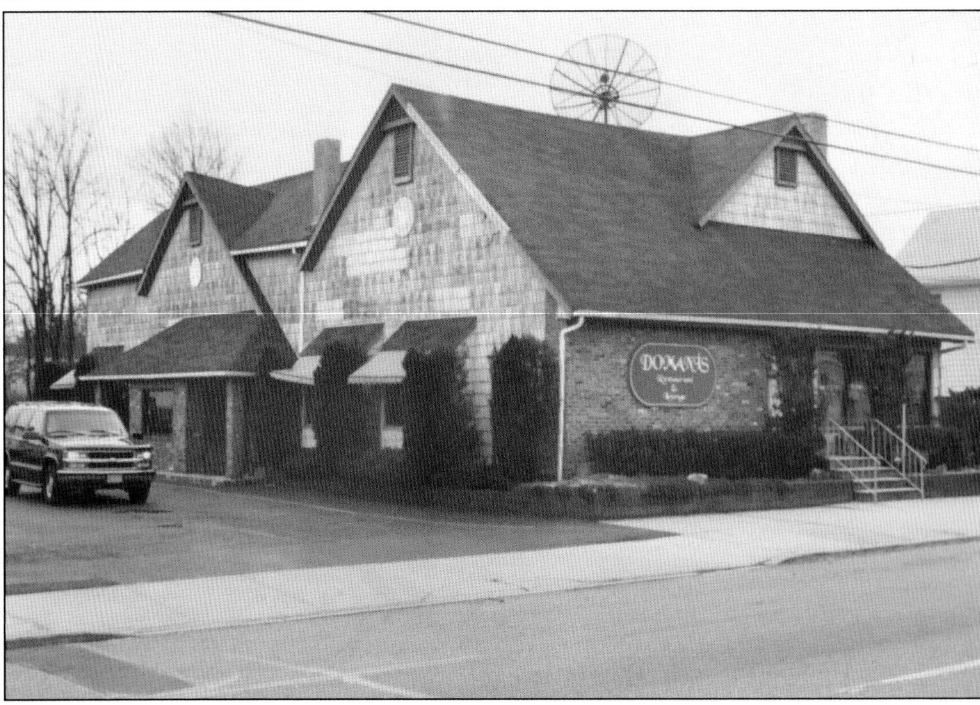

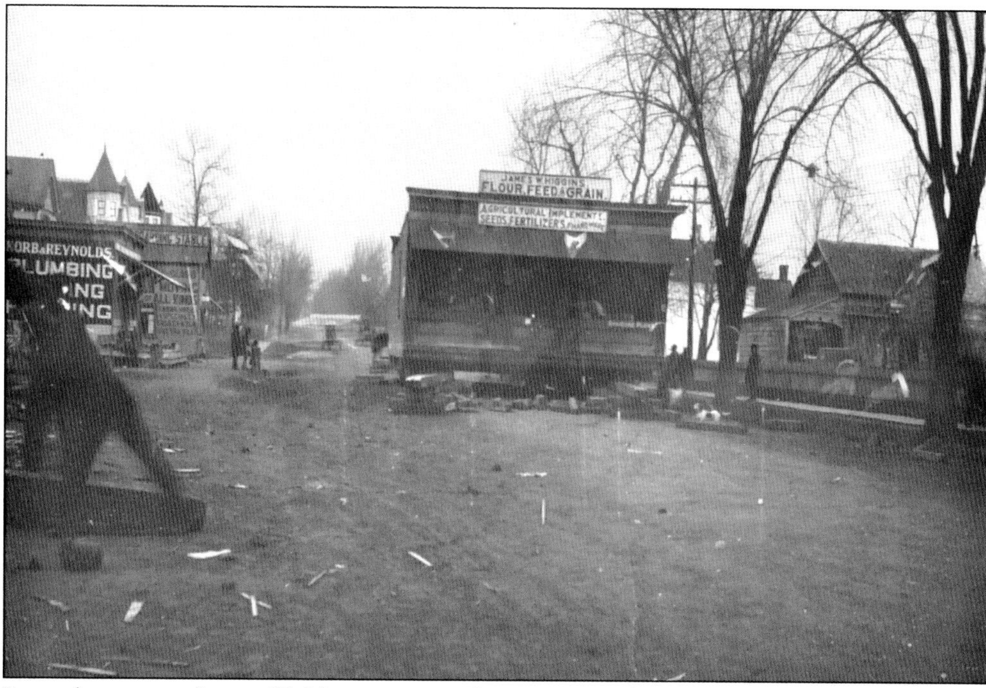

Passersby gape as James W. Higgins moves his store up Chestnut Street near the corner of Westfield Avenue. Business demands of the pre-turn-of-the-century Roselle Park area were heavy on flour, feed, and grain. Higgins sold agricultural implements, seeds, fertilizers, and hardware. The same peaked roofs of yesteryear's storefront homes have survived and are still behind the facade of today's business.

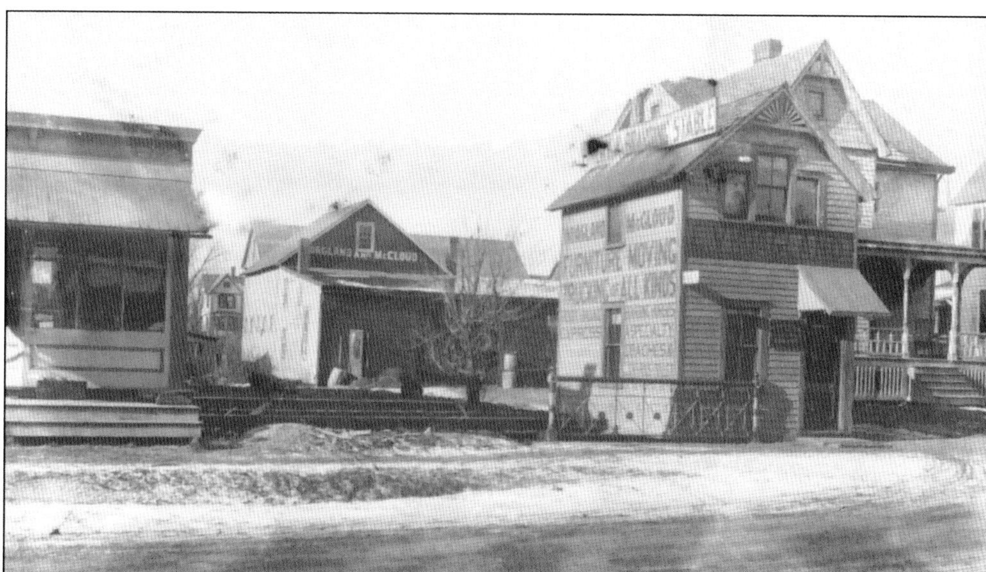

On the west side of Chestnut Street is Korb & Reynolds Plumbing. Next door is Hoagland & McCloud's Livery and Boarding Stable. Their diversified market included furniture moving, trucking of all kinds, freight, package express, boarding horses (their specialty), and coaches and light rigs to let.

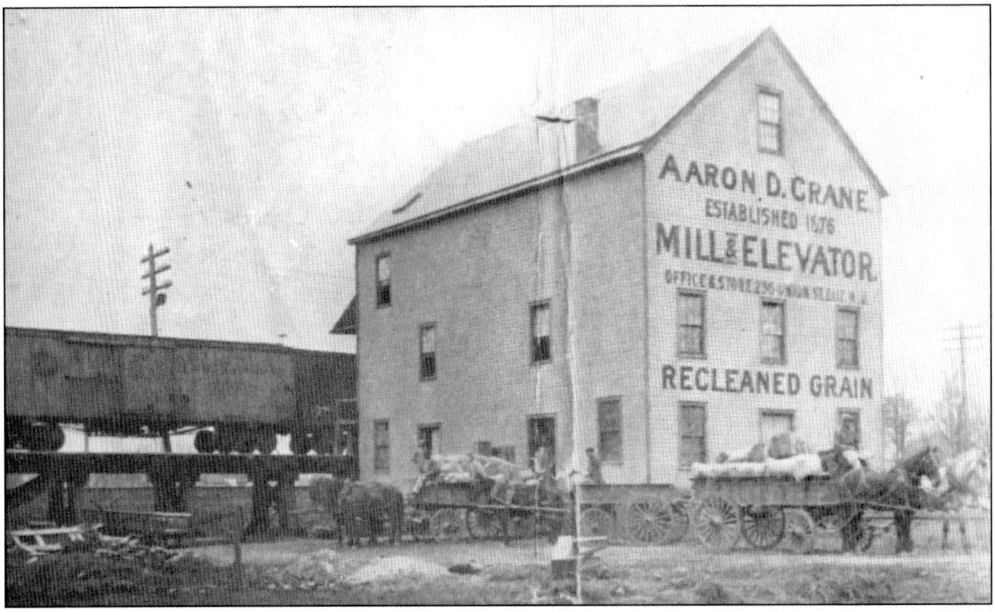

Aaron D. Crane Mill and Elevator was located along the railroad tracks on East Westfield Avenue below Linden Road. Recleaned grain is being hauled from the mill by teams of horses and wagons.

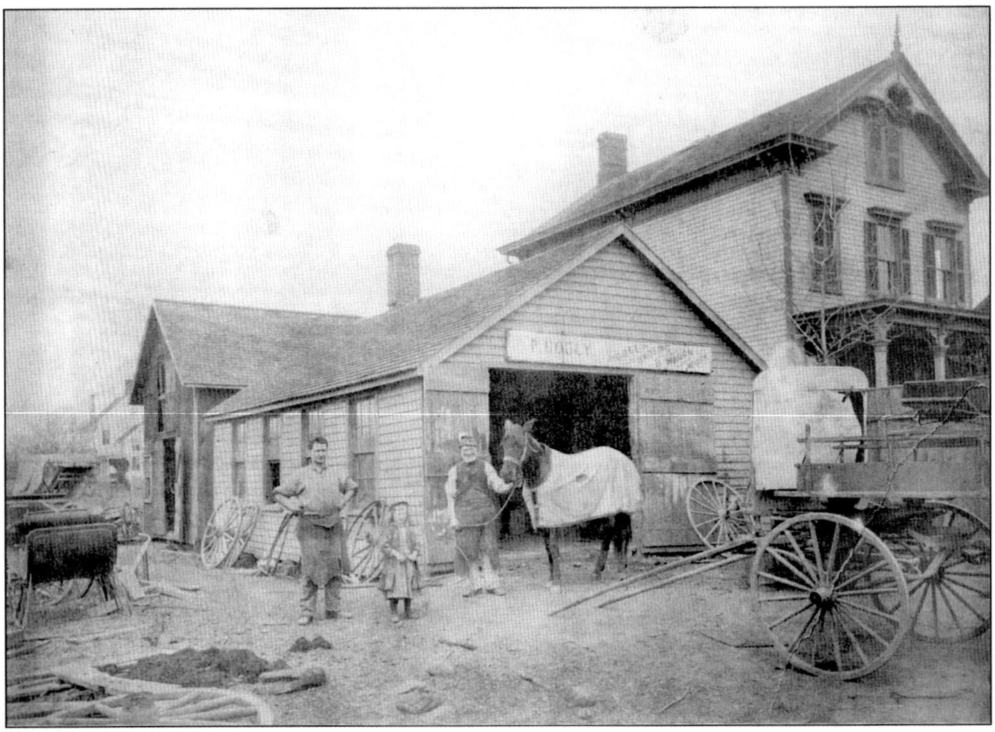

Patrick Cooley's Blacksmith Shop and Wagon Repair, *c.* 1890, was on Westfield Avenue and is believed to have been near the Park Cinema. Pictured here are Patrick Cooley, his son John, and a worker. Mrs. K. Shriner, who moved to Roselle Park in 1902, recalls watching the fire and hearing the hammer as they shoed the horses.

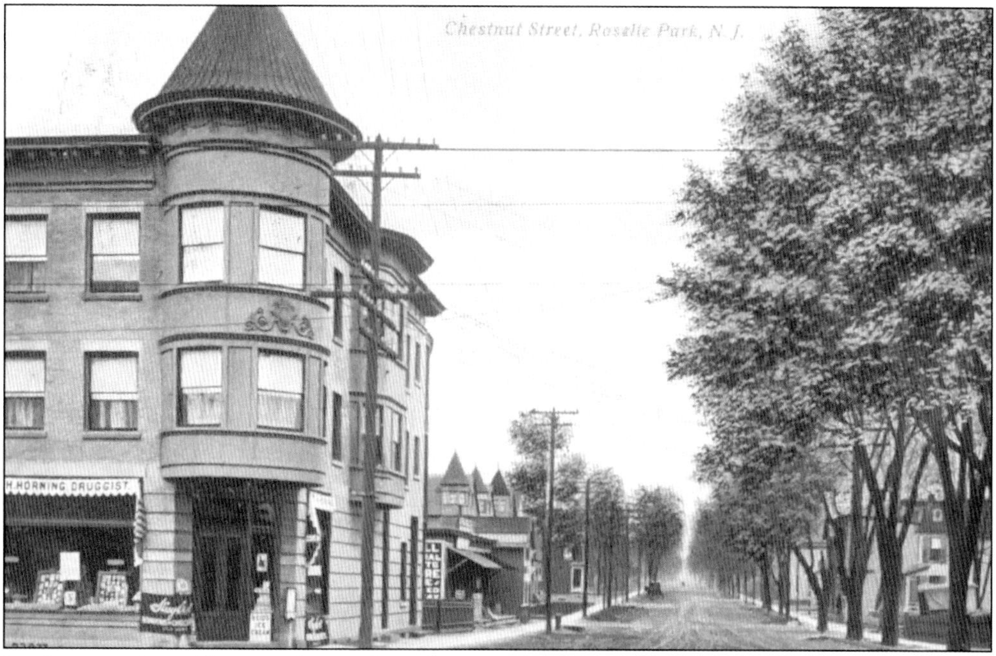

Looking north up Chestnut Street, from the corner of Westfield Avenue, is the "center of town," c. 1900. The Queen Anne-style building, a classic landmark for more than 100 years with its familiar peak, housed Horning's Drugstore. Mrs. K. Shriner describes the interior decorated with vases strung with gold cord, round tables, and tiny chairs: "If you had the money, you could get a sundae in there." Its neighbors were a plumbing shop, a livery stable, and residences. Tall trees lined the unpaved road.

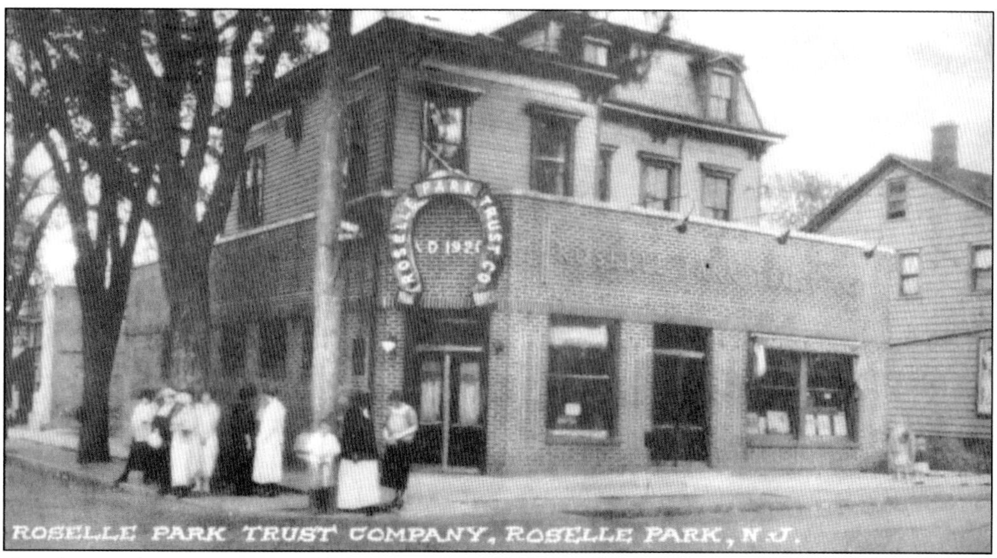

On the northeast corner of Chestnut Street and Westfield Avenue was Woodruff's Butcher Shop. Early residents remember the meat hooks, heavy chopping block, and sawdust covering the floor. Out back were pens for chickens, pigs, and other animals. The building was remodeled and opened in 1920 as the Roselle Park Trust Company with Aaron D. Crane as president.

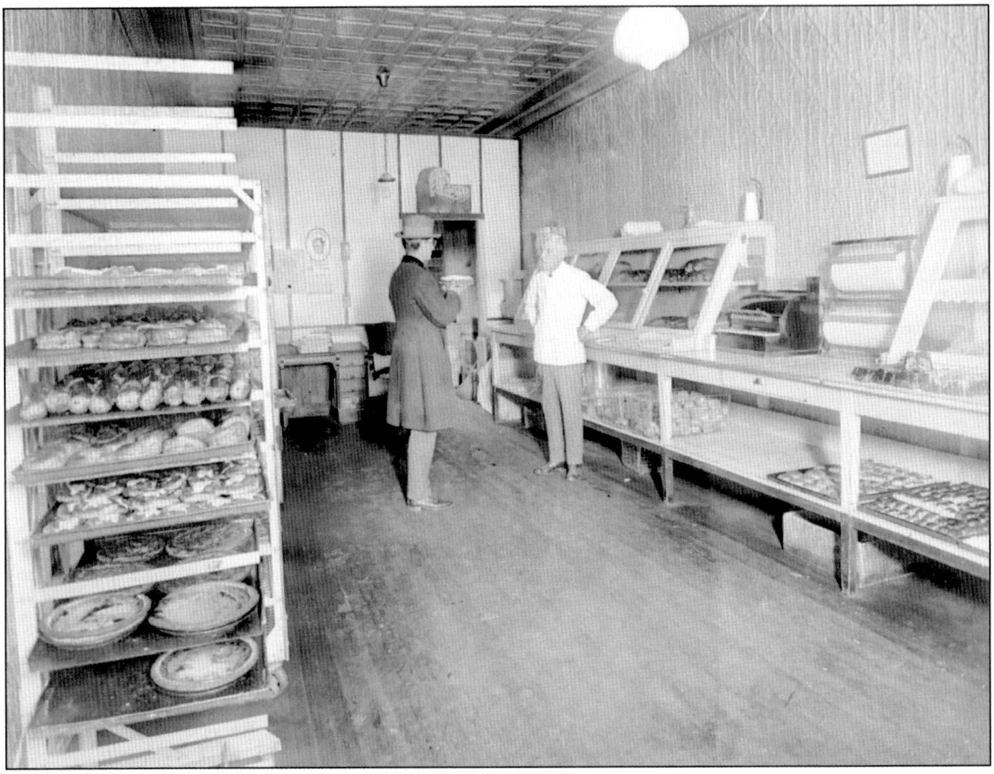

Bill McCloud proudly displays his baked goods as a gentleman selects a pie in his shop, located on the east side of Chestnut Street. Note the tin ceiling. Sadie Wilson remembers working in this bakery shop in the early 1920s.

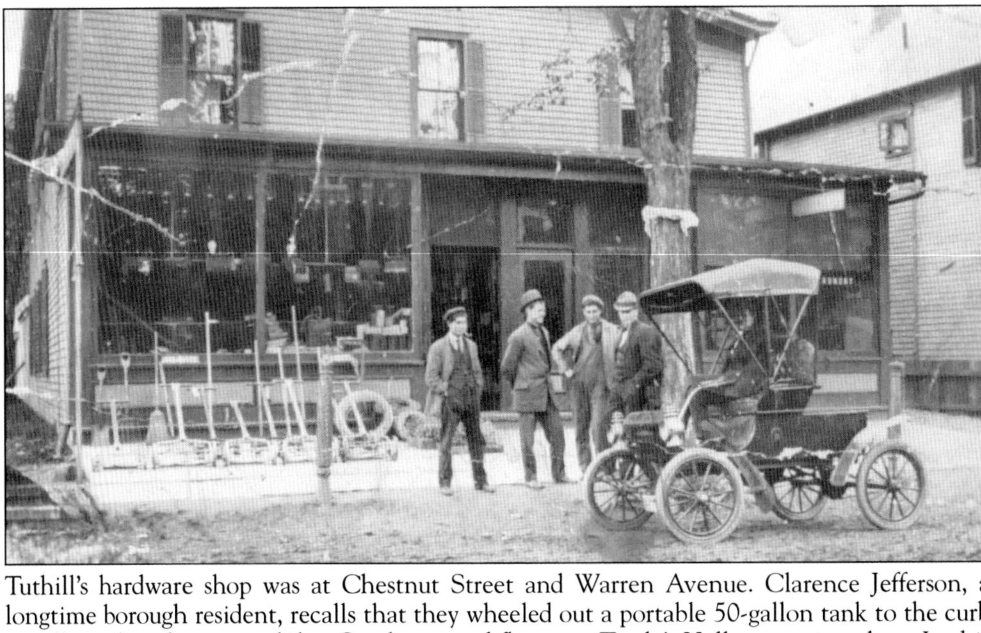

Tuthill's hardware shop was at Chestnut Street and Warren Avenue. Clarence Jefferson, a longtime borough resident, recalls that they wheeled out a portable 50-gallon tank to the curb to sell gasoline for automobiles. On the second floor was Tuttle's Hall, a meeting place. In this image, John Cooley is driving the first electric car in Roselle Park.

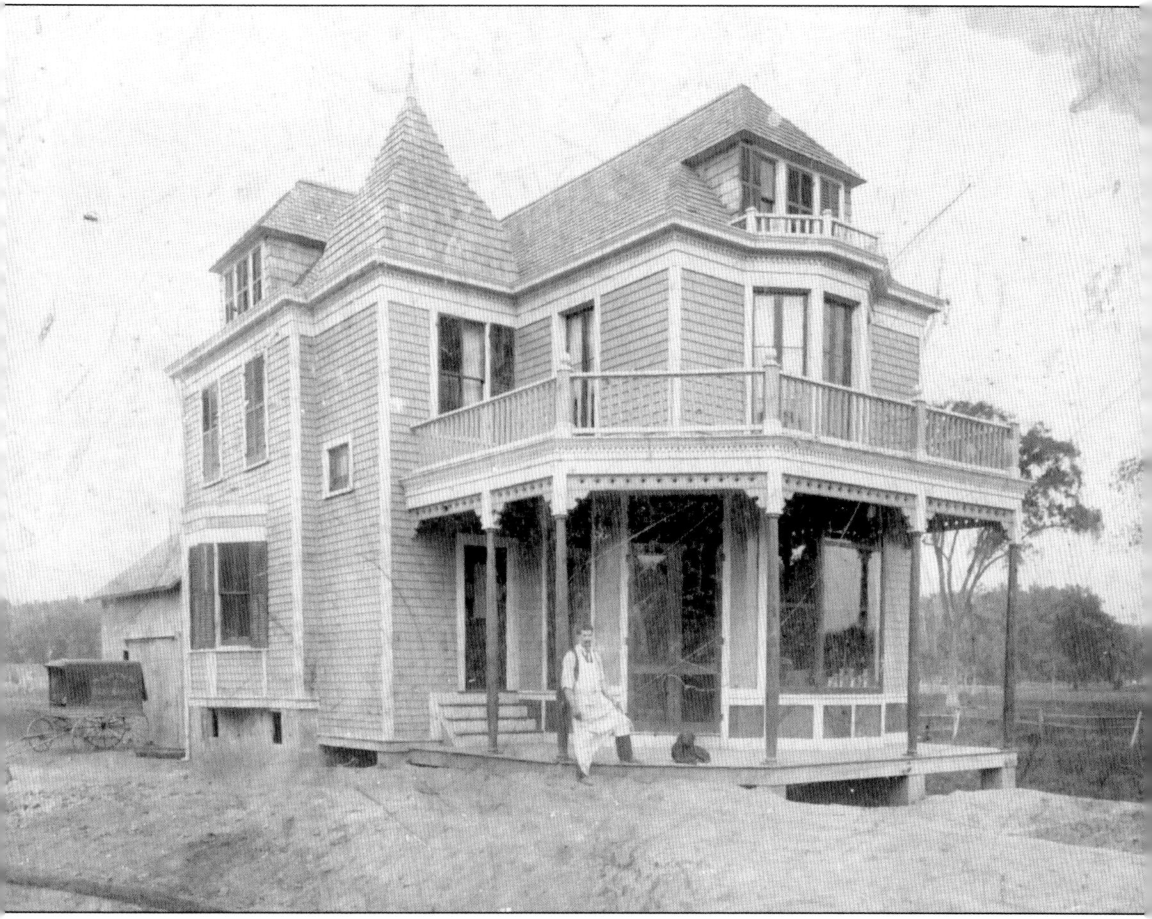

Joseph Riccatelli stands in front of his meat market and home on the corner of Chestnut Place (now Columbus Place) and Westfield Avenue. He started his business in Roselle Park by selling meat door to door. He also sold real estate and cement blocks. Joseph Riccatelli was the first fire marshal in the borough and one of the organizers of the volunteer fire department. He donated funds and property to build the first Roman Catholic church in Roselle Park, behind his market.

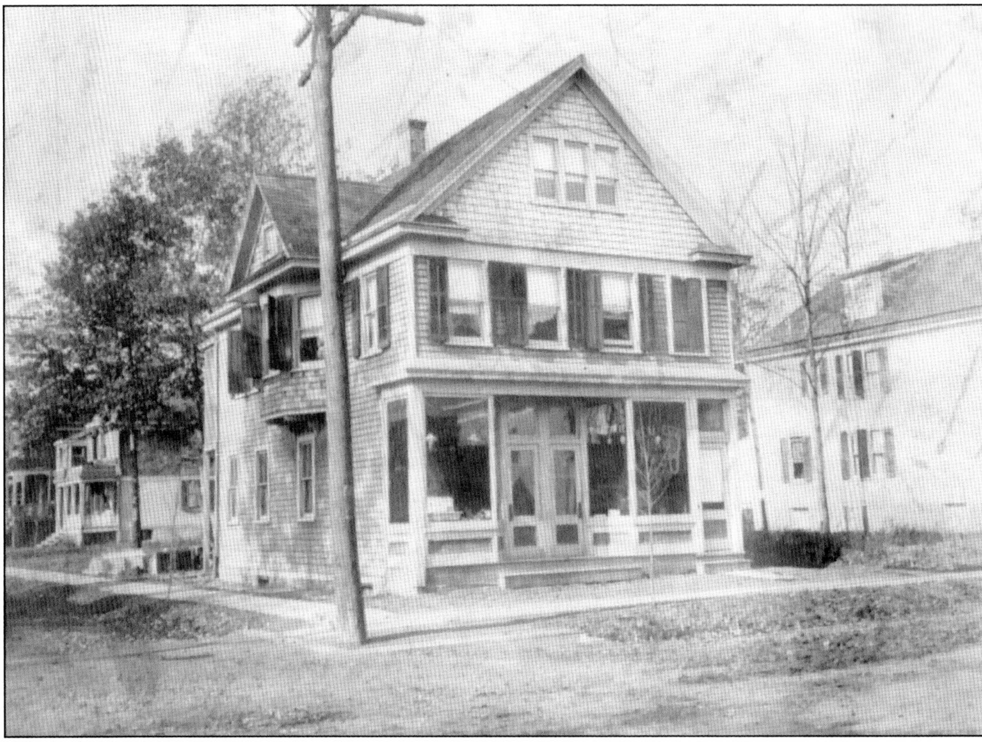

Fred Vanderwig's Plumbing & Heating business, at Chestnut Street and Warren Avenue, served home improvement needs for homeowners who were converting from outdoor to indoor plumbing and from wood to coal furnaces to meet demands of the 20th century. Succeeded by First Class Chinese Hand Laundry and Lettieri Real Estate, the building was demolished and replaced by Rita Pharmacy. A grassy drainage ditch runs along the dirt road in this turn-of-the-century photograph.

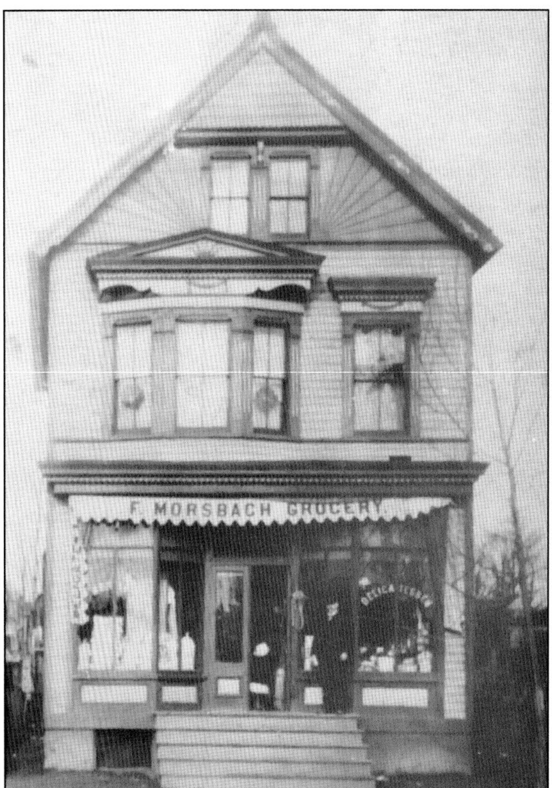

F. Morsbach's grocery store was located on the north side of West Westfield Avenue near Filbert Street in the early 1900s. The wooden steps leading into the shop with living quarters on the upper floors was typical of this era.

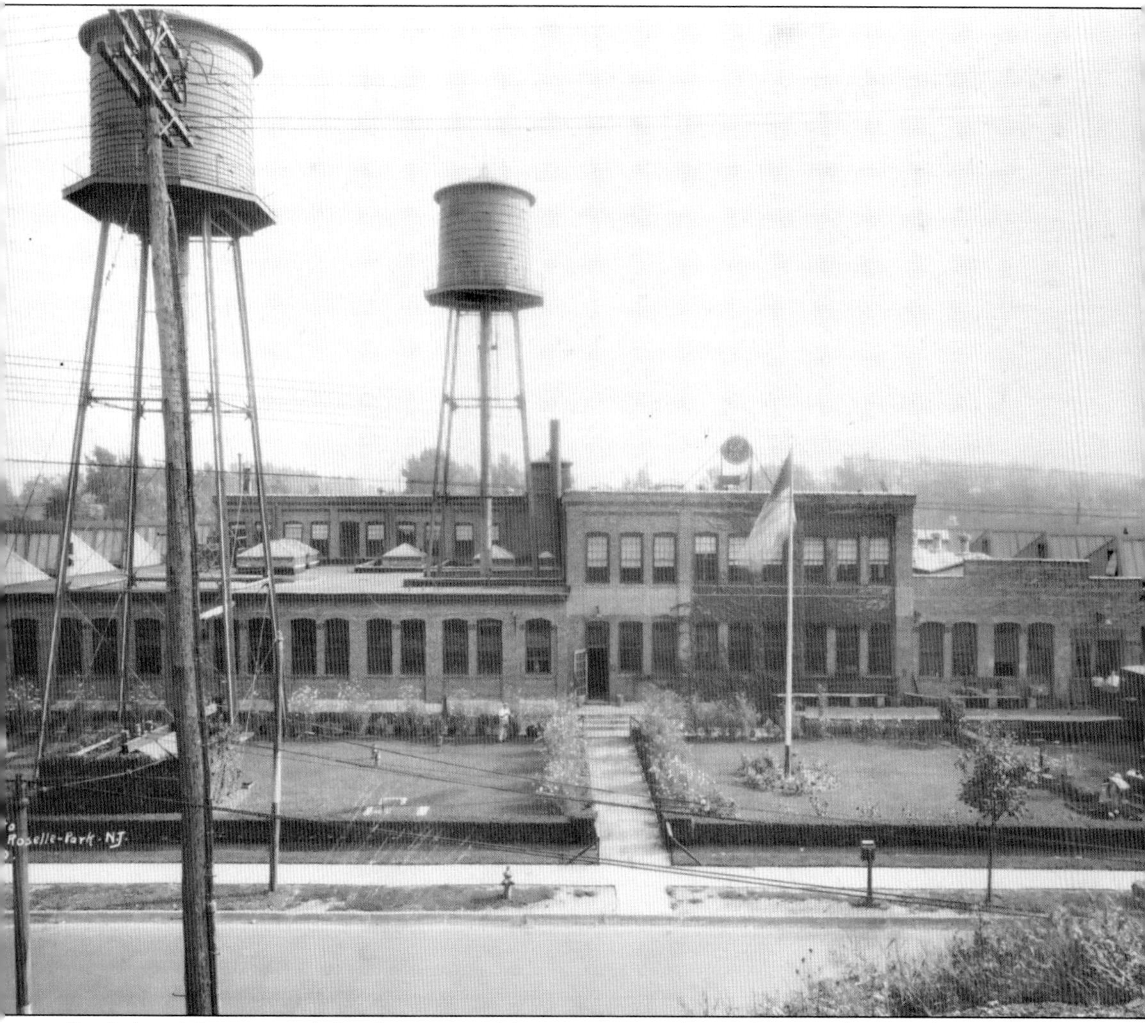

Guglielmo Marconi made his first successful transmission of a wireless signal across the Atlantic Ocean in December 1901. In 1912, his American Marconi Company purchased property at Aldene and built a 20,000-square foot manufacturing plant. Employing 200 people, the company rented and sold wireless equipment to the U.S. Navy. Two transmission towers for testing were installed. During World War I in 1917, the plant doubled its footage and tripled employment to provide equipment for the war effort. U.S. troops stationed at the Gordon Street Bridge protected the vital facility from sabotage.

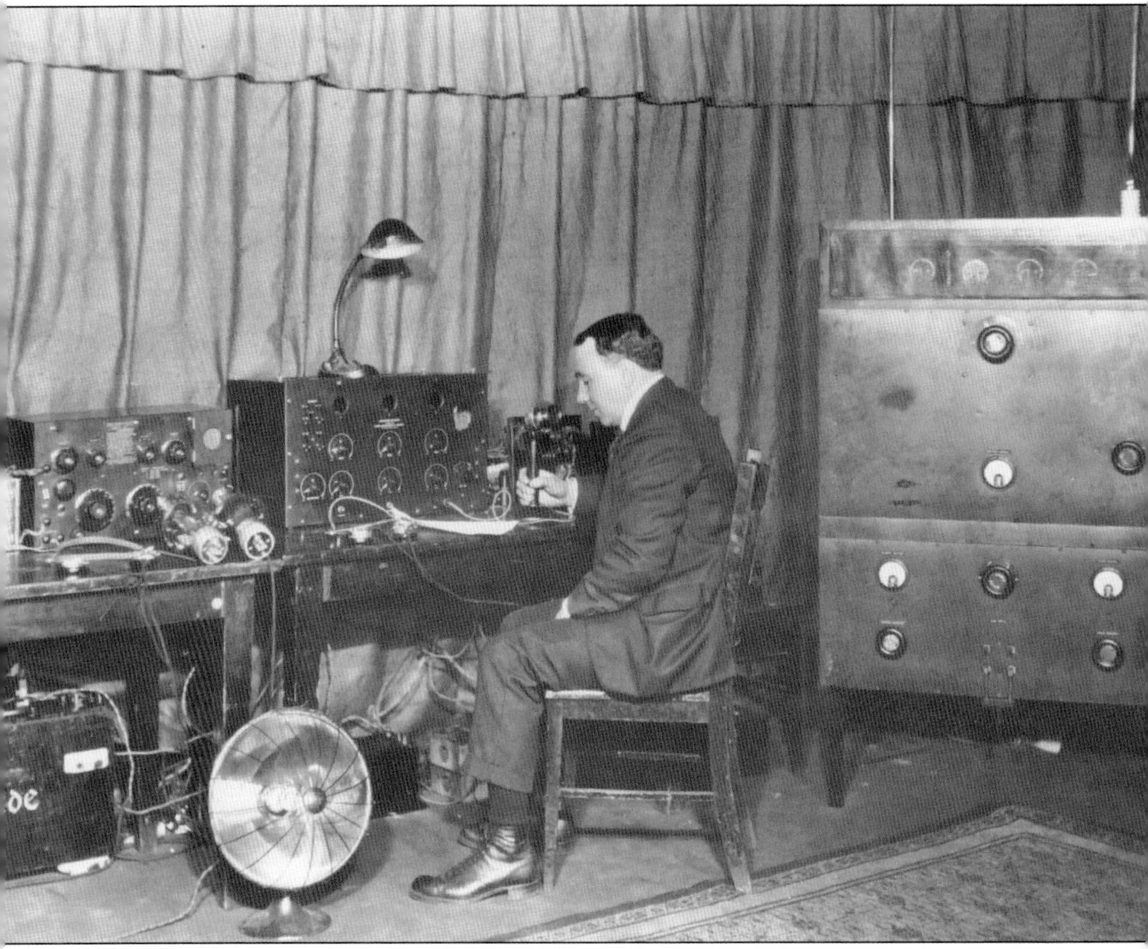

According to the February 1922 edition of *Wireless Age*, "the Radio Installation at WDY is located in an artistically appointed studio which occupies a room at the old factory of the Marconi Wireless Telegraph Co. at Roselle Park, once filled with a maze of precision machine tools used for the construction of model radio equipment." David Sarnoff, a radio pioneer, started as Guglielmo Marconi's office boy. He initiated radio communications as manager of the Marconi Company, which became part of RCA. Later, he became president of the Radio Corporation of America (RCA), organized National Broadcasting Company (NBC), and was elected NBC president.

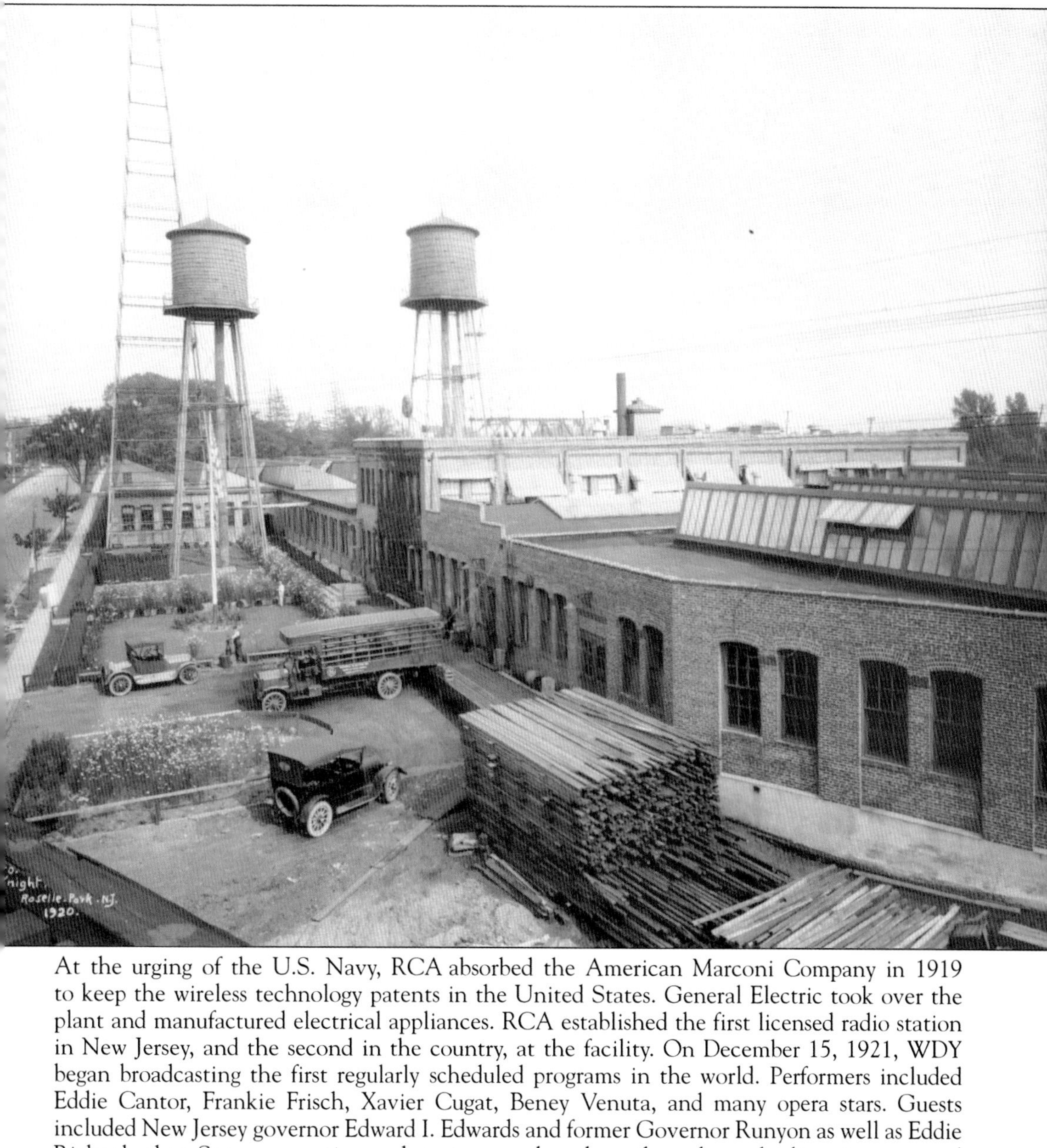

At the urging of the U.S. Navy, RCA absorbed the American Marconi Company in 1919 to keep the wireless technology patents in the United States. General Electric took over the plant and manufactured electrical appliances. RCA established the first licensed radio station in New Jersey, and the second in the country, at the facility. On December 15, 1921, WDY began broadcasting the first regularly scheduled programs in the world. Performers included Eddie Cantor, Frankie Frisch, Xavier Cugat, Beney Venuta, and many opera stars. Guests included New Jersey governor Edward I. Edwards and former Governor Runyon as well as Eddie Rickenbacker. Sermons, parties, and stories were broadcast throughout the listening area and reached as far as Puerto Rico, Canada, Florida, and Nebraska. Tenants of the building on West Westfield Avenue that followed were the Karagheusian Rug Company, makers of the famous Gulistan Rug, and Romerovski Brothers, textile recyclers and exporters.

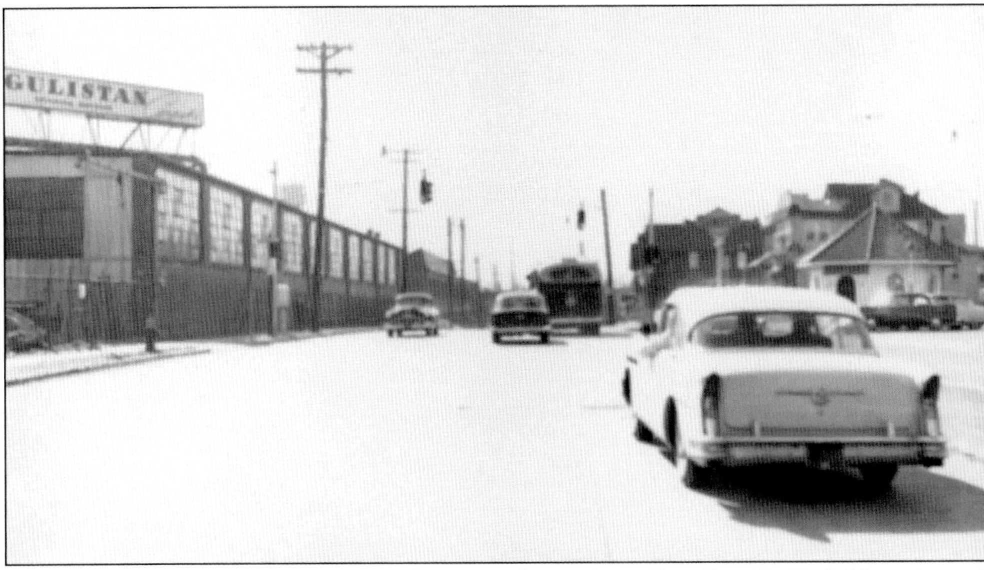

Mr. Karagheusian called his spinning division "the Little Mill in Roselle Park," but the mill became famous as the House of Quality carpets, producing yarns for suppliers of Gulistan Carpets to Radio City Music Hall and the Supreme Court Building in Washington, D.C. Interacting with the community, the Karagheusin Scholarship provided full four-year college tuition to a Roselle Park High School graduate annually and supported their own softball team.

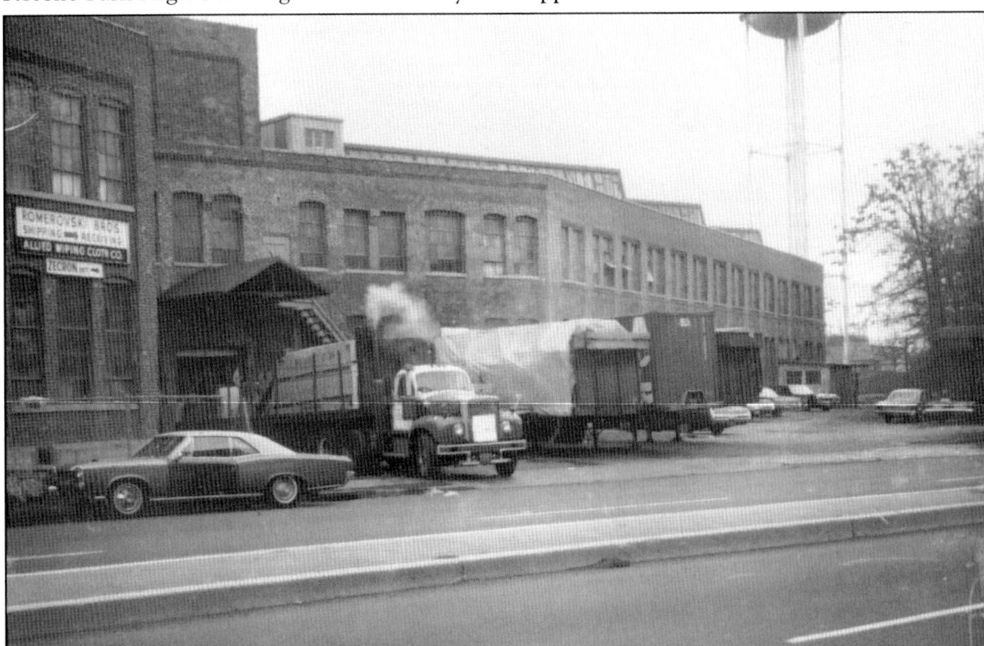

Romerovski Brothers buys, grades, and sorts mostly used clothing and irregular textiles for export to developing countries. Some materials are shredded to produce wipers. Mr. Romerovski is proud that his business helps the environment by keeping 90 percent of the fiber material he receives "out of the landfill." After taking over the former Karagheusian site in 1962, the company became locally known by the nickname of the Rag Factory. This is a 1971 photograph.

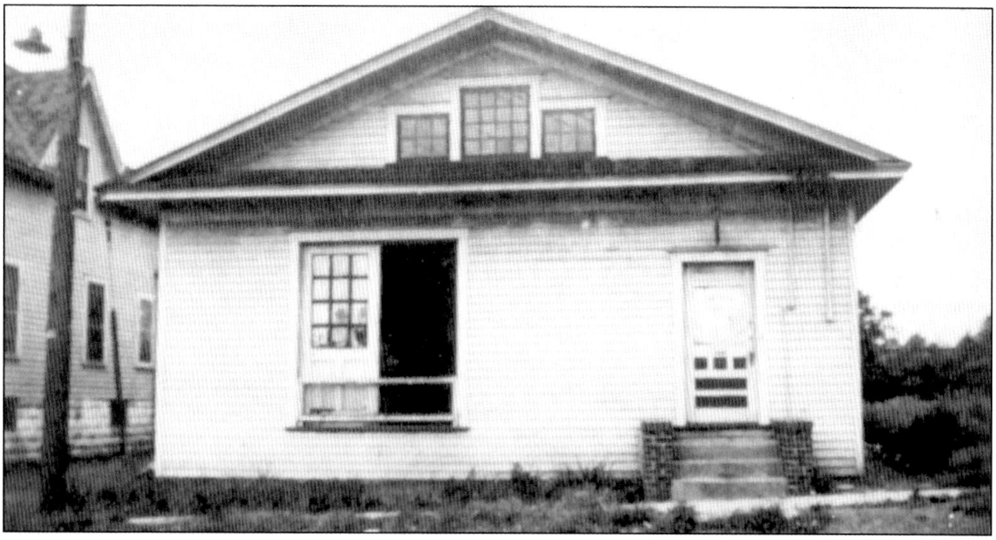

Hexacon was founded by Arthur and Elizabeth Johnson in this small workshop in 1932. It remained a family business during nearly 70 years of operation on West Clay Avenue. The electrical manufacturing plant was passed down to their sons, Robert and Richard, and then to Richard's daughter, current president Cathy (Johnson) Schlinger. Hexacon has drawn many employees from the available workforce of Roselle Park. The modern facility produces soldering irons and related electrical components.

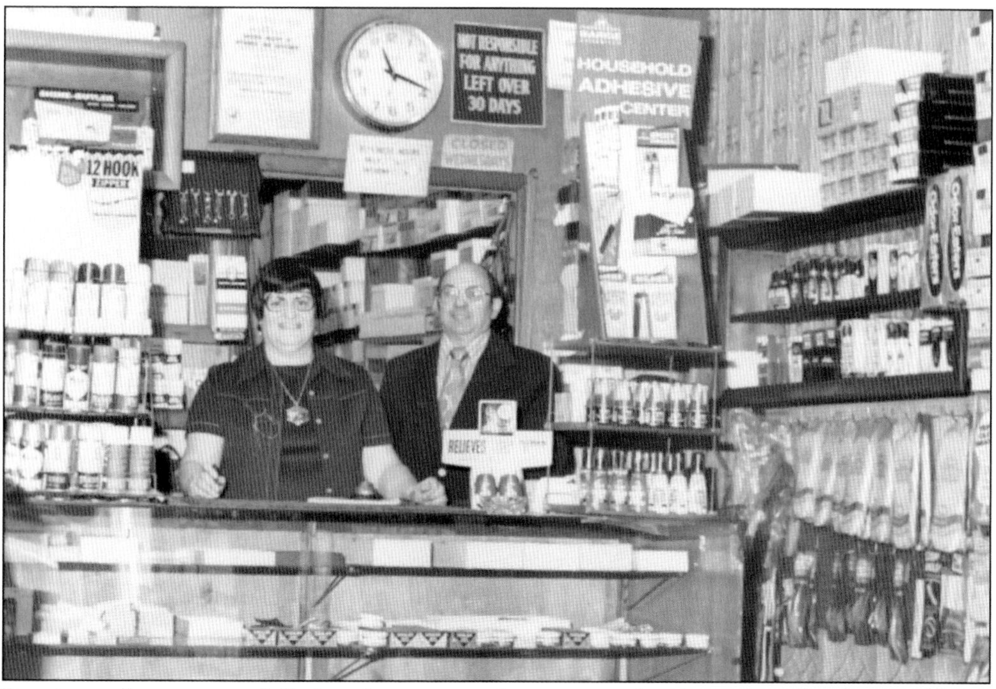

Repairing shoes was a skilled and important business in the days when families could not afford to replace worn ones. Footwear was taken to the local shoe repair shop, where new soles and heels were added to extend their usefulness. Frances and Patrick DeMarco are seen working at their shop at 208 Chestnut Street. They retired in 1990 after 65 years of service to the community.

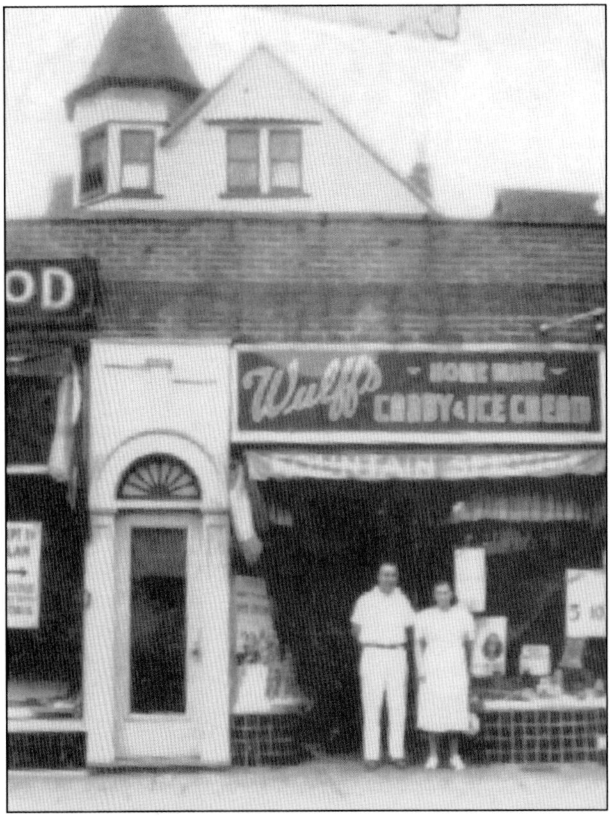

Herman and Emma Wulff are in front of Wulff's confectionery store at 126 Chestnut Street. Except for some penny candy, the Wulffs made all of the ice cream and candy on the premises. This business was in operation from the end of 1937 to the end of 1948. The family lived in the apartment over the store.

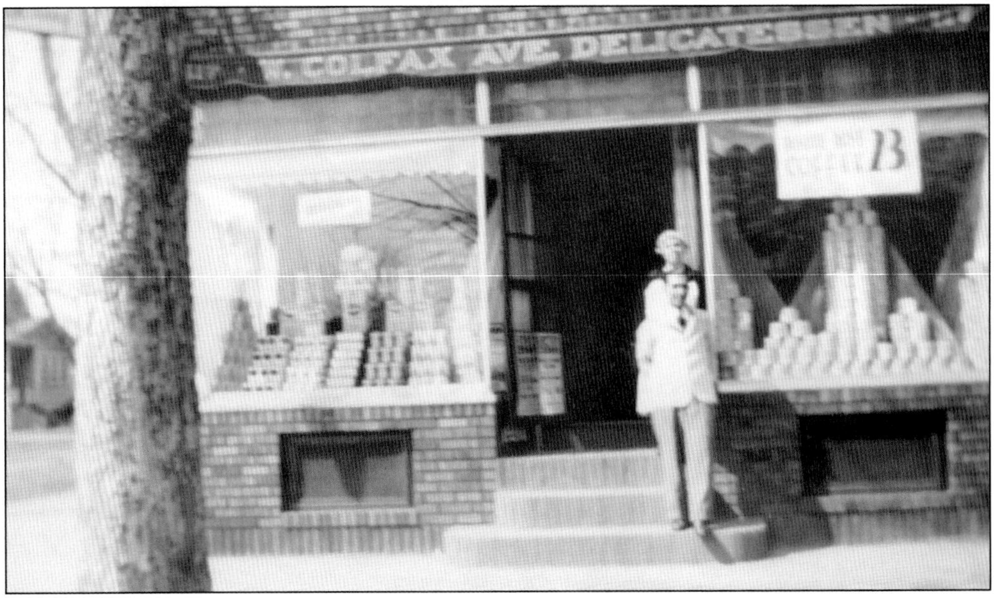

DiStefano's liquor and grocery store has served the community since 1929 as a family business at 117 West Colfax Avenue. In 1932, the store was issued the first liquor license in Roselle Park after the repeal of Prohibition. Charles DiStephano poses with his aunt, Mrs. Marian Donato, in front of a window sign advertising White Rose Coffee for 23¢ per pound.

Owner of Larry's Sub Shop, Larry Torino (right), warmly greets one of his faithful customers, Lou Burnet. Since 1946, the shop on the corner of Locust Street and West Grant Avenue has satisfied three generations of hungry students and their teachers from four schools. Torino still identifies school children by their family names, linking familiar faces to his memories of their parents and grandparents.

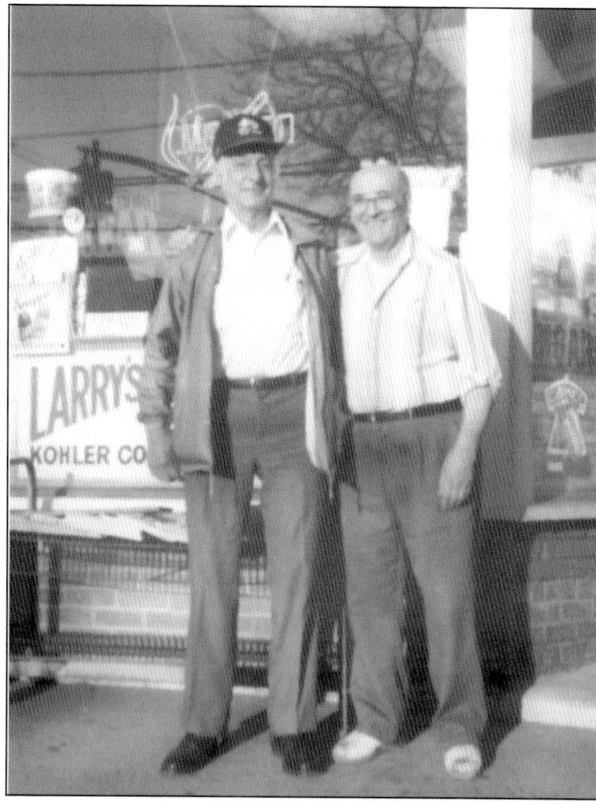

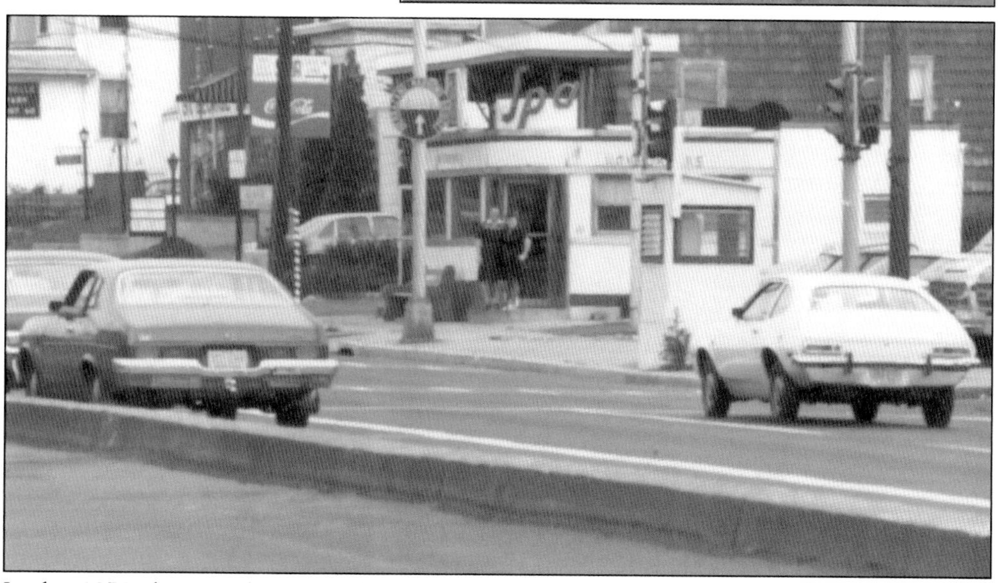

In this 1978 photograph, owner Chris Shealey and longtime waitress Cleo Borre stand in the door to the Spa Diner, a place where "everybody knew your name" on busy Westfield Avenue at Chestnut Street. Opened in 1947 by Chris and Jerry Shealey, the Sunday Special in 1958 included 10 hamburgers for $1. In 1960, the 49-cent breakfast special included eggs, ham or bacon, toast, potatoes, juice, and their famous coffee. Borre was a waitress there from 1947 to 1986. Her most important rule was to "keep grudges and arguments outside."

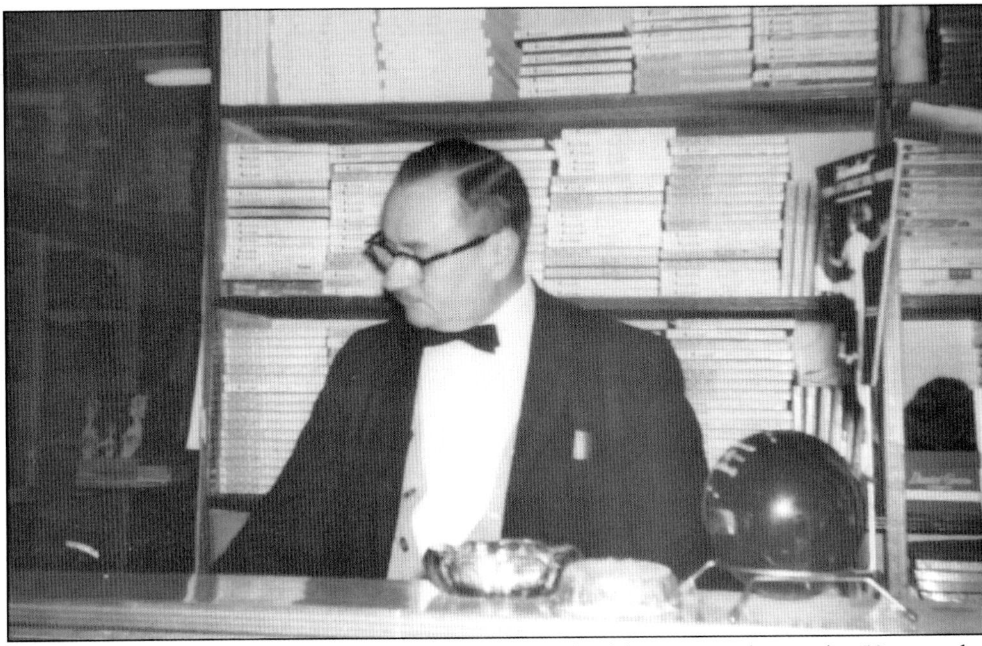

Jerry Goll, a familiar businessman, was the epitome of public support during the 53 years that he and his wife, Celia, owned Jerry's Department Store. He immigrated here from the Ukraine in 1924. Whether behind the counter in the lingerie section, or behind the local baseball team cheering them on, he was known as a patriot and a friend, frequently donating his time, money, and goods to borough causes. Interesting in this photograph are the ladies' stocking boxes.

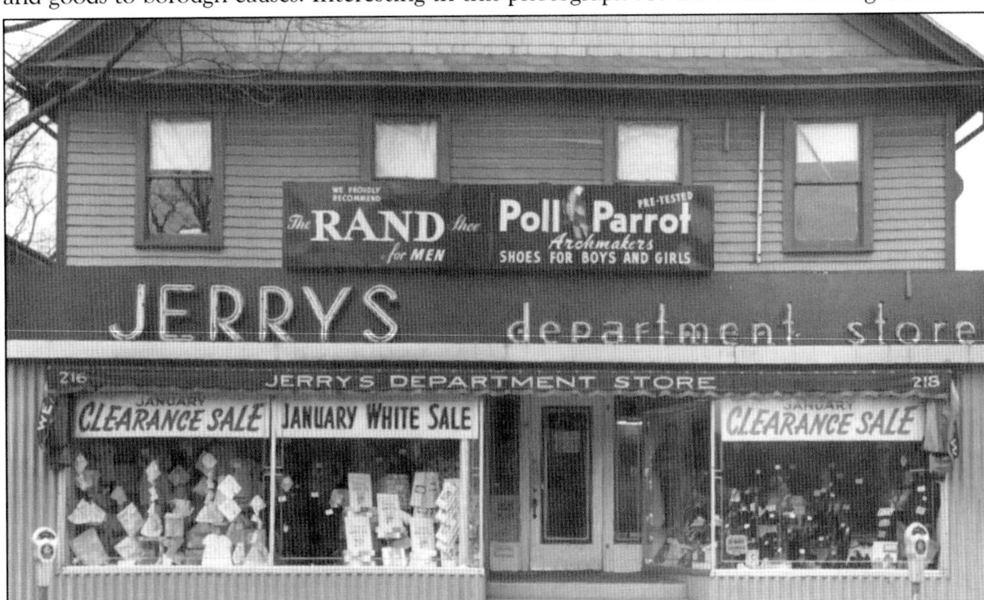

The building at 216–218 Chestnut Street housed Jerry Goll's first store in 1932. He moved down the block to 110 Chestnut Street several years later. In addition to quality merchandise, Goll stocked vintage goods not available at malls, but still in demand by his regular customers.

Hap's-an-Kap's evokes many memories of the "happy days" of the 1930s through the 1950s, when local youths hung out at 3 West Westfield Avenue. Five-cent hot dogs, a soda fountain, toys, cigarettes, cigars, and newspapers attracted many customers. Highway signs indicate that U.S. Route 22 and New Jersey Route 28 ran parallel along the main drag in this 1936 photograph.

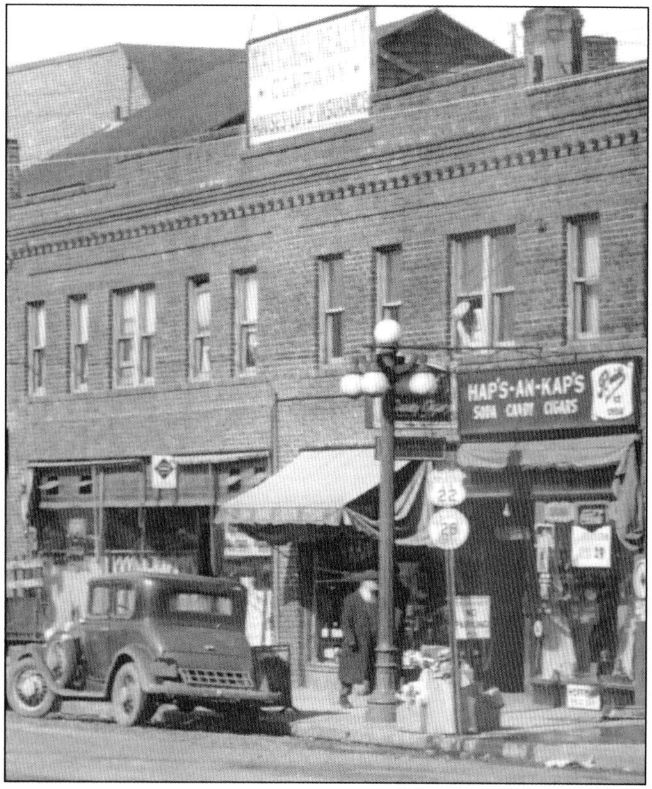

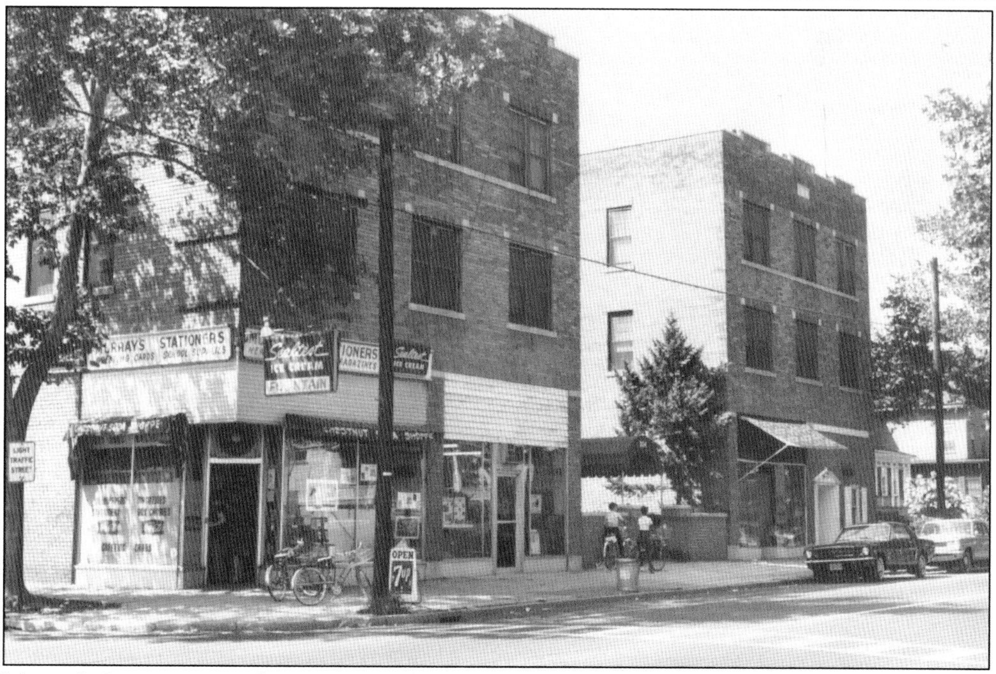

Murray's Stationers in the corner of the Washington apartments was a landmark soda shop within a landmark building. In September 1965, biking to Murray's for a soda at the fountain or a comic book was a pleasant after-school treat. Next-door was Engelmann's Realty Company.

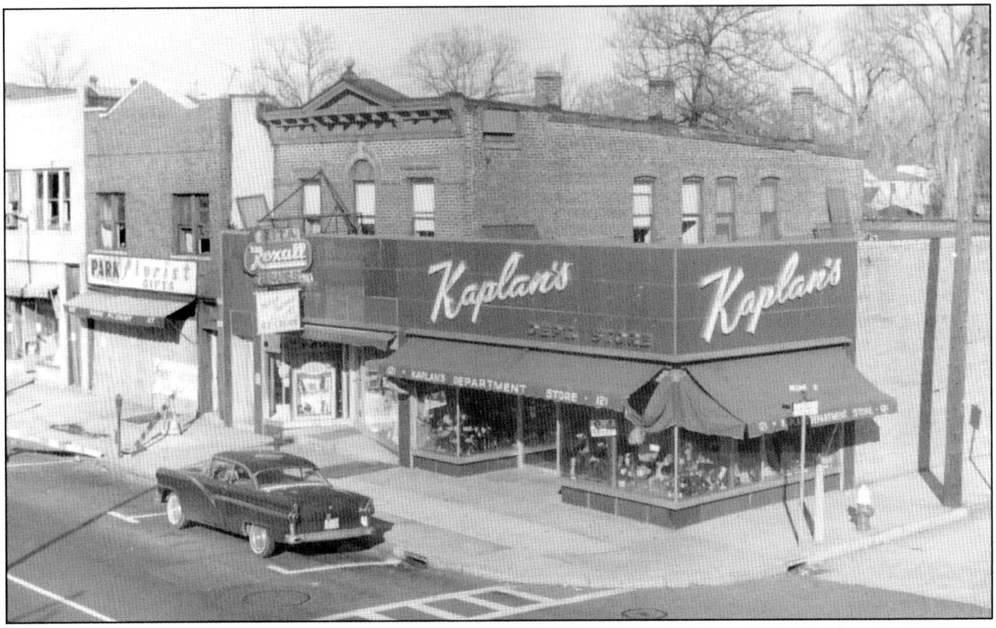

Old-timers once tied their horses in front of Dowers Clothing Store at 121 Chestnut Street. Then it became Kaplan's Department Store, where they sold clothing as well as thread and notions for 46 years. Ryan's Liquor Store moved in, and later Jeannie's Flower Shop occupied the premises. The photograph was taken in 1967, after the Chestnut Street fire.

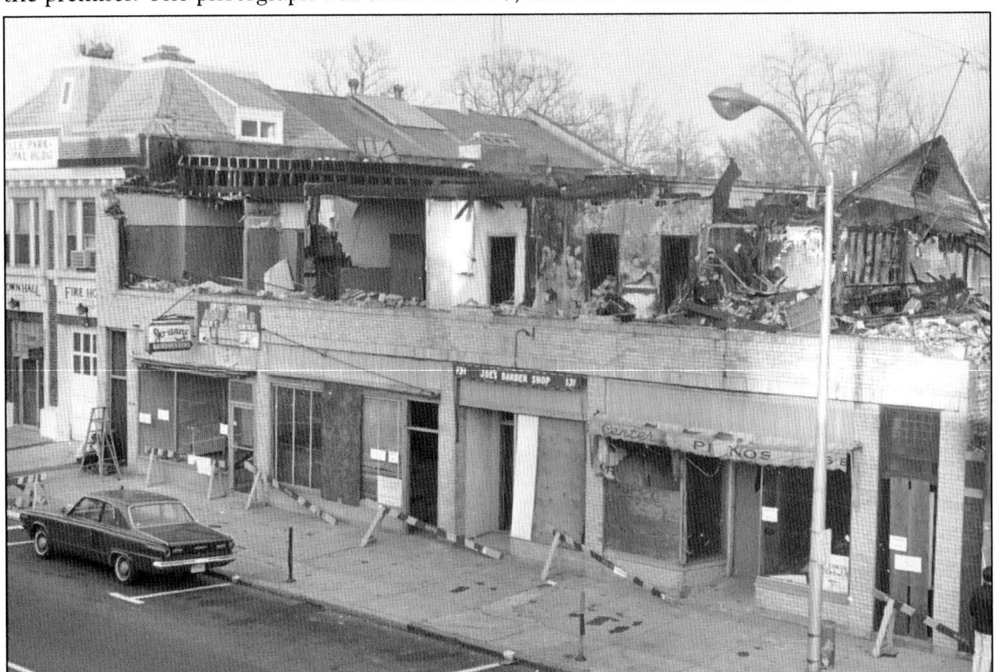

In October 1967, a devastating fire ravaged a large portion of Chestnut Street. The borough hall was so endangered that heroic volunteers rushed to save important records, carrying them to the Methodist church. Destroyed businesses included Jo-Anne Hairdresser, Joe's Barber Shop, Hensler's Music Shop, a dentist's office, and Park Florist.

Eight

Sports

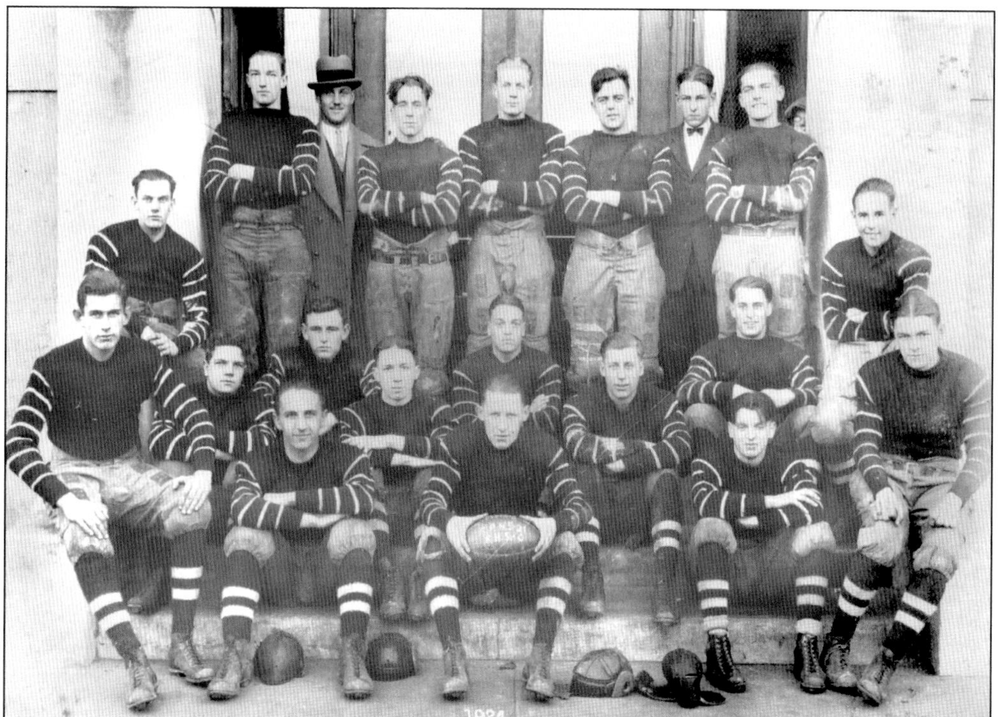

One of the oldest sports rivalries in the state is the annual Thanksgiving Day football competition between Roselle Park and its neighbor to the south, Roselle. In 1924, Roselle Park triumphed with a score of 21–0. Uniforms were canvas belted pants, wool jerseys, footwear with cleats, and soft leather helmets without face masks. Team members included John Dalton, Donald Dill, Fred Cummings, Edward Richards, Raymond Ruth, Frank L. Pita, Kaizmer Stupak, Edward Hopkins, William Bauman, Edward Dill, Lyle Bannam, Theodore R.Stiles, Henry Glowka, and Charles Bagley.

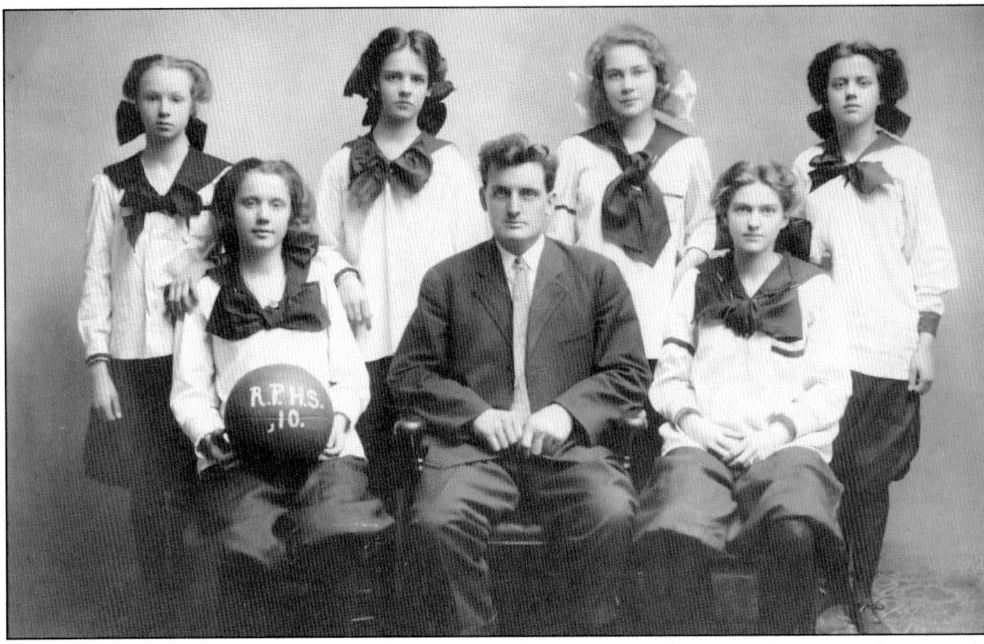

One versatile advisor served as the all-sports coach in 1910, as shown in these two photographs of the girls' and boys' basketball teams. The members shown from the girls' team, from left to right, are the following: (front row) Clarice Hunt, forward and captain; Roy Starry, coach; and Lenora Dennick, forward and manager; (back row) Pauline Worth, center; Isabell Miller, guard; Luella Stryker, guard; and Grace Van Wagner, guard. The members shown from the boys team, from left to right, are the following: (front row) Lloyd Lewis, coach Roy Starry, and Earl Stanton; (back row) Judson Van Wagner, Phillip Fraley, and Harry Lewis.

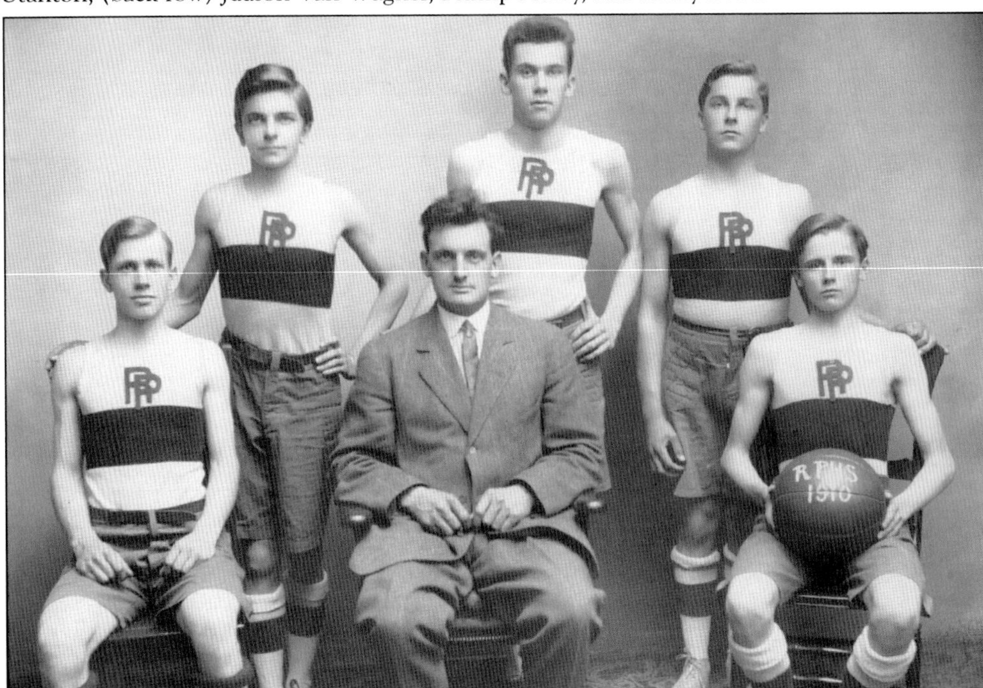

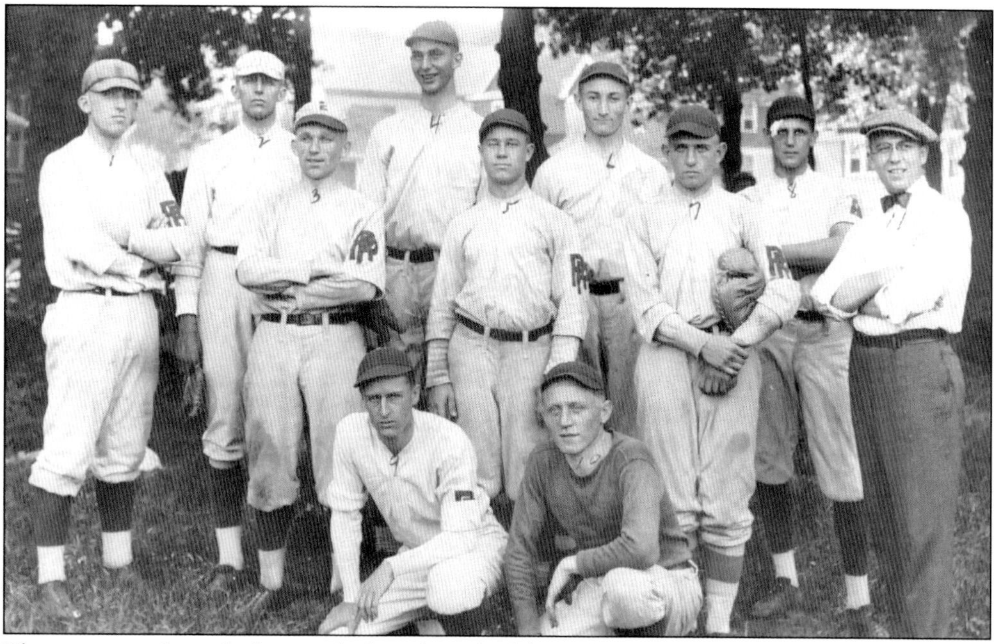

They may not have had a coach, but they "had lots of natural ability and a strong desire to play baseball," according to Pug Williams. The Roselle Park Baseball Club, a semi-pro team "played all comers, winner take all" in 1914 at the corner of Clay Avenue and Walnut Street. Big leaguers sometimes joined them, and the hat was passed to collect money. Shown, from left to right, are the following: (first row) B. Streffler and H. Hansen; (second row) C. Mutch, C. Ern, M. Lindon, and C. Hayes; (third row) R. Hayes, R. Shaw, C. "Stretch" Montgomery, J. Vachal, and D. Boeller.

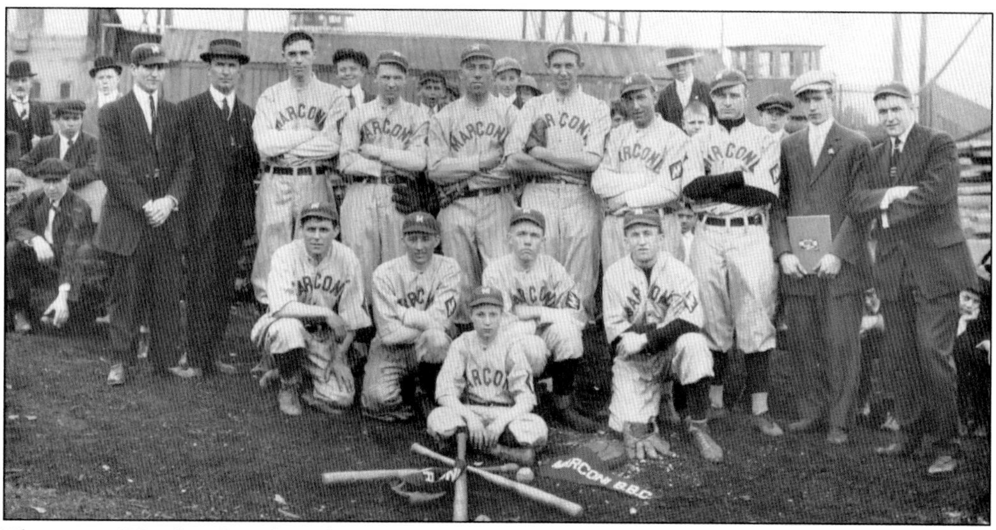

This was a "Hustling bunch at the Marconi Wireless factory, Aldene," according to a 1914 sports item in the *Elizabeth Daily Journal*. The Marconi Baseball Club was one of the best around, playing mostly on the road. Shown, from left to right, are the following: (first row) M. Tomasulo, bat boy; (second row) F. Lenihan, F. Wahl, C. Marsden, and H. Decker; (third row) Manager H. Kreis, P.J. "Paddy" Collins, club president; F. Washburn, F. Boettner, J. Reichart, R. Schuyler, J. Mason, ex-boxer C. "Kid" Beck, G. Kacheireiss, scorer; and W.J. Bennett, secretary.

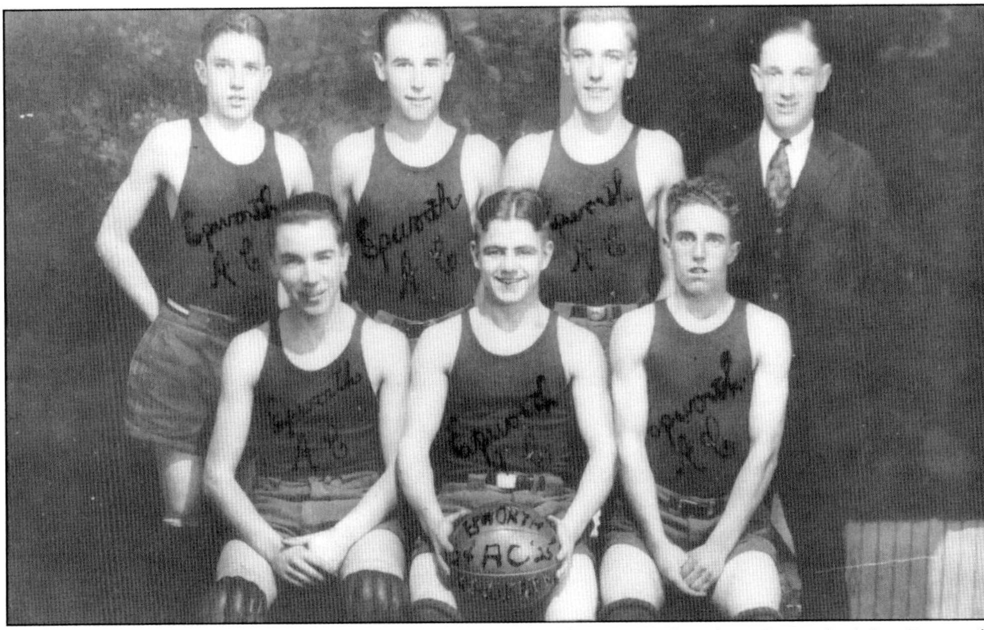

In 1923, a group of local youths who started shooting hoops in the church yard of the Epworth Methodist Episcopalian Church in Elizabeth chartered the Epworth Athletic Club and enjoyed not only a sports league but lifelong friendships.

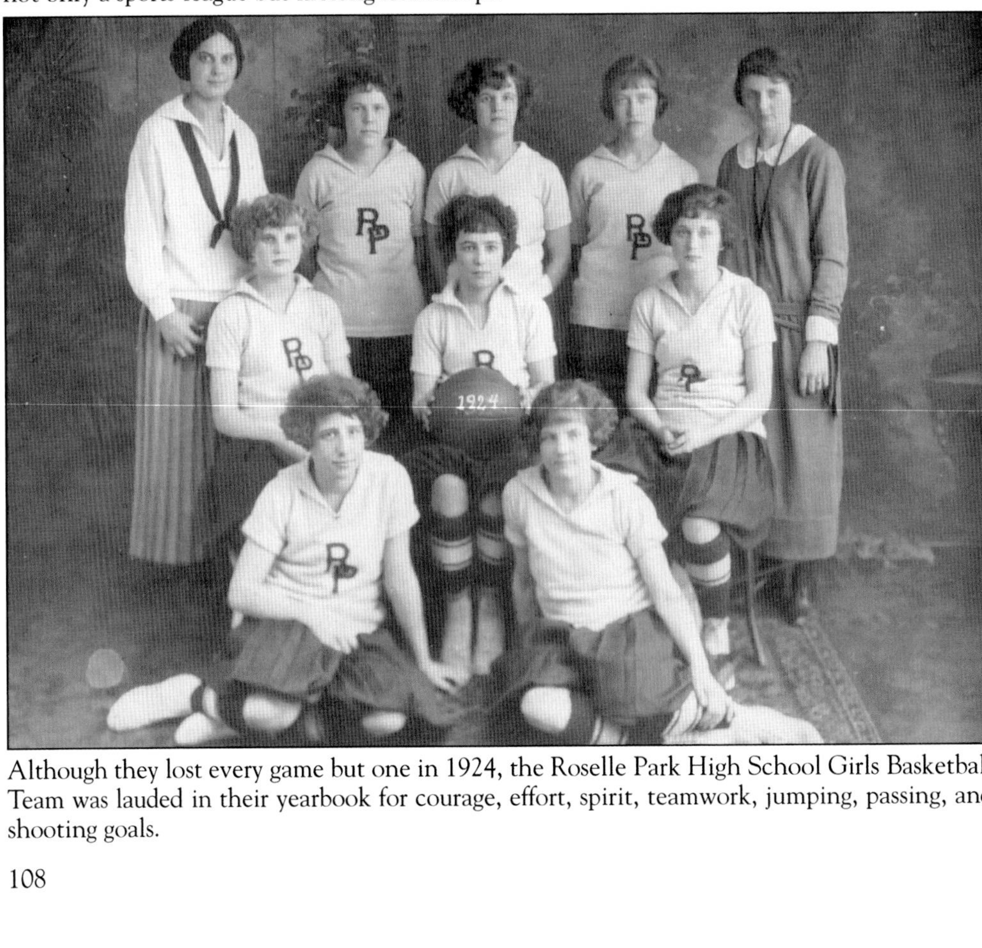

Although they lost every game but one in 1924, the Roselle Park High School Girls Basketball Team was lauded in their yearbook for courage, effort, spirit, teamwork, jumping, passing, and shooting goals.

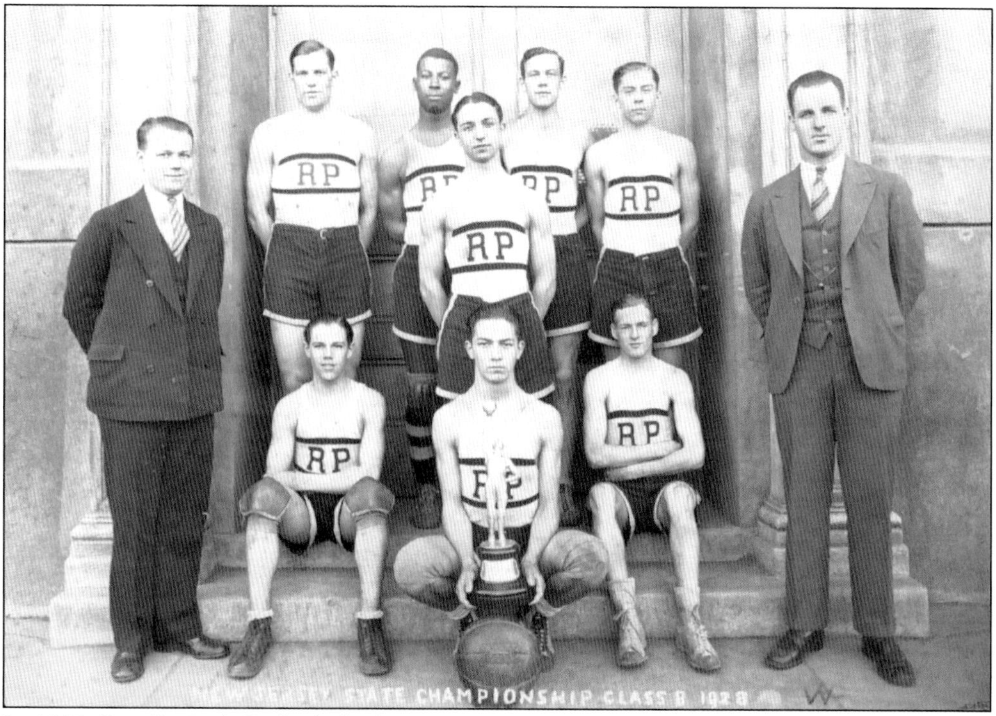

In 1928, Roselle Park Basketball players took the New Jersey State Championship, Class B. At the right front, a young coach Herm Shaw beams. In the last row, second from left, is Tom "Tank" Conrad, who also excelled at football, baseball, and track, and achieved Black All-American as captain at Morgan State in 1931. Tank played professional football with the New York Brown Bombers and coached and taught at Delaware State and Winston-Salem. He was inducted into the Douglas Hall of Fame, which honors black athletes. In the middle of the picture is Frank Tomasulo, who later became a dentist.

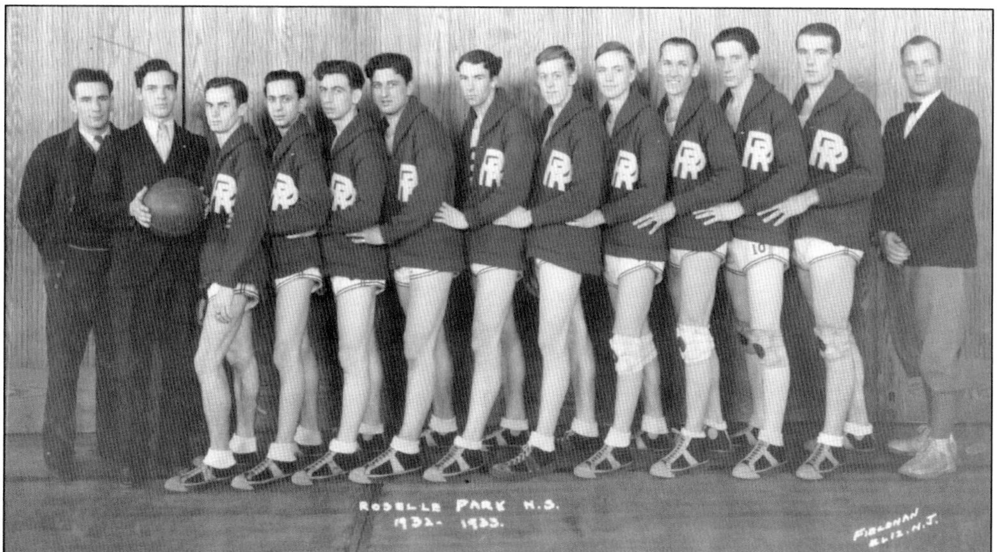

The boys on the Basketball Team of 1932–1933 strike a pose different than the usual sports group. The only identity known is that of coach Herm Shaw on the far right.

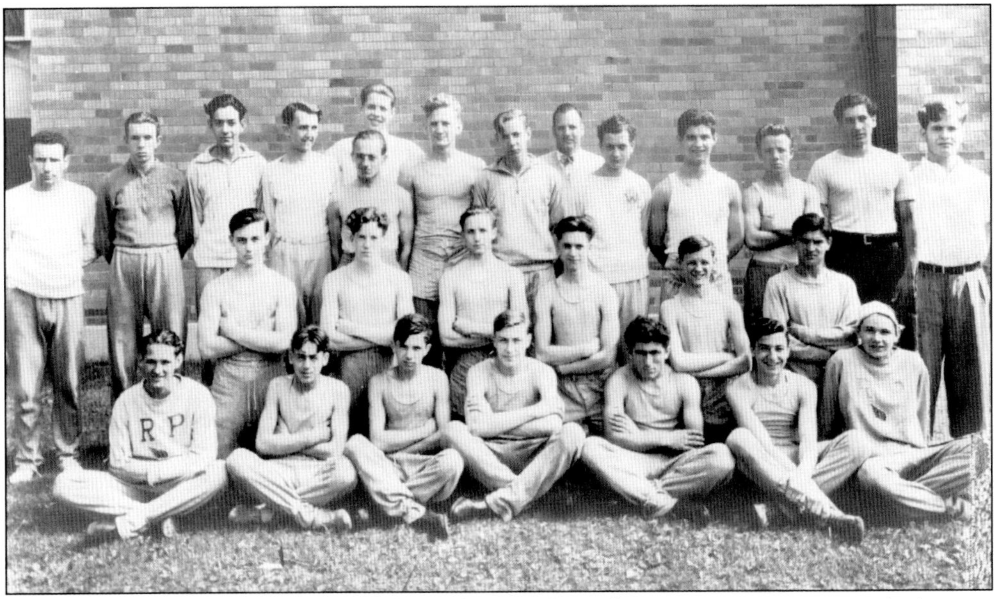

Undefeated in 1934, the Roselle Park Track Team beat their opponents in seven dual meets and one triangular. They pose on the west side of their new high school, which is now the Middle School.

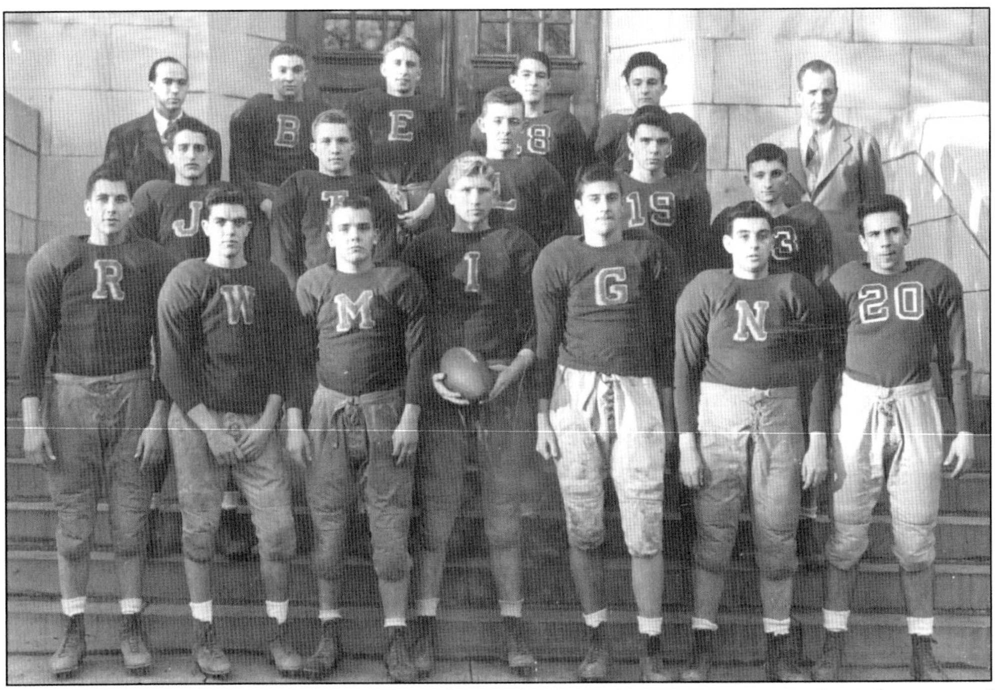

Although the school only had 190 boys from which to draw, its team was hailed as one of the best in Roselle Park history. The members shown, from left to right, are the following: (first row) Joe Rafalowski, Ted Wieber, captain Jim McKay, Herm Hering, Charles Casmer, Robert Towey, and Freddy Klett; (second row) John Artuso, Sandy Thompson, Don Langstaff, captain-elect Dan Woolley, and Paul Rafalowski; (third row) assistant coach Harry Munkel, Jim Collucci, Don Brown, Rocco Collucci, Anthony Lugara, and coach Herm Shaw.

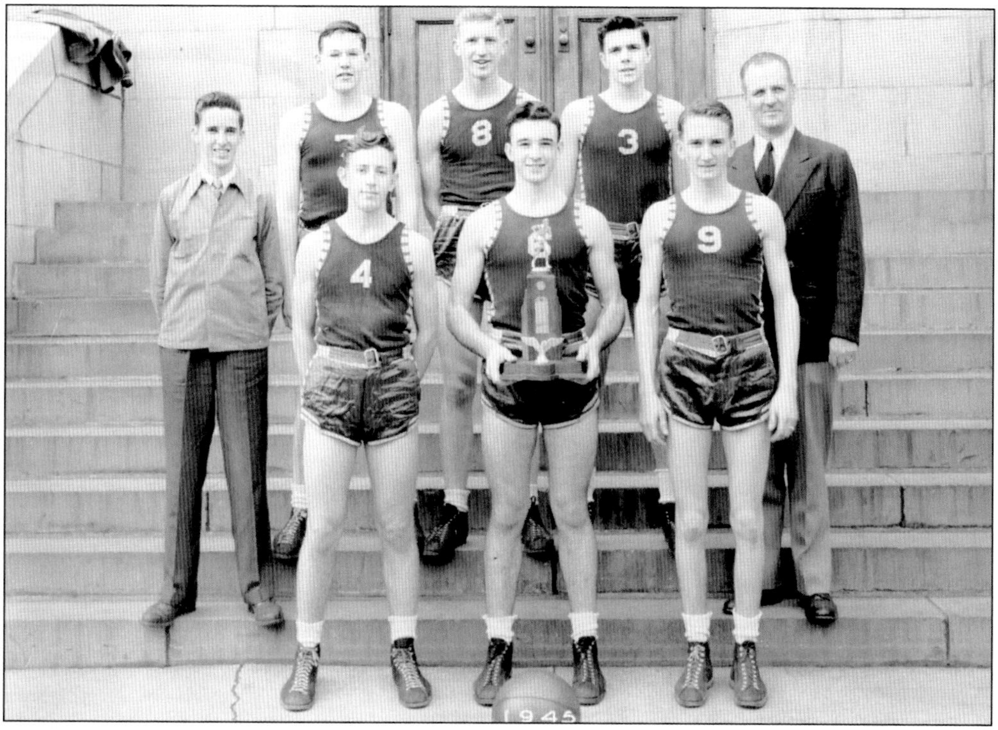

Frank Burns proudly displays the 1945 State Basketball Championship Group II Trophy. Later named to the Roselle Park Hall of Fame, he became football coach at Rutgers for nearly 35 years. Victors that year included Sal Bunin, Frank Burns, Bill Felton, manager Dick Graham, Bill Wichelhaus, Herm Hering, Dan Woolley, and coach Herm Shaw.

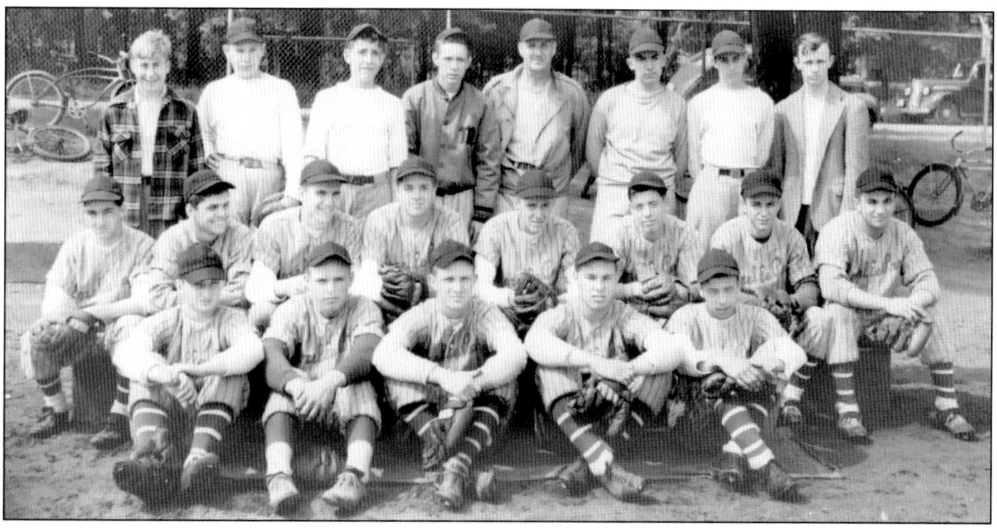

Roselle Park High School's baseball team won the North Jersey Group II Championship in 1947. Shown, from left to right, are the following: (first row) Paul Rafalowski, Bob Shriner, captain Sandy Thompson, Rudy Schultz, and Fred Jeffreys; (second row) Dick Wall, Dick Majesky, Dan Woolley, Ray Parenteau, Bill Jones, Ed Mack, Joe Rubino, and Jim Colucci; (third row) Don Unbekant, Bruce Kymer, unidentified, Durwin Dawson, coach Herm Shaw, George Ledder, unidentified, and Bob Cale.

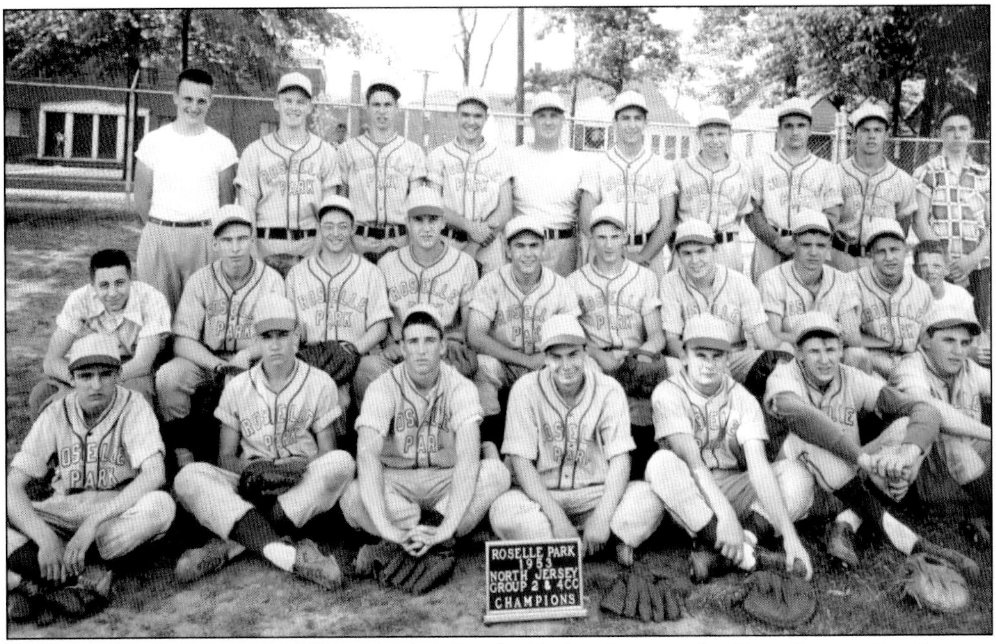

A memorable win in June 1953 resulted in Roselle Park's claiming the Four County Conference Championship as well as the Group II New Jersey State Championship for the second year in a row. Included on coach Herm Shaw's team were J. Partilla, R. Hennessey, V. Lanza, J. Triano, J. Appello, D. Gucker, M. Belford, J. Lupo, T. Seippel, R. Schmidt, R. Heal, R, Hunte, D. Szymanski, R. Lipari, and J. Nardiello. The team-autographed ball resides at the Roselle Park Museum.

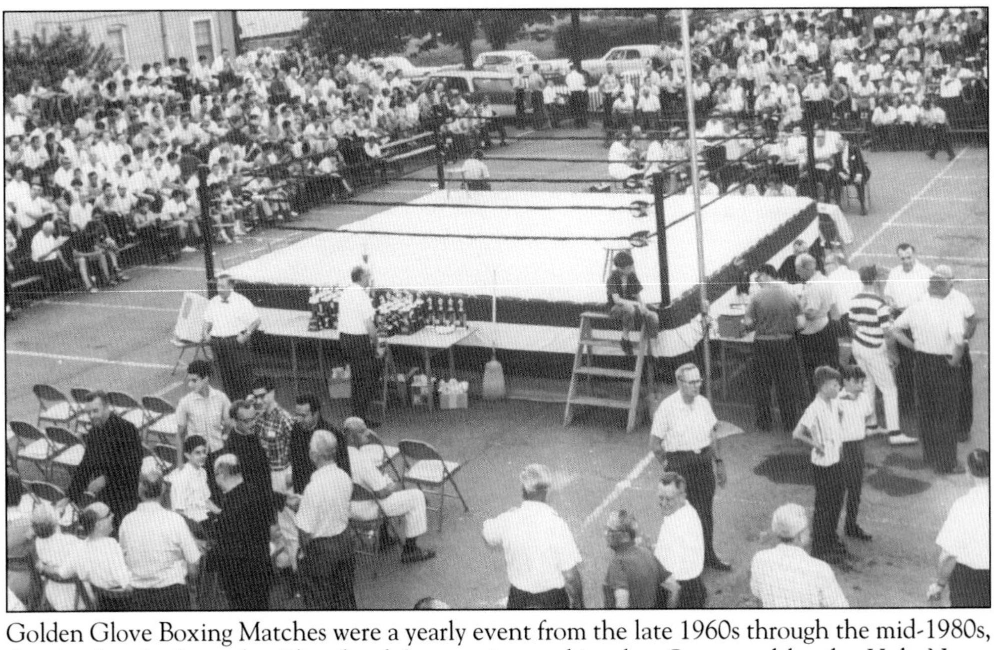

Golden Glove Boxing Matches were a yearly event from the late 1960s through the mid-1980s, drawing hundreds to the Church of Assumption parking lot. Sponsored by the Holy Name Society, they were directed by Frank Orlando Sr. In this photograph, parish priests in the lower left corner include Fr. James Garvie, Fr. Sebastian Chiego, and Fr. Joseph Loreti.

Home-grown Juline "Jujie" Brazinski Simpson won a Gold Medal at the Pan American Games in Mexico in October, 1975, on the undefeated Women's International Basketball Team, and the Silver Medal at the Universe Games in Moscow. In this photograph, mayor Eugene Carmody admires her Gold Medal.

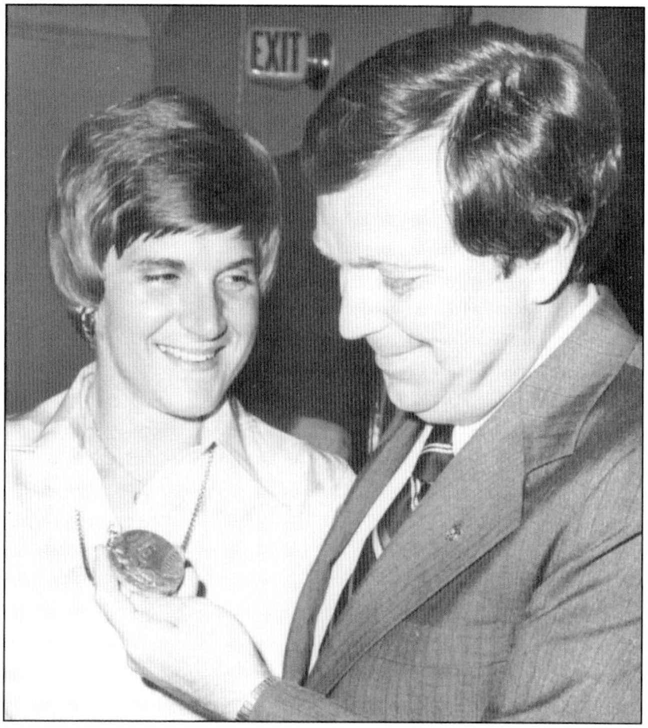

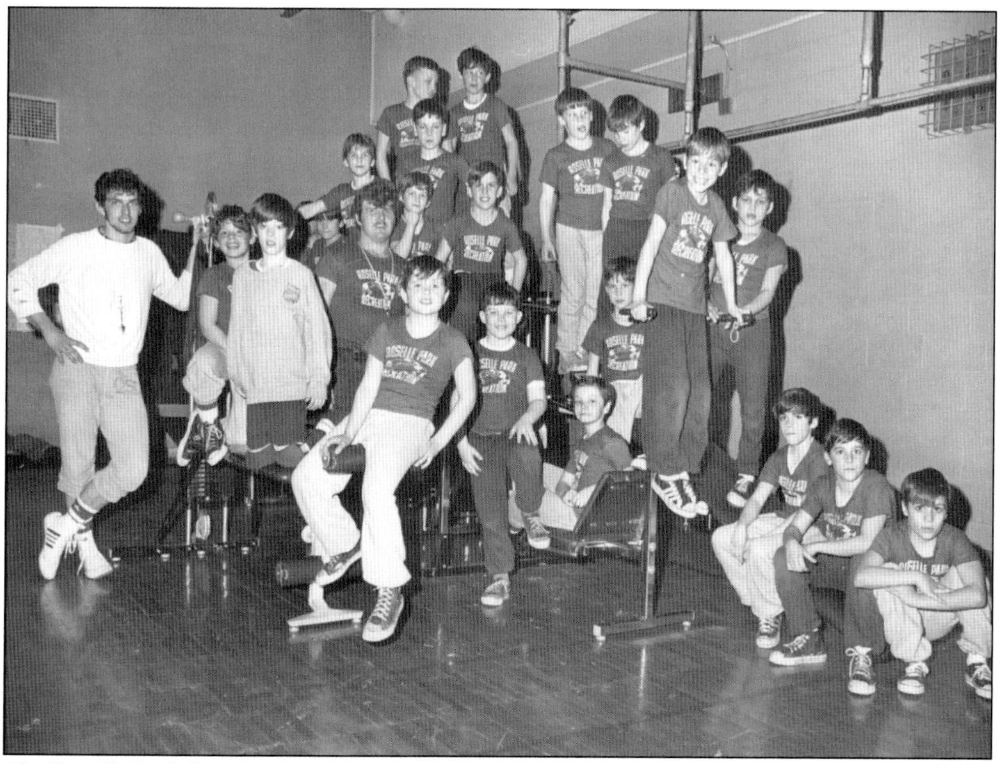

The Roselle Park Recreation Committee celebrated the dedication of new universal equipment at the high school in 1974.

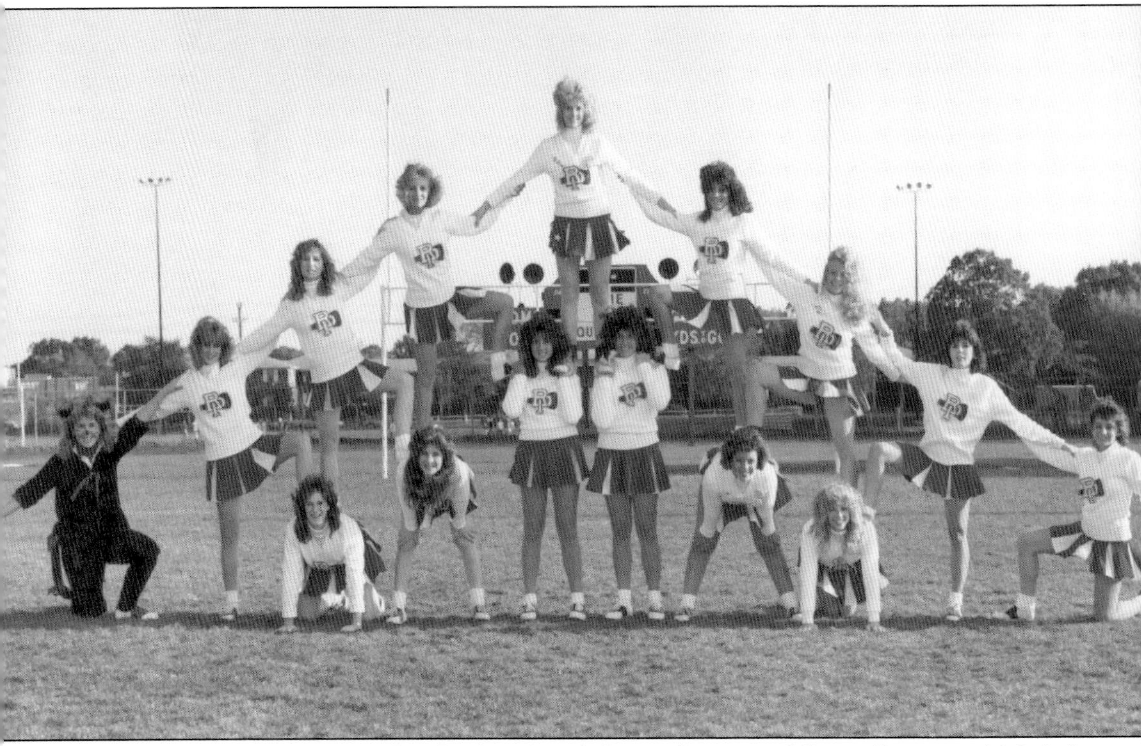

The 1985 Panthers varsity cheerleaders, from left to right, are as follows: (lower row) Michele Keller, Kathy Pagnetti, Sandra Gasorek, Jennifer Rock, Lisa Gallicchio, and Amy Feith; (upper row) Kim Kuterka, Jaimie Breen, Lisa Hofmeister, Sue Keller, Jamie Gronoistasky, Tiffany Manzo, Tana Sabatino, Lisa Barz, and Lori Siter.

Nine

CELEBRATIONS

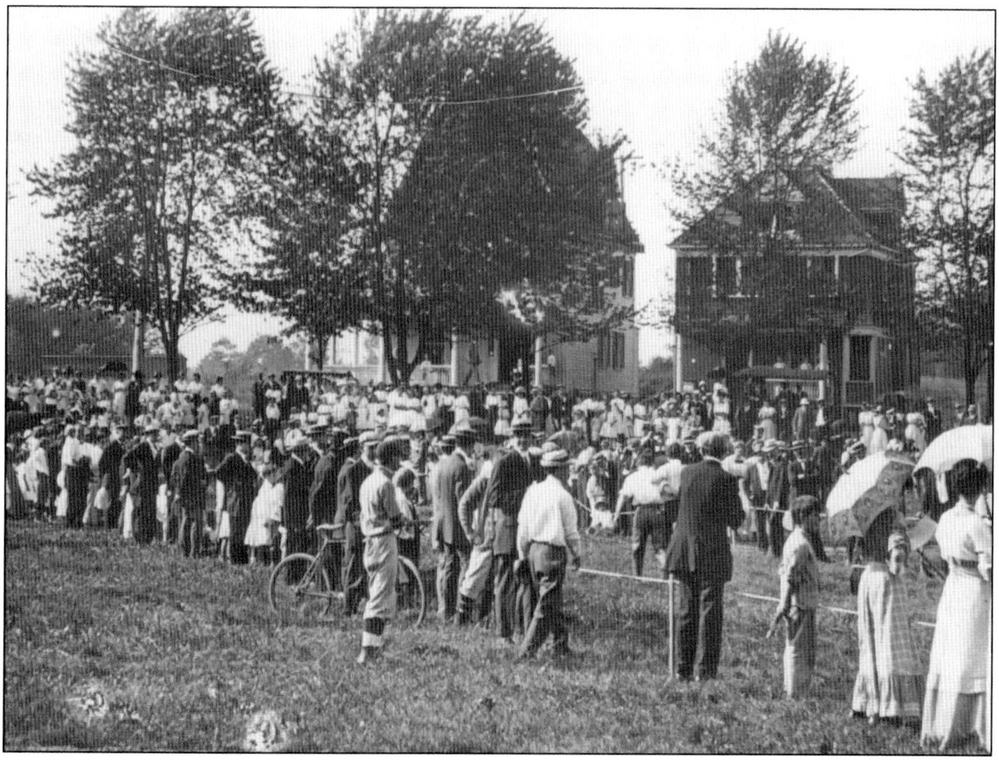

Everyone would look forward to Annual Home Day Games, when townspeople of all ages joined on a mild autumn day to participate or just to watch the games of the day. On September 2, 1911, local gentry mingled and enjoyed each other's company. They are sporting umbrellas or hats to shield complexions in the sunny field behind the newly built Robert Gordon School.

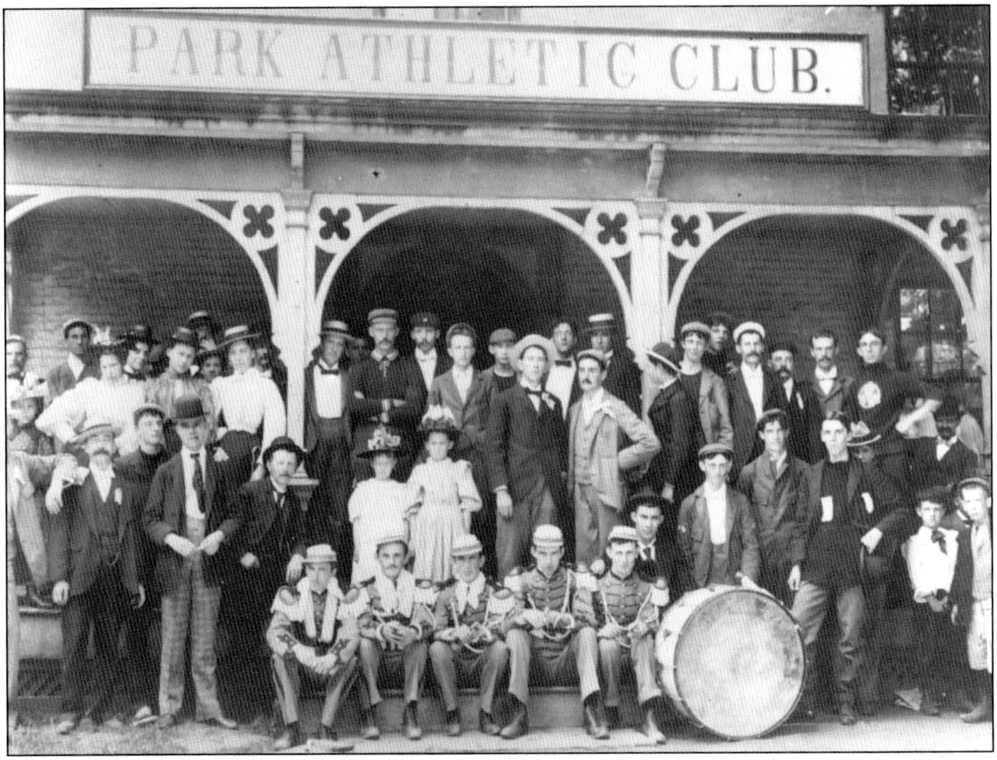

An all-purpose center during the earliest decades, the Park Athletic Club was the "in" place to meet, organize, and socialize in the middle of the newly formed borough. Members, friends, and families surround their five-piece uniformed band. Wearing fine suits, straw hats, or leg o' mutton sleeves, this gathering pauses to create a memory on a gingerbread porch.

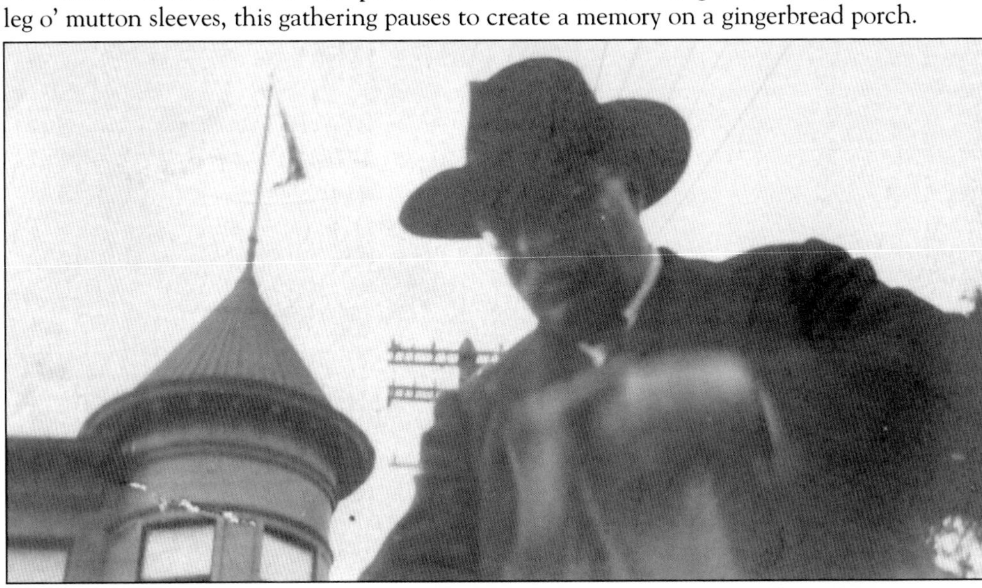

Theodore "Teddy" Roosevelt came to Roselle Park and spoke to residents who crowded the Oval to catch a glimpse of the famous president. In 1912, Roosevelt campaigned throughout New Jersey for reelection on his "Bull Moose" ticket. Oval Park, at Central Railroad Station, was the place for town celebrations until it was bought from the borough by Sullivan Chevrolet.

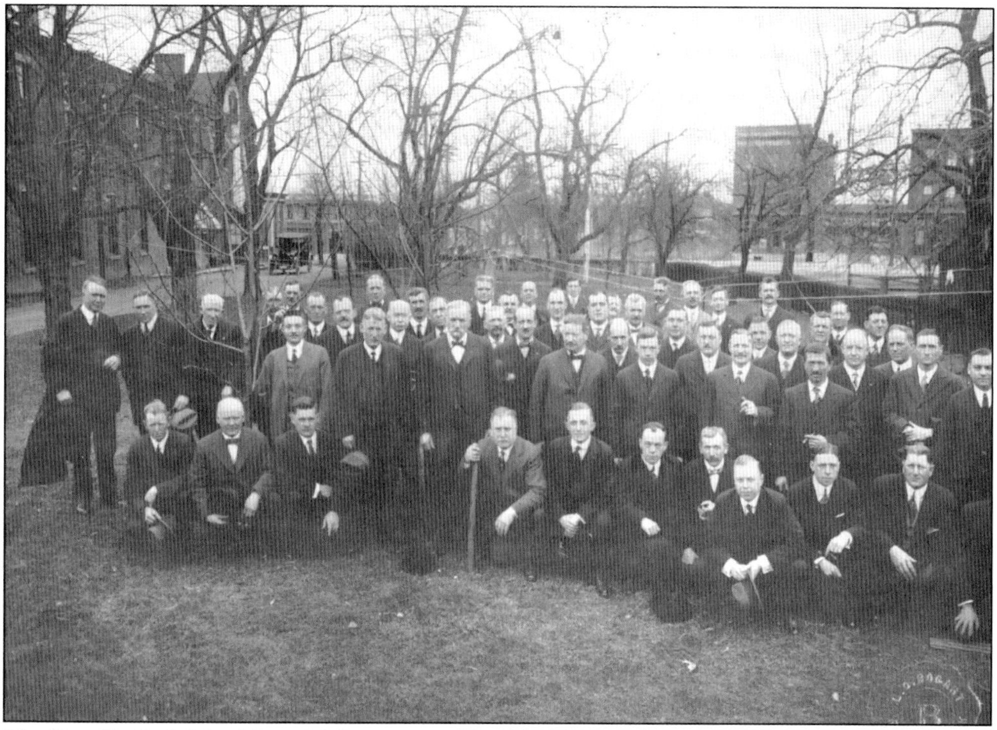

The Roselle Park Neighbors Club, organized by John C. Bender, meet at Bender's Grove in this 1915 photograph. Lorraine Hotel, which later became the Bender Slaughterhouse and Butcher Shop, is on the left. The Roselle Park Animal Hospital is behind the automobile. Stores and apartments at 400–404 East Westfield Avenue are beyond the trees.

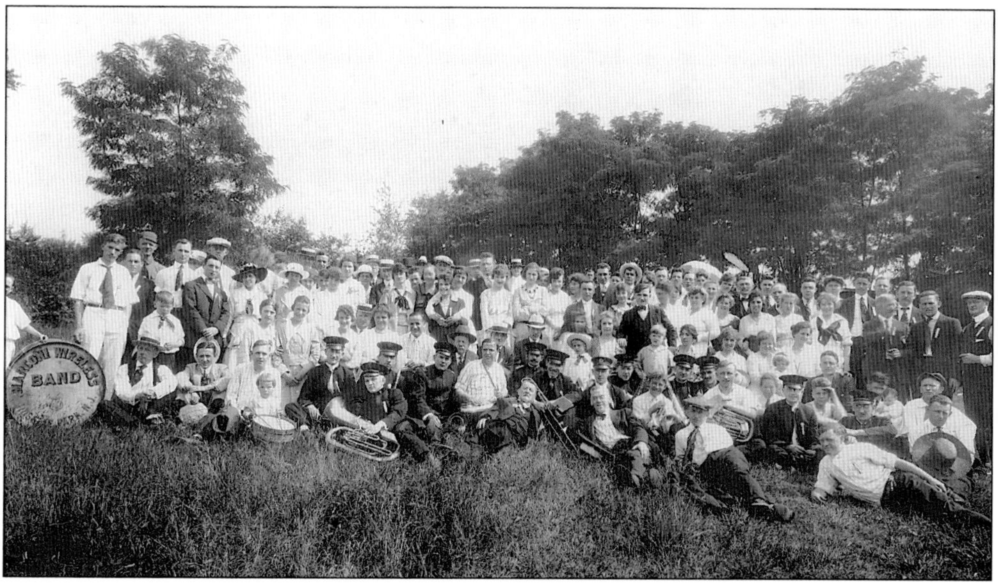

Marconi Wireless employees and their families gathered for an outing on a fine summer day. They were entertained by their own Marconi Wireless Band. The company was a forerunner in providing leisure activities for workers. In 1917, plant employees numbered 400, many of whom resided locally.

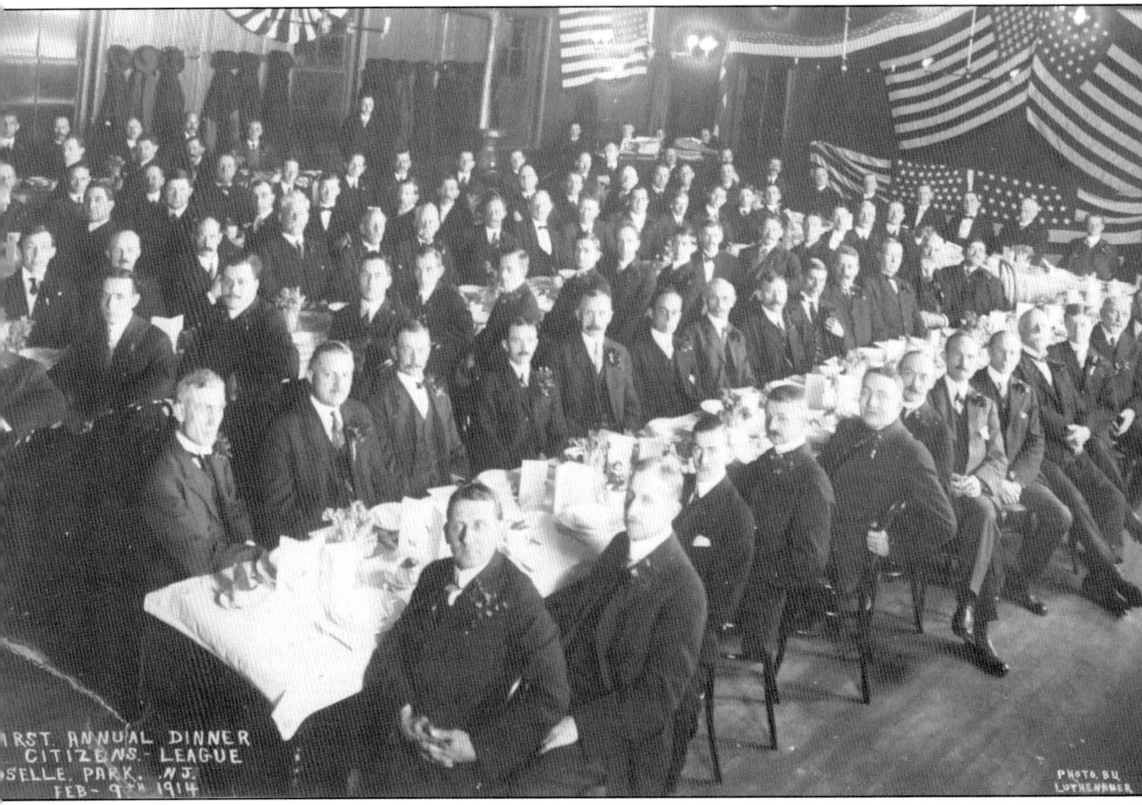

On February 9, 1914, the Citizens League, including many founding fathers, celebrated its First Annual Dinner when Roselle Park was less than 13 years old. Fixtures used to illuminate the affair were both electric and gas lamps, and a pot-belly stove warmed the room. All men, some renowned attendees included Harwood Fish, W.I. Finkle, Abe Woodruff, William Hale, Robert Gordon, Dr. J.A. Jones, F. Armstrong, Aaron Crane, Noah Woodruff, James Ratchford, Simon Birmingham, Jerry Mariano, Samuel Kline, Edward MacNaughton, Charles Renton, Arthur M. Crane, Dr. F.H. Brown, Charles E. Van Doren, Alex Cummings, John Wilson, George Whittaker, George Horning, William Bainbridge, Bartley Tuthill, Arthur Churchill, Wallace Higgins, S.W. Kingsland, John Bender, and Frank Feirer.

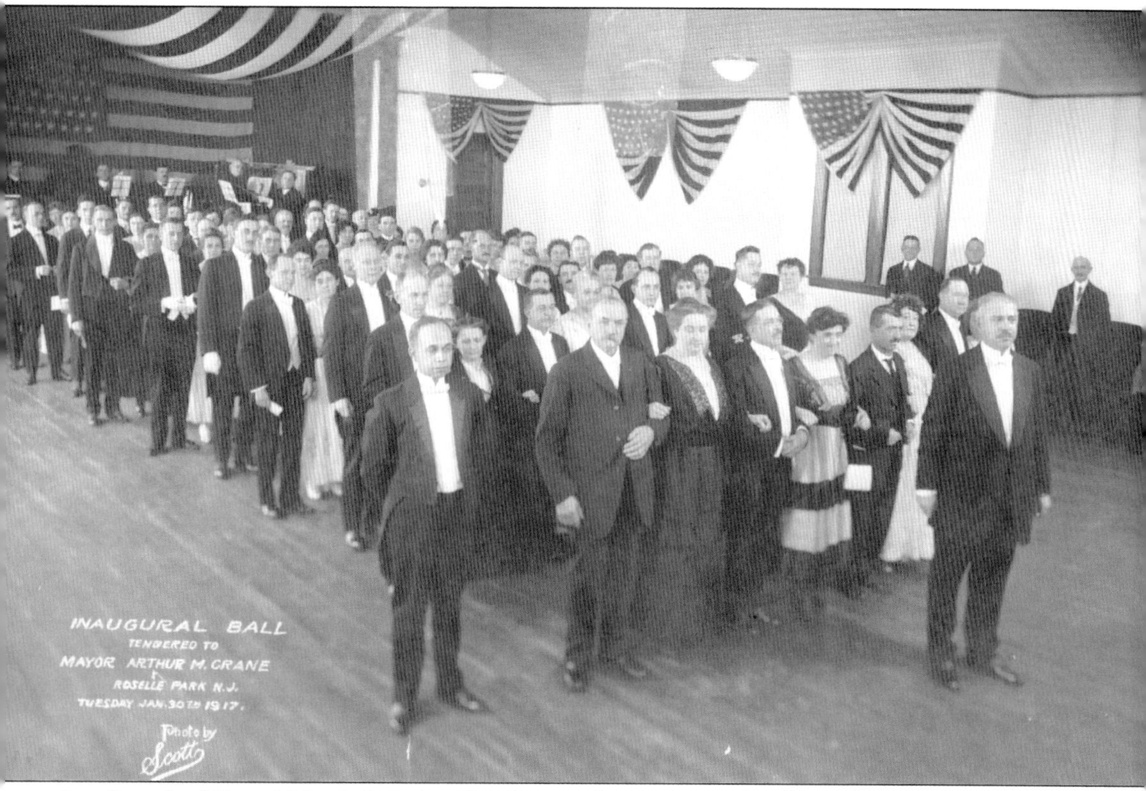

Leading the "Grand March," Arthur M. Crane, the sixth mayor of Roselle Park, celebrated his inauguration on June 30, 1917, with a formal ball in the town hall. He assumed the seat of chief magistrate after one of the hottest confrontations for the mayoralty against incumbent Harwood Fish. One of the highlights of the aggressive campaign was a float driven around town depicting a crane with a fish in his beak. Crane came to be known as the "war mayor" because his term of office was during World War I. His administration was largely concerned with war activities.

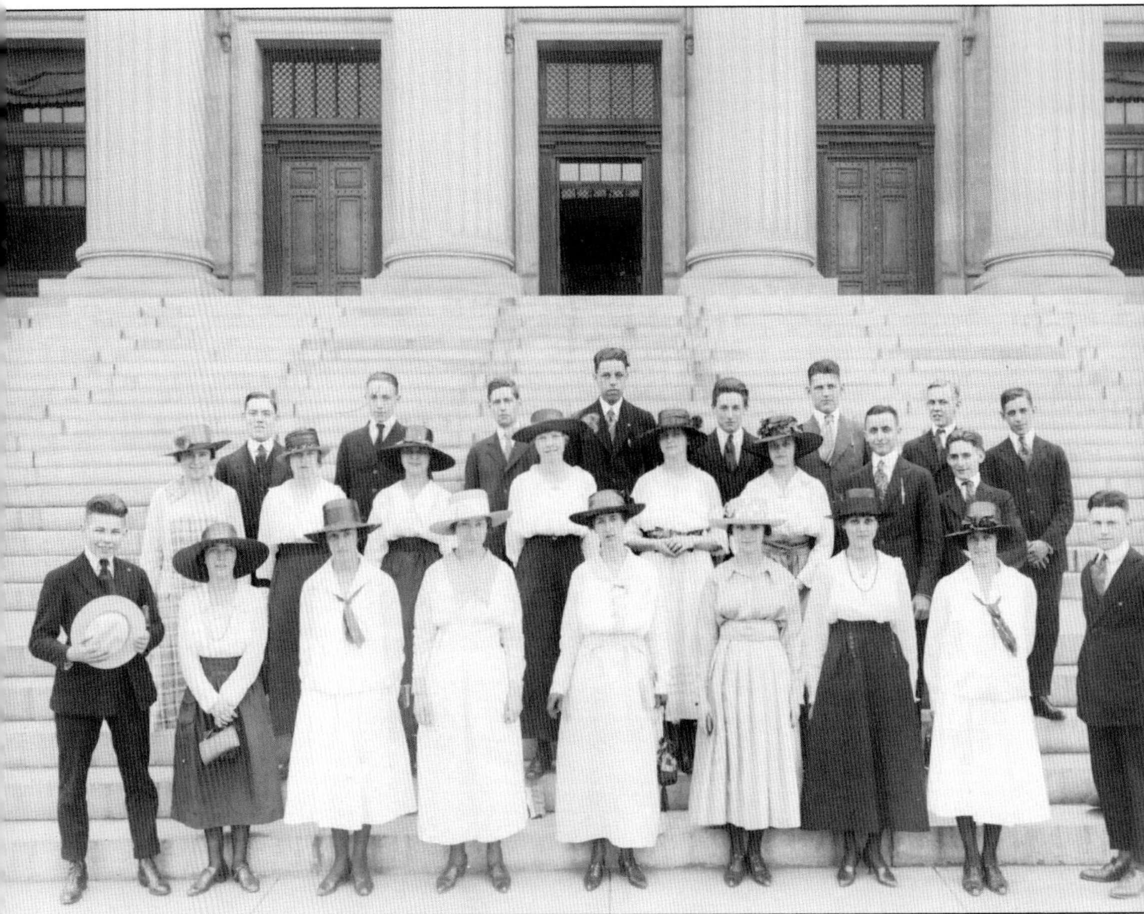

The members of the Class of 1919 would be centenarians in the 21st century. Roselle Park High School seniors on their traditional class trip to Washington, D.C., from left to right, are as follows: (first row) Chester McCloud, Anita Valdes, Maria Jack, Miss Ober, Mrs. Suy, unidentified, Gertrude Wariecke, Josepha Valdes, and Kieth Moore; (second row) Evelyn Payne, Leonore Kay, Elsie Albach, Alida Kjielinack, Kathleen Brown, Mildred Gathberg, unidentified, and one unidentified student; (third row) Albert Kohler, unidentified, George Faint, Richard Pfairer, Donald Collins, Nelson Skaarup, Walter Hamilton, and one unidentified student.

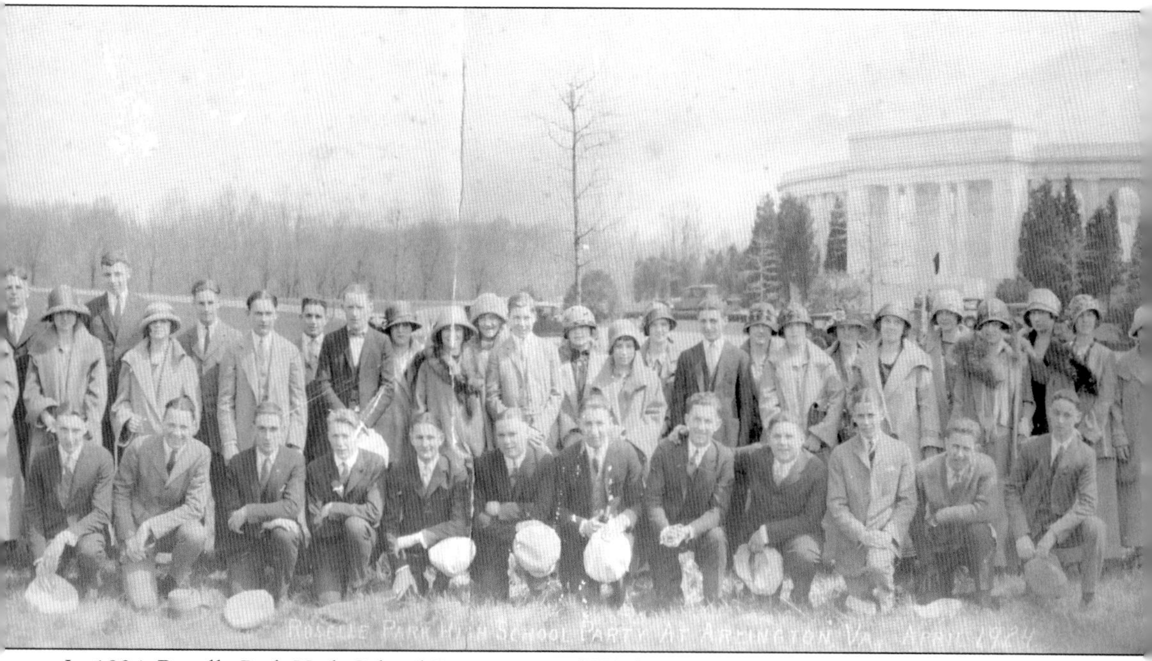

In 1924, Roselle Park High School Seniors visited Washington, D.C., and stayed at the Capital Park Hotel. They toured the Capitol, the Smithsonian Institute, the Treasury Building, and Mt. Vernon. They also climbed to the top of the Washington Monument. This well-dressed group poses on April 16, 1924, at the Amphitheater in Arlington, Virginia.

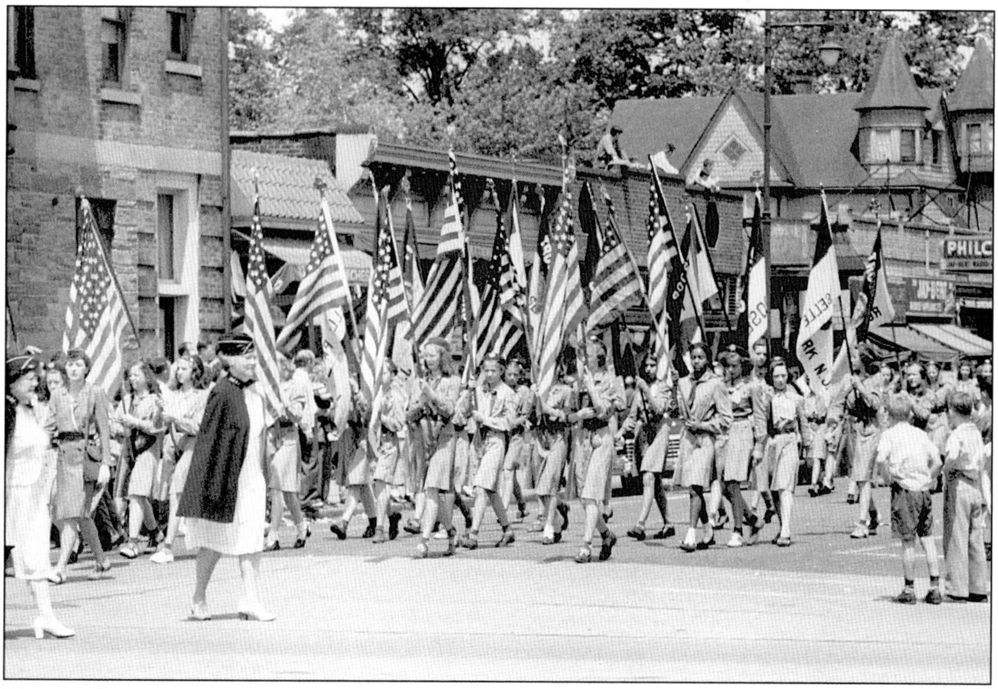

Memorial Day and the holiday season are two annual occasions that rouse spectators and marchers. This c. 1940s photograph shows girl scouts rounding the corner at Chestnut Street and Westfield Avenue. Although the background has changed, the patriotic spirit remains the same.

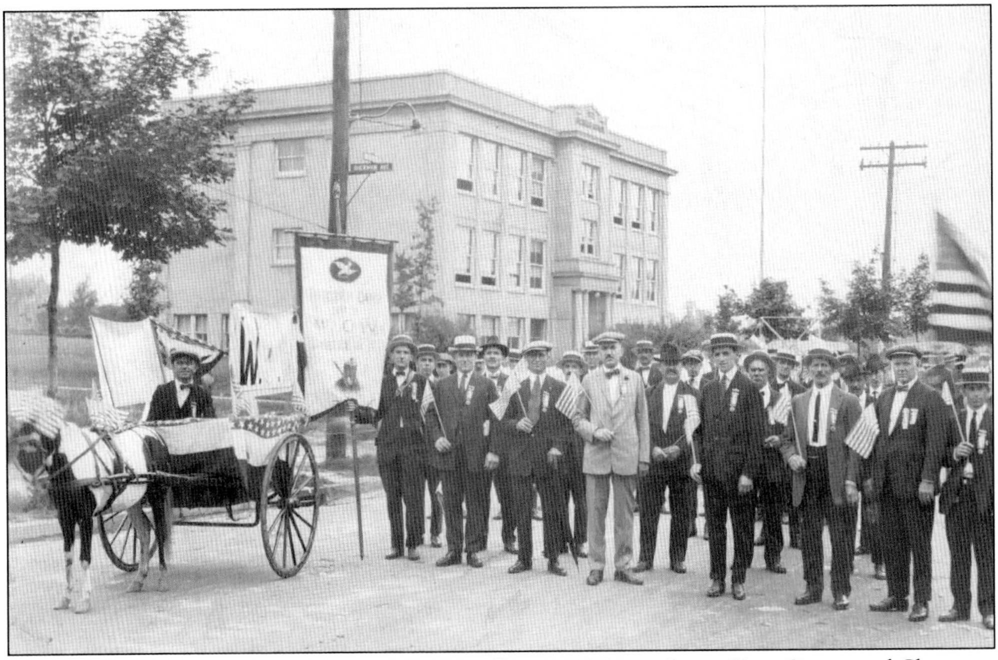

The Woodsmen of the World (WOW) step off in a 1922 parade on East Grant and Sherman Avenues. Anthony J. Salerno of Seaton Avenue leads the parade in the cart and pony he won in an Eagles (FOE) raffle. Behind the WOW banner in the second row is Armando Finizio, grandfather of Ernest Finizio Jr, the superintendent of schools.

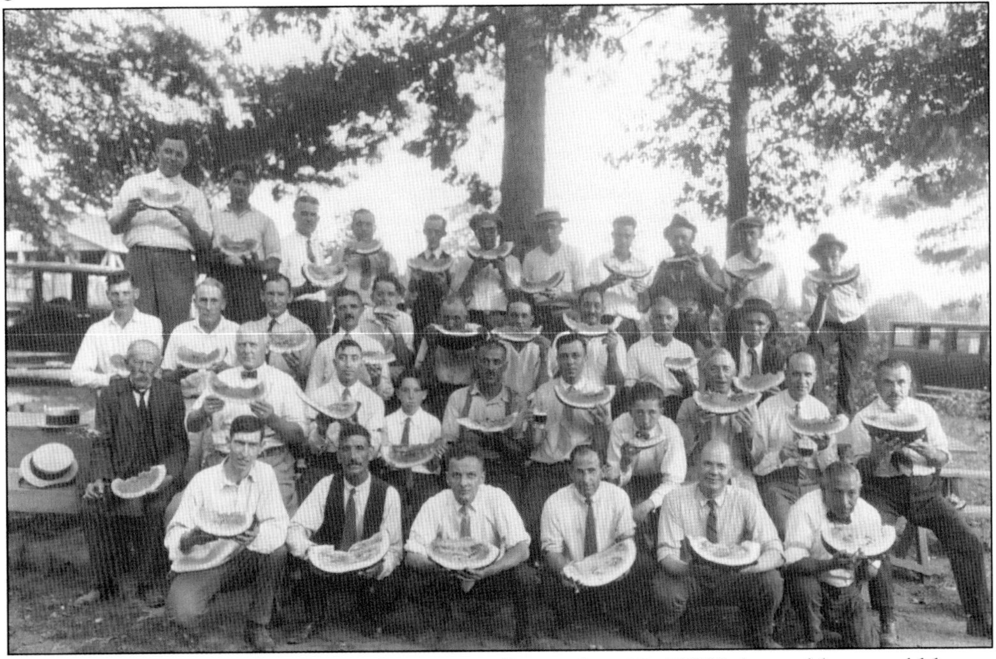

Who won the Watermelon Eating Contest on September 12, 1925? A good bet would be on the gentleman in the middle, still eating the big slice. Roselle Park Progress Camp No. 36 WOW members competed enthusiastically at their annual outing and clam bake at Patrylos Grove, Kenilworth.

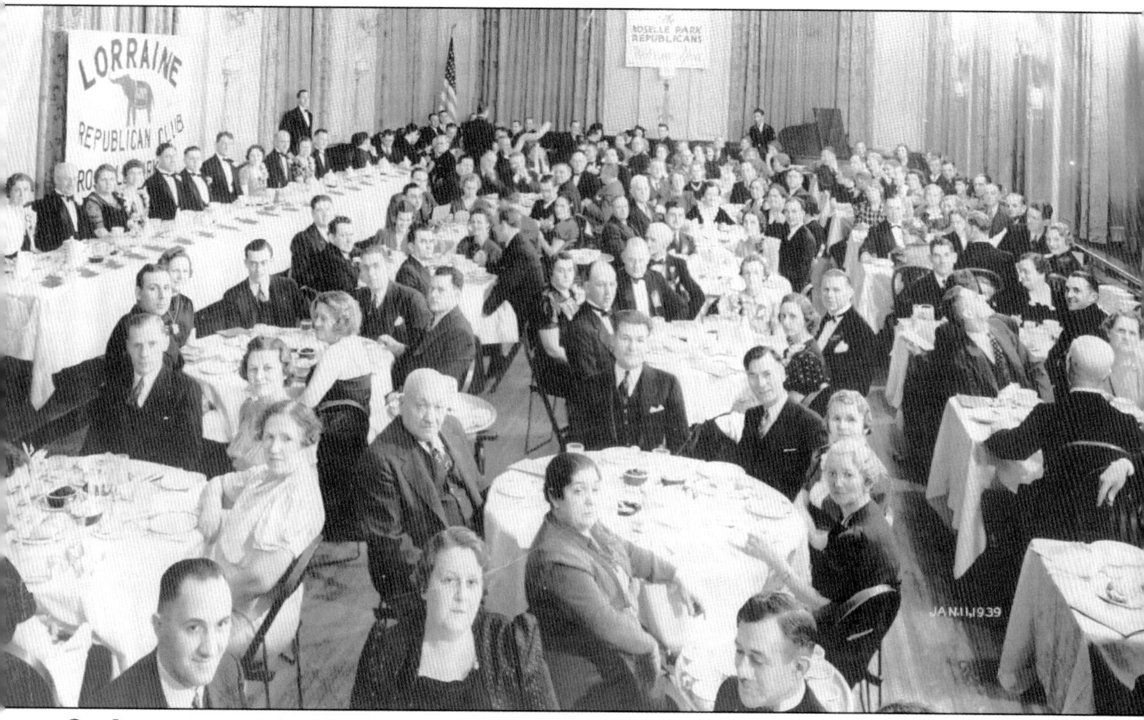

On January 11, 1939, Lorraine Republicans gather for a dinner sponsored by their club. The Lorraine section is made up of the eastern end of the borough. Those identified in the photograph include the following: (first table) Mr. and Mrs. Joe Soehl, Mayor and Mrs. H. Soehl, Charles Teller, Liz Peterson and her husband, Rose Glabb, Dr. Gledear, Dr. Nelton Leiberman, John and Doris Neusteader, and Dr. Frank and Mildred Pita; (second table) Wes Price (who later became police chief), and Hazel Houck and her husband; (center table) O'Connor and Joe Lettiere; (last table) Anthony and Mary Colucci; (next table to the right) Mr. and Mrs. H. W. Bollwage, daughter Louise and her husband Ralph Glover, Ada and Paul Soxer, and Mr. and Mrs. Al Price; (front far right table) Henry Otzman (who was nicknamed "Charlie Chaplin").

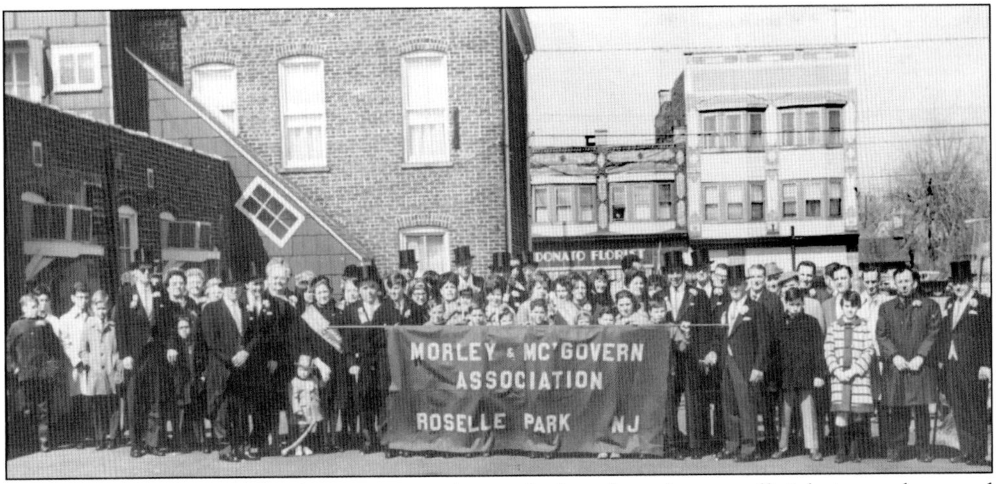

The Morley & McGovern Association gather with friends and town officials in top hats and tails before marching in Newark's 1969 St. Patrick's Day Parade. The building on the left is the back of Morley & McGovern's Tavern, a vintage pub popular with those celebrating the Irish holiday. Many believe that the district's first schoolhouse, Cedar Grove School, was located on or near this site on East Westfield Avenue near the Walnut Street Bridge.

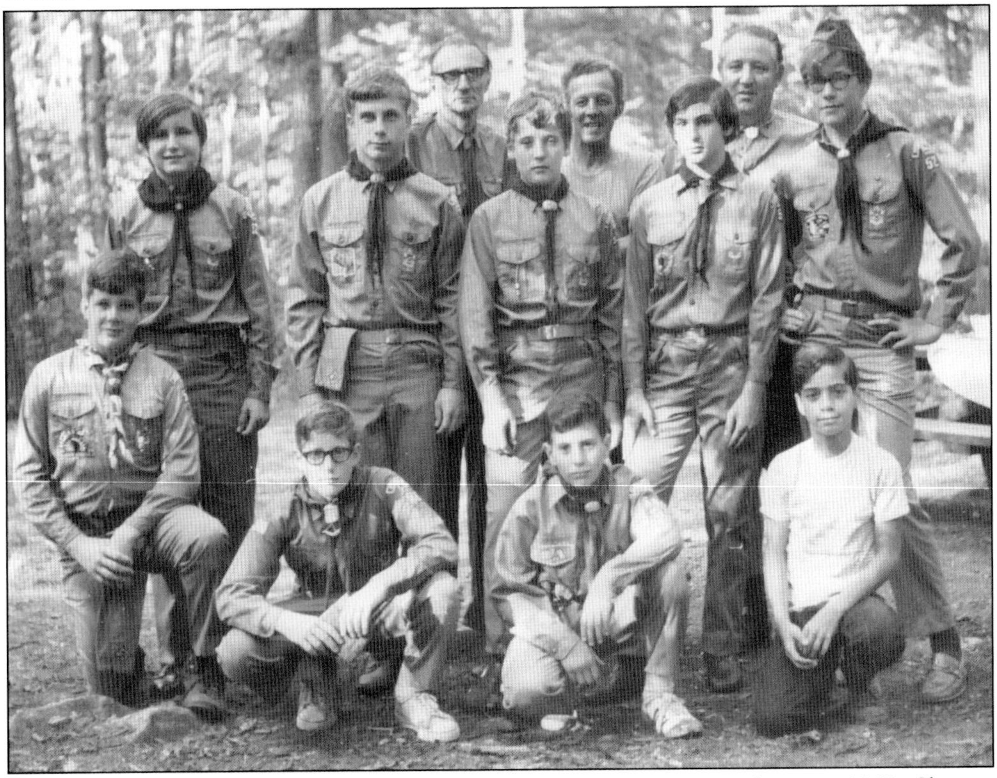

Boy Scouts and leaders of Troops 52 and 59 stayed at Camp Winnebego in 1969. Shown, from left to right, are the following: (first row) Thomas Cummings, Matthew Webb, Arthur Hardardt and Peter Monti; (second row) Gerald Robbins, William Reeves, Todd Morgan, Louis Citera, and Peter Gardner; (third row) Jacques Moritz, scoutmaster; Arthur Hardardt, assistant scoutmaster; and Robert Morgan, advancement chairman.

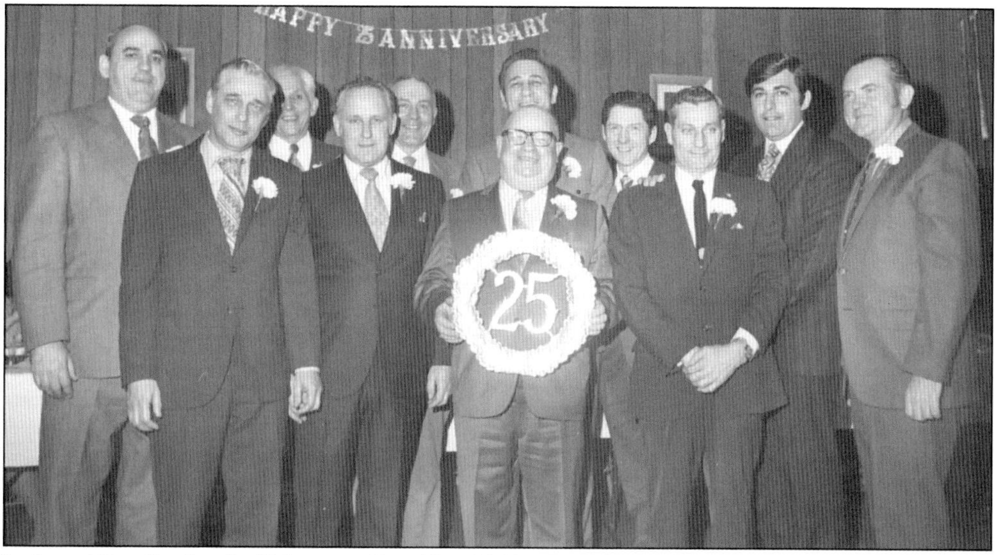

Jack and Lee Ragland of Veterans Post No. 9119 were silver anniversary celebrants in March 1972. Shown celebrating, from left to right, are the following: (first row) Peter Koerner, Joseph Gabriel, Robert Belcher, Clyde Saunders, and Larry Koffall; (second row) Paul J. Endler, Henry Mueller, Herbert Heipertz, Frank Rafferty, Roland Wilke, and John D. Mollozzi.

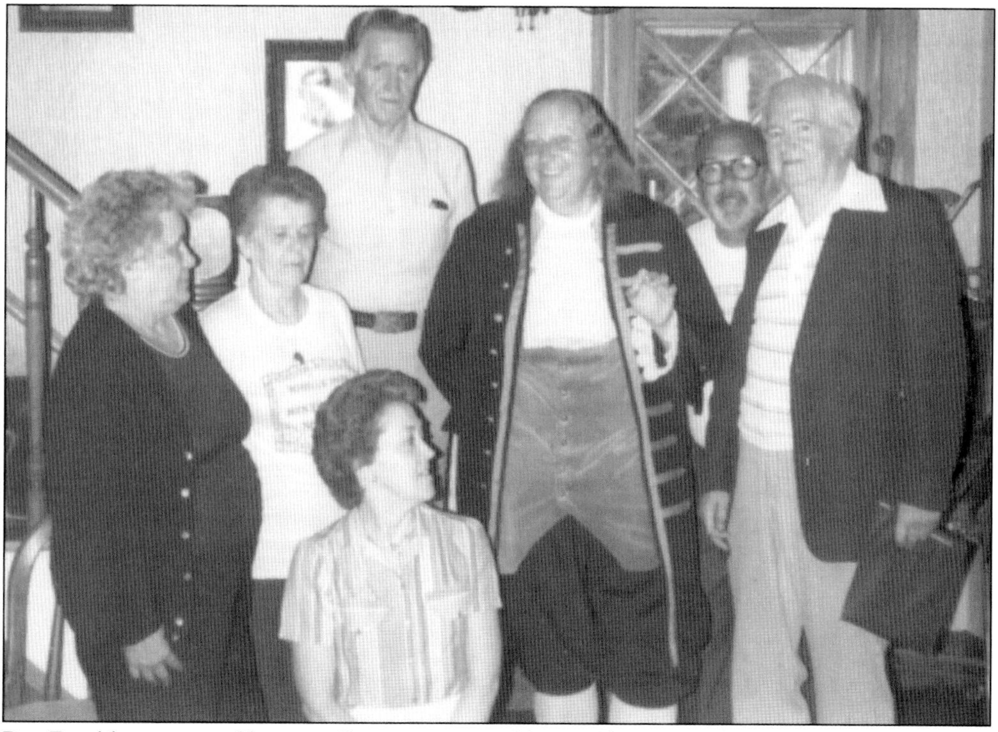

Ben Franklin portrayed his era of history to assemblies at Sherman, Aldene, and Robert Gordon school students on June 11, 1985, sponsored by the Roselle Park Historical Society. Shown in this photograph, from left to right, are the following: (front row) Clem Powers, Audrey Morgan, Pat Pagnetti, Ralph (Ben Franklin) Archbold, and Bob Lehr; (back row) Dave Keenan and Vince Parlapiano.

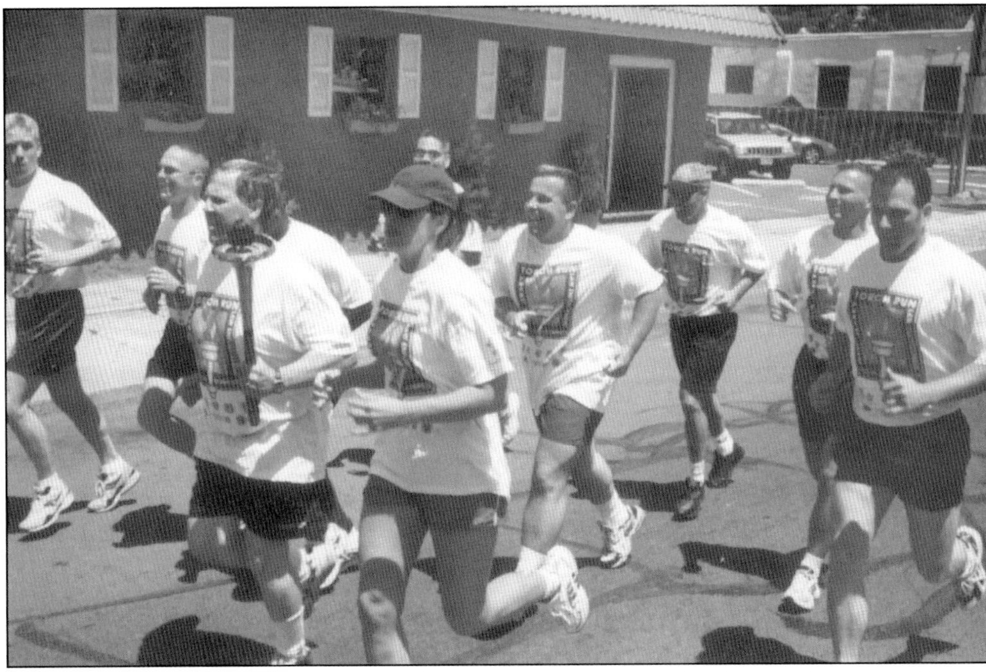

The Roselle Park Patrolmen Benevolent Association raises funds for Children's Special Olympics in the New Jersey Law Enforcement Torch Run. Running past Tavern in the Park on June 4, 1999, are officer Danny McCaffery, New Jersey state trooper Mike Small, officer Carl Hokanson with the torch, officer Brian Thomas (hidden), officer Jenny Keesler (the first female police officer in Roselle Park), detective Manny Jimenez, officer Nick Adamski, officer Sam Assad, officer Dave Pitts, and officer Harold Breuninger.

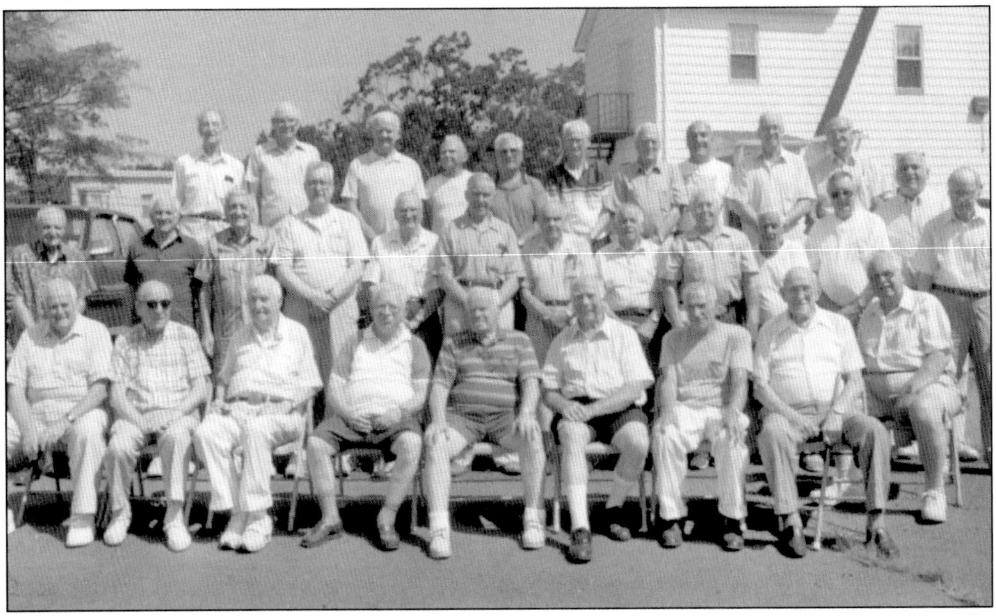

In September 1960, a group of middle-aged gentlemen created the Retired Associates of Roselle Park for the purposes of mutual assistance, recreational companionship, and social activities. Members are gathered in this photograph in July 1999 at Church of the Assumption.

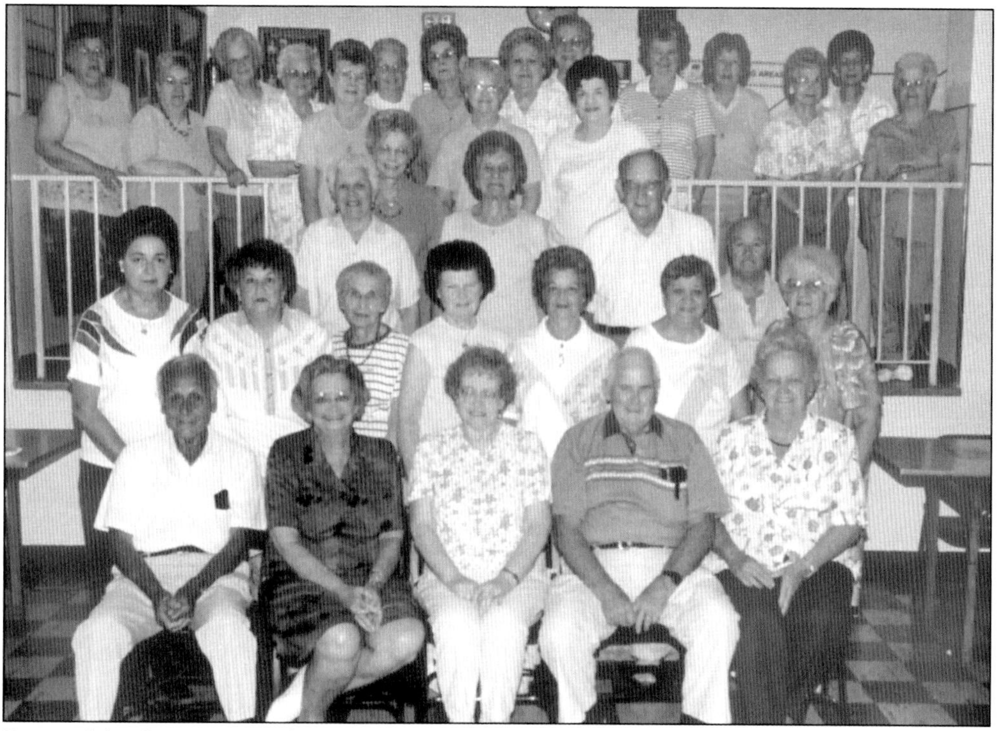

Some of the 58 seniors in these two photographs have witnessed up to nine decades of events and changes during their lifelong residencies in the area. The Roselle Park Senior Citizen Association gathered in July 1999 at Assumption Church to represent for this publication the people who, over the past century, did so much to enrich and populate the borough.

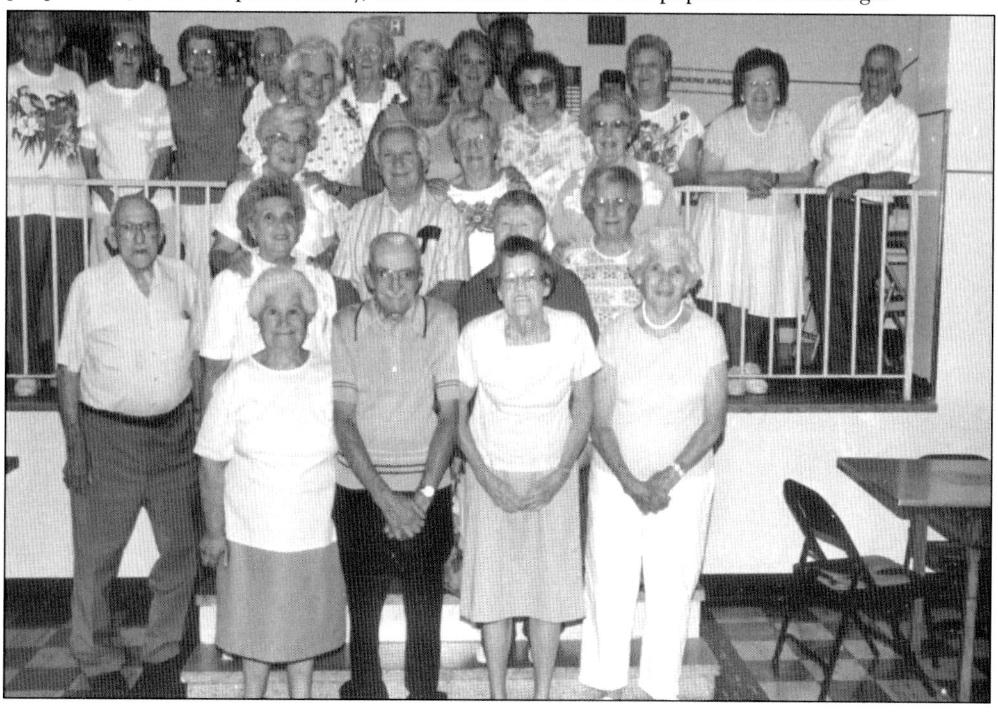

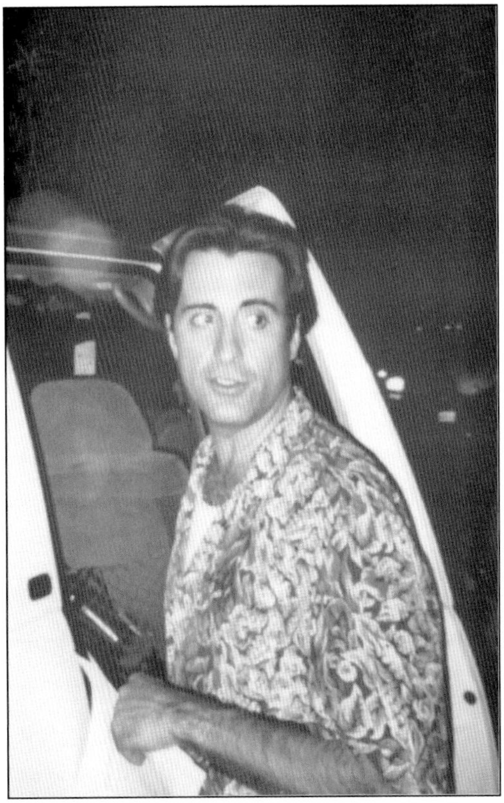

Actors Andy Garcia and Andie MacDowell, co-stars in the romantic comedy *Just the Ticket,* performed in Roselle Park where several scenes were filmed in July 1997. Other actors in the film included Elizabeth Ashley, Richard Bradford, Wally Dunn, Abe Vigoda, Chris Lemmon, and Laurie Harris. Directed by Richard Wenk, who has family in Roselle Park, the film was released by MGM-United Artists and premiered at the Park Theater on February 26, 1999.

New Jersey governor Christie Whitman toured the center of town on April 14, 1997, as she kicked off her reelection campaign. During ceremonies at Michael Maury Park, the governor was serenaded by this group of Roselle Park students. She was reelected in November of that year.

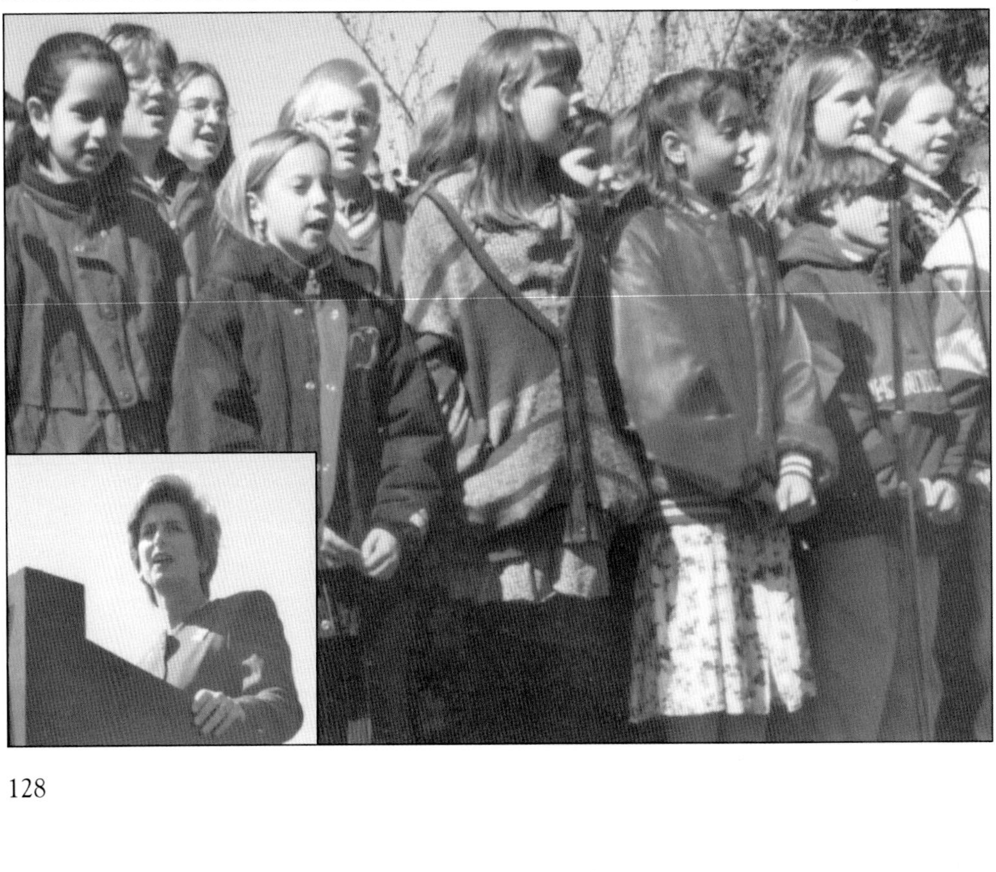